6 STEPS TO A STRONG SCHOOL CULTURE

A Leadership Cycle for Educational Success

Samuel Nix

Solution Tree | Press

Copyright © 2024 by Samuel Nix

Materials appearing here are copyrighted. With one exception, all rights are reserved. Readers may reproduce only those pages marked "Reproducible." Otherwise, no part of this book may be reproduced or transmitted in any form or by any means (electronic, photocopying, recording, or otherwise) without prior written permission of the publisher.

555 North Morton Street
Bloomington, IN 47404
800.733.6786 (toll free) / 812.336.7700
FAX: 812.336.7790

email: info@SolutionTree.com
SolutionTree.com

Visit **go.SolutionTree.com/leadership** to download the free reproducibles in this book.

Printed in the United States of America

Library of Congress Cataloging-in-Publication Data

Names: Nix, Samuel, author.

Title: Six steps to a strong school culture : a leadership cycle for educational success / Samuel Nix.

Description: Bloomington, IN : Solution Tree Press, 2024. | Includes bibliographical references and index.

Identifiers: LCCN 2024003799 (print) | LCCN 2024003800 (ebook) | ISBN 9781960574527 (paperback) | ISBN 9781960574534 (ebook)

Subjects: LCSH: School principals--United States. | Educational leadership--United States. | School management and organization--United States. | School environment--United States. | Academic achievement--United States.

Classification: LCC LB2831.92 .N58 2024 (print) | LCC LB2831.92 (ebook) | DDC 371.2/0120973--dc23/eng/20240207

LC record available at https://lccn.loc.gov/2024003799

LC ebook record available at https://lccn.loc.gov/2024003800

Solution Tree
Jeffrey C. Jones, CEO
Edmund M. Ackerman, President

Solution Tree Press
President and Publisher: Douglas M. Rife
Associate Publishers: Todd Brakke and Kendra Slayton
Editorial Director: Laurel Hecker
Art Director: Rian Anderson
Copy Chief: Jessi Finn
Production Editor: Gabriella Jones-Monserrate
Text and Cover Designer: Kelsey Hoover
Acquisitions Editors: Carol Collins and Hilary Goff
Content Development Specialist: Amy Rubenstein
Associate Editors: Sarah Ludwig and Elijah Oates
Editorial Assistant: Anne Marie Watkins

— FOR —
EBONI NIX, STEVIE NIX, AND **SAM NIX III**

ACKNOWLEDGMENTS

Solution Tree Press would like to thank the following reviewers:

Doug Crowley
Assistant Principal
DeForest Area High School
DeForest, Wisconsin

Amber Gareri
Instructional Specialist, Innovation and Development
Pasadena ISD
Pasadena, Texas

Louis Lim
Principal
Bur Oak Secondary School
Markham, Ontario, Canada

Christie Shealy
Director of Testing and Accountability
Anderson School District One
Williamston, South Carolina

Ringnolda Jofee' Tremain
Director of Professional Learning
Texas Leadership Public Schools
Arlington, Texas

Steven Weber
Assistant Superintendent
Fayetteville Public Schools
Fayetteville, Arkansas

Visit **go.SolutionTree.com/leadership** to download the free reproducibles in this book.

TABLE OF CONTENTS

Reproducibles are in italics.

About the Author xiii

Introduction 1
    Institutions of Learning 2
    The Journey of Leadership 4
    About This Book 6

1 Succeed by Investing in Others 9
    The Biggest Lessons 10
        Pay Attention to the Process 10
        Invest in People 11
        Apply Research Effectively 13
    How to Invest in People 15
        Understand How Experience and Beliefs
           Inform Performance 16
        Prioritize Personal Interactions 17
        Be Consistent 20
        Recognize the Consequences of Not Investing
           in Others 21

Ensure Success by Investing in Others 22
  Key Points 23
  Reflective Activity: Investment 24

2 Empower Learners 25

  Clarifying What It Means to Ensure Learning 26
    Establish Relevance 26
    Encourage Self-Acknowledgment 27
  Managing Individual Expectations 28
    Limitations of the Term Students 28
    Potential of the Term Learners 29
  Re-Envisioning Classroom Success 30
  Ensuring Learning for Independent and
    Dependent Learners 32
  Key Points 34
  Reflective Activity: Ensuring Learning 35

3 Establish Quality Instruction and Learning 37

  The Outcomes and Assessments of
    Ensuring Learning 38
  Misconceptions About Learning Assessment 39
    Assessment and Evaluation Are the Same
      Exact Thing 39
    Data Inform Best Decisions 39
    Most Assessments Are Summative 40
    Assessment Is One-Way Communication 41
    Assessments Are for Grading Purposes 41
    Everything a Learner Does Needs a Grade 42
    Grades and Test Scores Maximize Student
      Motivation and Learning 43
    An Assignment Turned in Late Should Not Count
      for Full Credit 43
  A Common Issue: Focusing on Action Over Learning .. 44

A Tale of Two Mindsets 45
    Fixed Mindset 46
    Growth Mindset 46
Two Types of Challenges 47
    Technical Challenges 47
    Adaptive Challenges 48
    Technical and Adaptive Challenges in Schools 49
Feedback 49
    Technical Teaching 52
    Technical Learning 52
    Adaptive Teaching 54
    Adaptive Learning 54
    Feedback in Action 55
Key Points 56
Reflective Activity: Adaptive Teaching 58
Reflective Activity: Where Is Your Focus? 60

4 Learn the Leadership Cycle 61

Processing as Part of Leadership 63
Learning the Leadership Cycle 64
    1. Clarify the Mission 65
    2. Plan Strategically and Make Decisions 66
    3. Empower Yourself and Others 66
    4. Measure and Gather Feedback 67
    5. Adjust and Improve 68
    6. Be Accountable and Give Rewards 69
Creating a Sustainable Environment for Success 70
Skipping Steps in the Leadership Cycle 70
Key Points 72
Reflective Activity: Leadership Cycle Analysis 73

5 Step 1: Clarify the Mission 81

Defining Clarity 82
Ensuring Clarity 85
Beginning With Vision 87
Sustaining the Vision 90
Distinguishing a Mission From a Vision 92
Clarifying the Mission 92
Fostering Buy-In 95
Prioritizing Consistency 97
Key Points 100
Reflective Activity: Determining Mission Clarity 101
Reflective Activity: Consistent Impact 102

6 Step 2: Plan Strategically and Make Decisions 103

Working Around Time and Change 104
Determining What Can Be Controlled 105
Redefining Strategic Planning 107
Planning Strategically Using the Seven Principles 108
Making Decisions Effectively 110
Incorporating Emotional Intelligence 112
Addressing the Roots and Fruits of the
  Decision-Making Process 114
Using Root Cause Analysis 121
Key Points 123
Reflective Activity: Planning Time 124
Reflective Activity: Strategic Planning 125

7 Step 3: Empower Yourself and Others 127

Two Focus Areas of Empowerment 128
  Self-Empowerment 129
  Empowerment of Others 131
Impact Without Imposition 133

Leadership and Emotional Security 135

The Relay Race 137

Key Points 138

Reflective Activity: Empowerment *140*

8 Step 4: Measure and Gather Feedback 141

Defining Measurement and Monitoring 143

Understanding Feedback 144

Receiving Feedback 146

Giving Effective Feedback 149

    Goal Referenced 149

    Actionable 149

    Timely 150

    Ongoing 151

    Pendleton Model Feedback 152

    Praise 153

Skipping the Step 154

    A Lack of Time and Attention 154

    Monitoring, Measurement,
    and Micromanagement 156

    A Lack of Metrics to Track Improvement 156

    Wasted Time 157

Key Points 158

*Reflective Activity: Determining
Measurement Challenges* *160*

*Reflective Activity: Measuring the Quality and
Frequency of Feedback* *161*

9 Step 5: Adjust and Improve 163

The Difference Between Adjustment
and Improvement 164

When to Make Adjustments 166

Six Questions for Adjustment Reflection 168

Key Points 170

Reflective Activity: Perspective for Adjustment *172*

10 Step 6: Be Accountable and Give Rewards 175

Accountability as a Positive Thing 176
A Culture of Accountability 179
    Two Questions That Impact the
        Accountability Process 180
    Three Major Accountability Inhibitors 180
    The Seeds of a Culture of Accountability 181
    An Accountable Leader's Mindset 182
    An Accountable Leader's Actions 182
When Ownership Is Dormant 183
The Differences Between a Culture of Accountability
    and a Culture of Nonaccountability 185
Reward and Recognition 187
Key Points 188
Reflective Activity: Culture of Accountability *190*

11 Hire With Precision 193

Hiring With Climate and Culture in Mind 194
Examining the Interview Process 197
Applying Emotional Intelligence in the
    Interview Process 198
Shaking Up the Interview Process 200
    Identifying Interview Red Flags 202
    Ensuring the Right People Fill the Right Seats 205
Key Points 206

Epilogue 209

References and Resources 211

Index 225

ABOUT THE AUTHOR

Samuel Nix, EdD, has been an educator for more than twenty years with a background as a teacher, middle and high school principal, and chief of schools in a variety of school settings. He has used his experience to design professional learning sessions for educators on topics ranging from maximizing the success of the entire organization, with an emphasis on raising the academic achievement of all students, to helping leaders re-envision their learning cultures, to promoting systems thinking that transforms organizations.

Nix loves to motivate, inspire, and encourage others to achieve greater success. Every session that he delivers is designed to give participants not just a clear understanding of the whys behind the ideas that he is introducing, but tangible examples of how to turn those ideas into collaborative practices that work.

While he served as a high school principal, Nix's campus was named one of the top thirty-two urban schools in America by the National Center for Urban School

Transformation. Nix has been awarded a Leadership in Education Award by the Texas House of Representatives. He received the NAACP's Mary McLeod Bethune Heritage Award for Education in 2010, the NAACP's Dr. June James Education Award in 2016, and the Future School Leaders Network's Leadership Legacy Award in 2019.

Nix received a bachelor's degree in history from the University of Texas at Arlington, a master's degree in educational leadership from the University of North Texas, and a doctorate in educational leadership from Texas A&M University-Commerce.

To book Samuel Nix for professional development, contact pd@SolutionTree.com.

INTRODUCTION

*Leadership is not something you do to people.
It's something you do with people.*

—Ken Blanchard

WHAT IS the purpose of school? Is it to prepare students for the future? Is it to teach students about themselves and the world around them? A traditional notion of education I would ask you to reconsider is that the purpose of school is to teach students. Millions of dollars are spent each year to train, develop, equip, and provide resources for teachers to become more skilled in their profession. Despite the investment, that particular goal is not the sole purpose of a school's existence. In every single school across America, there is a lot of teaching going on. However, students are not always learning, even though teachers are teaching their hearts out. In fact, many students are struggling to learn.

The purpose of school is not just to teach students. The purpose of school is to ensure that students are learning. Everything we do as educators should always go back to demonstrating evidence of student learning. Schools are supposed to be institutions of learning, not institutions of teaching. However, these organizations are perfectly designed to get the results they continue to get. To break schools free from their self-imposed limitations, leaders must overhaul their strategic-thinking paradigm, replacing reactive patterns with proactive and deliberate planning. But this is no small feat. The most hazardous threat to the future is the safety of the past. It is human nature to cling to the familiar and to duplicate actions that have produced favorable results. It is comfortable to rely on the lessons of yesterday for the test of today. But that mindset produces a dependence on the familiar and reduces leaders' ability to leap through the wall of uncertainty toward improvement and progress. What is learning if not progress?

The leadership cycle introduced in this book is more than just a framework; it's a catalyst for transformative thinking. It empowers leaders to shift their mindset from reactive firefighting to proactive planning and action. By emphasizing clarity, strategic vision, empowerment, measurement, and accountability, the cycle equips leaders to challenge the status quo and develop a future-oriented vision that people will strive to achieve.

Institutions of Learning

I realized my intention to achieve clarity in my work when I was teaching, and it has stayed with me throughout the years. As a young teacher, I came into a school and requested for other teachers to give me students they deemed "challenging." Some of these students were behind grade level, some had reading deficiencies, and most were labeled *special ed*, or *504*, which referred to students who had defined disabilities.

But none of those concerns was the biggest issue. The majority of my students did not enjoy their learning environment. They hated school. Most teachers have had this experience and been faced with the questions, "What should I have done? What do I do now?" When this happens, some will dig into what they were taught before their teaching careers started, pondering their textbooks for hours to determine the best way to teach and reach their students so that they can excel. I always start with observation.

For example, one of my history students struggled to read on grade level. How does one teach complex history material to a young person who is struggling to read and conceptualize the content? Sad to say, but my student, like many students, did not enjoy history or school in general. What the student did enjoy, though, was tapping out beats on his desk with a pencil and freestyling raps to go along with the beats. That student could recite complex rap songs verbatim and wrote original works right off the top of his head. It takes a smart mind to expertly rhyme words and match the syncopation of pencil percussion.

The student engaged in that activity frequently. Other teachers viewed the behavior as a distraction, and even a reason to send the student out of the classroom with a referral. What some saw as a distraction, I saw as an opportunity. If the student enjoyed rapping and making beats, maybe blending history with rap would make the lessons relevant and interesting. I had an idea. I asked a friend to help me compose music to accompany a rap that I would write pertaining to our next unit of study on the U.S. Bill of Rights. I was stepping completely out of my comfort zone with this attempt to delve into a world with which I was unfamiliar. But my passion to ensure the student was learning superseded my pride and fear of failure.

My friend and I worked on the lyrics to that song into the early hours of the morning. Satisfied with the end result, I burned the finished product onto a CD and presented it to the student the following day. After he listened to the history mix, my student's entire demeanor changed. I could see enthusiasm start to radiate from him. Confident about the material and excited for the test, my student requested another mix for the next section we would be covering. I was not *teaching* the Bill of Rights to this student. I had discovered a way to *ensure learning*.

I spent the next five years doing everything I could to make sure every student experienced the best education they could when they set foot in my class. And they did! It had nothing to do with what I taught and everything to do with how my students learned. Understanding how people learn positions you to set clear goals and create activities that focus on their needs. It also helps you identify their strengths and weaknesses and make use of them as learning opportunities (Şener & Çokçalışkan, 2018).

Think about it. We all have our own personal styles of learning, right? Some of us like visual learning. Some of us prefer to read over material. Some of us like to be immersed in the learning process through tactile or kinesthetic methods. As a result, education requires differentiation. The term *differentiation* is often found embedded in well-written lesson plans; it is the subject of many professional development sessions. But more than just understanding how students learn, it is about understanding their experiences. It is about tapping into their beliefs. Differentiation is applicable at any level of a school organization, but to have it takes a commitment to invest the time, energy, and effort that, unfortunately, some are not willing to make.

Had I not taken an interest in my student's beat-tapping hobby and simply presented the material and tested the student like everyone else, that student would have failed. Quite possibly, he would have had to repeat the grade. What does that kind of failure do to the human spirit? Learning feels out of reach, and students give up. Traditionally, teachers are taught that their job is to provide information, resources, and opportunities for students; if students cannot conform to those opportunities or they continually struggle, then the failure is their fault. That technical approach to educating students often results in frustrated teachers and students.

We do a really good job teaching the students who need us the least. The students who need us the most are the ones who aren't on grade level, who are struggling, who have no parental supervision, who are going hungry, who have disciplinary problems, and so on. My initial teaching experiences enabled me to learn early on that the traditional way of accomplishing instruction is not working. We have to step outside our own perspective, listen with the intent to understand, ask the right questions, and observe before acting on any issues. Easier said than done. Believe me, I know. Despite learning that valuable lesson on the teaching side, I had a bigger lesson waiting for me in the leadership arena.

The Journey of Leadership

Embarking on the path of leadership requires a special mindset—one that prepares you to face rejection and persist despite setbacks. Allow me to guide you through the necessary mental framework for success, using a story that illustrates the development of such a mindset.

While I was a teacher, students might find buckets of ice, or the lights off, or a big ball leaning against my desk when they walked into my classroom. Surprises were the norm, and surprises can be exciting. To engage students, I had to make my class an exciting place to be. So, when a student once asked me, "Why can't every class be like this class?" I knew it was time to expand my influence beyond one classroom.

Like most teachers, I struggled with the idea of "leaving my students." But wise advice from a mentor helped me understand that I was not *leaving* my students; I was going to *lead* my students. Once I made the decision to become an assistant principal, I reenrolled in school to earn an administrative leadership degree. It was a time-intensive grind that demanded more dedication than anything I'd ever done. Two years later, my efforts paid off—an exhilarating phone call informed me of an opportunity to interview for my dream position. I vividly recall the nerve-racking interview, where thirteen individuals intently scrutinized my every word, evaluating my fit for the role. Despite feeling intimidated, I believed I had aced the interview.

I did not receive the position. And I did not receive the one after that. Or the one after that.

So often, rejection humbles us or hardens us. How many times have you found yourself qualified and positioned for a promotion but not received the opportunity? I refused to quit. Rejection fueled me to read more, to reflect on ways to continue to improve, until I finally earned an assistant principal position at a school that was struggling more than most in the state.

I was so excited and optimistic on my first day. Tragically, there was a shooting near the school, and we had to lock down the campus, on the first day of my dream job.

Nevertheless, on day two, I recognized that achieving the impact I desired would require elevated levels of preparation, understanding, and strategy. A level of preparation accompanies success in any endeavor. And so, I devoted myself to these endeavors. As an assistant principal, I read every book I could find on how to turn a school around. I sought counsel from accomplished principals, constantly self-reflected on my influence, and diligently attended every school board meeting for two years. I wanted to understand the politics, procedures, and hidden agendas of my school system and those surrounding it.

Over that period, I realized the only way I could ensure that every student enjoyed every class was if I held a position that gave me input on every teacher hire. I needed to become a principal. My philosophy would ensure that new teachers would be hired not just to teach, but to make the subjects relevant for the students by making real connections between the material and the students' lives.

I was rejected for ten principal positions in my district, yet I never lost that desire, passion, and commitment. And most importantly, I maintained a growth mindset. Deep down, I knew that a single yes was all I needed. And one day, that call arrived—an invitation from the superintendent to meet at 1 p.m. I was nervous. Curious if I had done something wrong, I entered the superintendent's office at 1 p.m. sharp, and to my surprise, he offered me the principal role at an underperforming junior high school. The superintendent expressed his frustration with the prevailing notion of limitations among the students and emphasized the need for effective leadership to showcase their true potential. Starting the very next day, I embraced this challenge.

How about that? Despite my having no executive principal experience, the superintendent referred to me as an effective leader. His investment in me instilled belief and breathed life into my aspirations, setting the stage for success in an improbable situation.

So, at the age of twenty-nine, I had a new job. I was the principal of a low-performing junior high school composed of 979 students, with an economically disadvantaged population of 95.4 percent, and I needed to get the teachers to respect my role. I was fired up. I had so many ideas and expectations, so many things I wanted to try. I knew we could turn the school around. I had been preparing for this moment for years. Or so I thought. I mistakenly believed that having knowledge would seamlessly translate into taking action. My assumption was rooted in the notion that my personal success journey could easily be replicated to help others achieve similar results. I thought the actions and mindset that had brought me success at previous levels would be sufficient for ensuring success at the next level. I still had a lot of lessons to learn—lessons I had to learn on the job—which I'll share with you in this book.

My story is simply an example of the leadership journey that so many experience. It illustrates the need to embrace rejection and persist despite setbacks. To succeed, aspiring leaders must cultivate a mindset that allows them to view rejection as an opportunity for growth and learning.

About This Book

Teachers, administrators, executive leaders, and school board members alike tend to target their concerns to the students they impact. I wrote this book because student success transcends the boundaries of the classroom, the confines of a curriculum, and the limitations of individual roles. It encompasses the holistic development of young minds—nurturing their curiosity, instilling a love for lifelong learning, and equipping them with the skills and knowledge to thrive in an ever-evolving world. It reaches beyond the walls of a school, embraces the larger community, and recognizes that education is a collective responsibility that requires collaboration, innovation, and a shared commitment to creating a brighter future for generations to come.

The success principles that I have learned and taught and that I present in this book are principles that anyone can adopt. Although the focus of this book is education, the outlined principles reflect how highly successful organizations of all kinds operate, make decisions, overcome problems, take care of each other, sustain themselves, and create opportunities for the future. This book and these principles are proven beacons that can determine your course through the daunting, changing educational landscape or any organizational challenge. This book is written for educators and educational leaders committed to making a positive impact on the lives of K–12 students.

I have used these principles to train hundreds of educators and leaders at all levels. Not every principle will be equally meaningful to you, and not all principles will be equally challenging to remember and practice. But I guarantee that you will not go wrong if you use these principles to guide you and your organization.

This book is a practical, reflective resource. It embarks on a transformative journey, guiding you through the key principles of empowering leadership and cultivating sustainable success. The chapters unfold in a natural, cyclical progression, building on each other to equip you with the tools and understanding necessary to create positive change, both individually and organizationally.

Chapter 1 lays the foundation, defining success as an outcome of investing in people, fostering collaboration, and embracing diverse perspectives. By understanding the profound impact that empathy and connection have on leadership, you'll begin to see the potential for positive change.

The focus then shifts to empowering learners in chapter 2. Schools are institutions of learning, not just places to teach. You'll discover how, by focusing on student-centered learning, you can unlock students' potential and ignite their passion for knowledge.

Chapter 3 delves deeper into the intricacies of quality instruction and learning. Here, you'll explore the crucial roles of assessments, feedback, a growth mindset, and challenges in shaping student achievement. By mastering the art of providing targeted and timely feedback, you'll equip learners with the tools they need to conquer complex obstacles and reach their full potential.

Chapters 4 and 5 tackle the leadership cycle itself, highlighting the importance of informed decision making and a clear, compelling vision. Specifically, chapter 4 introduces the whole leadership cycle, while chapter 5 covers step 1. You'll learn how to break down ambitious goals into actionable steps and effectively communicate progress to ensure buy-in and sustainable change.

Strategic planning and informed decision making take center stage in chapter 6. You'll gain valuable insights into understanding time, change, and the root causes of issues, enabling you to navigate uncertainties and make data-driven choices that drive meaningful progress.

Chapter 7 champions the power of empowerment, differentiating it from mere entitlement. By harnessing the potential of proactive learning and self-responsibility, you'll prepare individuals to confidently face present and future challenges.

Measurement and feedback are essential to effective leadership, as discussed in chapter 8. Actively seeking insights and fostering a culture of open communication are crucial for making informed decisions and ensuring continued progress.

Chapter 9 emphasizes the dynamic nature of leadership, advocating for adjustment and improvement based on data and feedback. You'll learn how to embrace change, overcome resistance, and optimize resource allocation to drive continuous growth.

Accountability and recognition are critical to success, and chapter 10 is dedicated to these vital concepts. You'll explore the detrimental effects of irresponsibility and discover how fostering ownership, celebrating achievements, and focusing on impact can elevate performance and cultivate loyalty.

The book concludes with chapter 11, which emphasizes the importance of emotional intelligence in effective leadership. By learning to assess and utilize this crucial skill, you'll significantly enhance conflict resolution, problem solving, and overall team dynamics.

By embarking on this journey through the chapters, you'll gain a comprehensive understanding of the principles and practices of successful leadership. You'll learn to empower individuals, navigate change, make informed decisions, and foster a culture of accountability and reward. Ultimately, you'll find yourself equipped to drive positive change in your personal and leadership endeavors.

Each chapter is enriched with thought-provoking reflective activities strategically positioned as reproducibles at the end of the chapter to amplify your engagement with the text. These purposefully designed questions aim to foster critical thinking, inspire personal reflection, and facilitate meaningful interaction with the presented ideas. Furthermore, each chapter concludes with a succinct summary of key points, serving as a valuable tool to reinforce comprehension and retention of crucial details. Deliberately engaging with both the reflective activities and chapter summaries not only enhances your overall learning experience but also contributes to deeper understanding and lasting retention of the material, making your reading journey more rewarding and impactful.

Now that I have laid the groundwork for our exploration, let's delve into chapter 1, where we examine success through the lens of investing in people and embracing diverse perspectives. It serves as the gateway to a deeper understanding of how these elements shape the trajectory of leadership for positive outcomes.

SUCCEED BY INVESTING IN OTHERS

*For our own success to be real,
it must contribute to the success of others.*

—Eleanor Roosevelt

NOW, I am not going to make you comb through these pages searching for the number-one secret to success. Instead, I am going to share it with you right here, right now. No matter what the issues are—be they systemic, funding related, or even faculty based—you already have everything you need to ensure transformation of your school. You don't need to invest in a fifty-thousand-dollar "teach the teachers" course. You don't need to get fancy gadgets or even hire a multitude of consultants (which means a lot coming from me since I am an educational consultant and a leadership consultant). You can develop quality teachers and ensure high-performing students with what you already have available. That's right; everything you need is already there, within you, within your staff, and within your students.

Notice I said "ensure transformation." There is a big difference between *doing* and *ensuring*. To do something means to take some sort of action. For our purposes, that action is to improve a situation. To ensure something is to make sure or guarantee it happens. Doing is activity focused. Ensuring is results focused. The wise words of John Wooden, one of the most successful basketball coaches in collegiate history, come to mind: "Never mistake activity for achievement" (Yaeger, 2016). Think about that quote for a moment. There is plenty of activity in education. There is plenty of "doing." But we are still suffering from a deficiency of student achievement. Student performance and achievement in mathematics and reading have shown consistent, widespread decline on the Nation's Report Card, part of a series of data from the National Assessment of Educational Progress (NAEP). For example, between the 2019–2020 and 2022–2023 school years, mathematics scores for thirteen-year-olds plummeted by nine points, marking the largest-ever drop in mathematics scores since the NAEP began monitoring long-term trends in student performance. Average reading scores saw a decrease of four points over that same period.

As leaders, we need to reflect on and potentially shift our focus to ensure learning. But first, you have to cast aside everything you know about education and leadership to start with a blank slate. In this chapter, you will start your journey by learning that investing in the right people in the right ways is the biggest lesson in ensuring success.

The Biggest Lessons

Imagine this: You're standing at a pivotal future point in your life, reflecting on the journey that brought you here. In this moment of introspection, you ponder three profound lessons that you wish you had learned earlier, lessons that could have transformed your path and brought you even greater success and fulfillment. Allow me to share these insights with you, for they hold the power to shape your future in remarkable ways.

Pay Attention to the Process

Begin by shifting your focus from solely fixating on end goals to appreciating the journey itself. While goals offer direction and purpose, the true magic lies in the process—each step, experience, and lesson learned along the way. Research in an article from *Organizational Behavior and Human Decision Processes*, titled "Step by Step: Sub-Goals as a Source of Motivation" (Huang, Jin, & Zhang, 2017), emphasizes that breaking down goals into manageable subgoals enhances the sense of attainability and boosts motivation.

Practically, this involves breaking down big goals into smaller, achievable steps, celebrating each completion as a mini-victory to foster a sense of progress and motivation. Keep a record of daily or weekly achievements, learnings, and experiences—whether in a journal, on a progress board, or as a simple list. Regularly reviewing your progress helps you appreciate how far you've come and identify areas for improvement. Make time for reflection, asking questions like, "What did I learn today?" and "What challenges did I overcome?" This reflective process helps extract valuable lessons from every experience.

By shifting your focus from solely fixating on the destination, you open yourself up to a world of growth and self-discovery. Embrace the process, cherish each moment, and relish the small victories. Recognize that every setback is an opportunity to learn, and every step forward, no matter how small, is progress. By immersing yourself in the process, you gain a deeper understanding of your own capabilities and strengths, unlocking your full potential.

Invest in People

Now, let's delve into the second and most significant lesson: invest in people. Throughout life, as you embark on various endeavors and pursue your goals, remember that success is not a solitary journey. Leaders, in particular, understand this fundamental truth. They recognize that greatness is accomplished not alone but rather with and through people.

In the world of finance, some savvy investors can strategically grow their money by choosing investments that will give them many returns. When they do this successfully over many years, they achieve the freedom to focus on the things they truly enjoy. It's an appealing concept, isn't it? You can apply the same principle to your relationships and interactions with others. Instead of simply *spending* time on people, I invite you to consider the power of *investing* time in people.

Just like money, time is a valuable resource, and how we choose to allocate it can make a significant difference. By investing time in others, you have the opportunity to cultivate meaningful connections and nurture personal growth. Think of it this way: When you invest your time in people, you are planting the seeds of knowledge, support, and encouragement. Over time, these seeds grow into strong and reliable relationships. The individuals you invest in become assets in your life, contributing to your personal and professional growth. They become sources of inspiration, guidance, and collaboration.

By consciously investing your time in people, you create a network of valuable connections that can benefit you in countless ways. These connections can open doors to new opportunities, help you navigate challenges, and provide you with diverse perspectives and insights. Moreover, by investing in others, you foster a culture of reciprocity, where your support and mentorship can be returned to you when you need them most.

As a young leader, I thought I knew it all. I thought I had the answers, as most confident, prepared, and ambitious leaders do. I went in full of thoughts, goals, and expectations that I lost sight of the people who could help me. I was trying to fix a school instead of investing in the people. I was taking the hard line of, "We are going to do this, and I don't care what you think about it. This is where we are headed. Get over it." And I was trying to accomplish a task without understanding the people who were integral to its success. The reality is that you do very little by yourself. You cannot fire your way to success. Principals do not teach mathematics or physics classes. It is imperative that you invest in and empower others so that you can work collaboratively in alignment with the vision.

I stayed at that school for a total of three years, the last two of which I spent investing in the people. By the third year, we experienced a complete transformation in the culture; the junior high staff were functioning as an aligned team focused on student learning. As a result, student achievement increased to such a degree that the campus earned three distinctions from the state in the areas of reading, mathematics, and top 25 percent student progress. My departure was a voluntary one to take a position at one of the same district's high schools.

Investing in others isn't complicated. Start by opening your decision-making process. Explain the intent and purpose behind initiatives and directions. Show genuine interest in people's aspirations, and offer support when applicable. True leadership involves helping people thrive at work and in all aspects of life.

Here's how to put this into practice.

1. Schedule dedicated time to build meaningful relationships. Get to know your people beyond their job titles.

2. Become an active listener. Open your ears and heart to understand their perspectives and experiences.

3. Share your knowledge and wisdom with those who can benefit from your guidance. Be a mentor, not just a manager.

4. Don't forget to show gratitude. Acknowledge and appreciate the contributions of everyone around you.

By taking these steps, you'll actively invest in your people, fostering a network of valuable connections and building a culture of mutual support and reciprocity.

Apply Research Effectively

Research alone does not change practice. That statement is true in any field, be it engineering, education, or law. Studies are not enough to change the day-to-day practice and habits of professionals. Just putting information into someone's hands does not help them understand how to use that information in order to improve their work. But empowering yourself and your team to best understand trustworthy, well-designed, and well-executed research founded on proven results can prepare you and them for sustained success.

In his fascinating book titled *What Got You Here Won't Get You There: How Successful People Become Even More Successful*, leadership expert Marshall Goldsmith (2007) says the research and practices that an individual uses to obtain a higher-level leadership role are not necessarily the tools they need once they achieve that role. In the educational leadership arena, talented assistant principals are often promoted to the role of principal when the opportunity comes. Most often, assistant principals are promoted because they were great at what they did. They supported district and campus initiatives with a positive attitude, managed student discipline, supported improvement in their academic department, managed the operations of the school, and effectively interacted with various stakeholders. A promotion based on previous performance—based on how good someone was—does not always translate to good work in a new leadership role. Simply put, what got you here won't get you there.

The newly minted principal faces an entirely new position. There are more people to manage, a new scope of work, different responsibilities, a bigger time commitment, unique priorities, and decisions that have more impactful consequences. The new principal must make decisions that positively affect students, faculty, and stakeholders while factoring in the political aspects of their decisions. Welcome to the leadership thinking game. If that new principal solely falls back on their past experiences as an assistant principal, the guidance and answers may not always be relevant to leadership situations. What does one do when faced with a problem they do not have the experience to solve?

The answer is research. The educational leadership arena is filled with best practices, tenets of leadership, case studies, and more. All new leaders know they can research tools for success. But not every new leader always puts those tools into practice.

This disparity is called the *research-practice gap* (Boser & McDaniels, 2018; Westerlund, Nilsen, & Sundberg, 2019). It is a gap where leaders know what the research says, but they fail to implement the best practices from that research. Principals say the gap occurs due to a prevailing sense of urgency and a lack of time compounded by scheduling demands. Instead of relying on evidence-based research to conquer leadership situations, principals feel forced to react to the situations rather than respond.

The research-practice gap is pervasive across professions. Airline pilots early in their careers spend a lot of time thinking about flying and learning how to fly. Veteran pilots spend less time in the *thinking* zone and more time *doing*. In his paper *How Expert Pilots Think: Cognitive Processes in Expert Decision Making*, Richard J. Adams (1993) states, "The mechanism behind this transition is not clearly understood and typically it has been assumed that learning to make good decisions could only be achieved through experience" (p. 6). Veteran principals, like seasoned pilots, operate in the doing zone, but those who are new to the job struggle.

When first-time principals credit scheduling demands, lack of time, and urgency as the root causes of the research-practice gap, they are not making up excuses. These are real problems. Huge demands are placed on principals and the profession itself. When the time comes, principals are expected to have the answer, to know what to do, to make the decision, and to move forward. Principals hire new teachers and staff, complete employee evaluations, develop professional development programs, and build the culture within a school. Those demands and that urgency create the perception of "I don't have time to engage in a process of thought because I have to give an answer and a solution."

It is worth mentioning that the aforementioned tendency to not have time to think or do research applies to nonemergency decisions. Clearly, when safety is a factor or an emergency situation arises, principals are absolutely expected to follow their protocols and gut intuition to mitigate the situation. But most issues that we're talking about here aren't emergencies. They are decisions that invite leaders to think, process, and consider multiple perspectives.

One reason that the application of learned information is so difficult is because change is difficult; that is human nature. Another reason is that it takes work to make a study relevant to what's happening on the ground. Plus, practitioners are often skeptical of experts. Academics, after all, often seem far removed from daily work experience.

However, as with anything that requires intentional action, practitioners must first make a decision that leads to action for impact. The decision that comes from a motivation to reach a destination can be guided by a research-based best practice such as the PDSA cycle.

The PDSA cycle is a four-phase, repeating process that evolved from the work of statistician W. Edwards Deming, whose goal was to use the scientific method to improve business processes. The letters of *PDSA* each stand for a critical phase in the cycle: (1) *plan*, (2) *do*, (3) *study*, and (4) *act*. To begin, a team develops a plan to test an improvement idea (plan), followed by a small-scale experiment and data collection (do). The team then observes and learns from the results (study) and decides whether to roll out changes or make modifications by initiating a new cycle of improvement (act; Moen, 2009).

Recognizing that change is challenging, the PDSA cycle serves as a structured framework for improvement. By conducting improvement investigations during the testing phase, practitioners, especially in education, can swiftly and affordably determine which interventions work and subsequently adapt and integrate them to achieve quality outcomes consistently and at scale (Bryk, Gomez, Grunow, & LeMahieu, 2015).

How to Invest in People

Whether you are a new leader assigned to a new school hoping to bring about positive change, or you are a seasoned veteran determined to transform your existing educational landscape, you need to listen, ask, and observe before acting on any issues (Karge, 2023). Dispel any notion in your mind that you know it all. Believe me, you probably do not.

Leaders can learn a lot from students, teachers, and the community by really listening, asking thoughtful questions, and keenly observing. This self-awareness proves crucial, as it helps leaders avoid being influenced by preconceived notions and personal biases, ensuring more effective decision making and change implementation.

When leaders truly get what others are going through, they can adjust how they do things and avoid repeating past mistakes. Leaders who prioritize personal interactions show that they care about different viewpoints, which helps create a community of people who work together and support each other.

Consistency forms the cornerstone of effective leadership. Leaders who maintain consistency in their practices, while also admitting that they don't have all the answers and remaining open to continuous learning and evolution, establish a stable and reliable foundation for leadership. This steady and flexible approach builds trust in the school community and shows that the leader is both reliable and willing to adjust based on new insights.

Understand How Experience and Beliefs Inform Performance

When you are building relationships with people, you first need to understand their current situation and how it came to be. Ask yourself, "What has this individual experienced that has led them to this belief or action and to the outcomes they are pursuing?" I firmly believe that your experience fosters your beliefs, your beliefs influence your actions, and your actions produce your results. It is really hard to change a person's belief system as to why they do their job, how they do their job, and what it means to them to do their job. Reconciling that complexity becomes a problem for leadership because leaders often deal with people from an action-and-result standpoint. For example, a principal might say to a teacher, "Try this plan (or try this strategy)," as an action to get a different result.

When you work with people from an action mindset, the relationship is superficial. You are focused on the outcome, not the person. You will have what I had during my first year as principal: compliance, but not commitment. By only focusing on actions and results, you ignore the fact that people think. (Guess what? There are reasons why people think the way they do.) Therefore, you leave unchanged the two elements that fundamentally affect performance: (1) experience and (2) beliefs.

People hold certain beliefs because they have been influenced by their past experiences and the information they have been exposed to. Confirmation bias, as identified by associate professor emeritus Shahram Heshmat (2015), is a person's tendency to accept information that confirms their views or prejudices while ignoring or rejecting contradictory information. This inherent bias can lead individuals to selectively focus on information that supports their existing beliefs, making it challenging for them to consider alternative perspectives objectively. Being aware of what people believe allows for a more empathetic and strategic approach. Instead of simply presenting opposing views or alternative actions, you can engage in a more nuanced and understanding conversation. Acknowledging people's experiences and exploring the reasons behind their beliefs helps build a stronger connection and opens the door for a more receptive dialogue.

If you can understand where a person is coming from and who they are, you will be in a good place to understand what it is going to take to relate to them. You will be well-positioned to create more sustainable and significant change, but it does take more effort.

Building relationships requires understanding where others come from, not just the actions they take. Instead of diving straight into action plans, start with experience. Ask curious, open-ended questions like, "What more can you tell me about the experiences that shaped your approach to this?" Truly listen, actively nodding and summarizing their points to show you're engaged. Seek common ground—shared challenges, values, or aspirations—to build trust and rapport. Remember, validation is key: acknowledge their experiences as valid, even if you disagree with their conclusions. Approach conversations with genuine curiosity, not the need to win a debate. This is not about changing minds instantly, but fostering open dialogue by respecting people's right to different beliefs. Be patient, start small, and reflect on each interaction. By prioritizing understanding over action, you pave the way for stronger connections, more receptive dialogue, and ultimately, more sustainable change. The journey of understanding is just as important as the destination, so invest the time and reap the rewards of deeper relationships and impactful change.

Prioritize Personal Interactions

In many instances, we encounter individuals who hold the title of leader but lack the true essence of leadership. Genuine leadership lies in prioritizing people. Indeed, time is the most important factor of your leadership. Nothing is more valuable. Giving someone your undivided attention and time is an essential component of investing in people. It demonstrates the value of the interaction. And the act can be as simple as projecting the right body language.

When someone comes to your office, do you stop everything, lock in, and make eye contact? Do you share that time with them no matter how busy you may be? If you do, then you must know that focus conveys a critical message. Your actions silently say, "You know I am busy, but right now, you are the most important thing in my life." That message alone means the world to people, and it is so simple to practice. To be the recipient of someone's time is a respectful gesture and an inspiring feeling.

Say you don't do those things. Maybe you check emails while meeting with someone or find it difficult to focus and maintain eye contact. What does that say? It says, "I do not value this time with you." It says, "There are other important things going on besides this." It is a surefire way to divest from people.

Another strategy is handwriting a heartfelt letter to someone on your team, expressing your appreciation and celebrating their accomplishments. Consider implementing a daily practice of writing a sincere note to at least one team member, acknowledging their efforts on various occasions. It could be as straightforward as recognizing their unwavering focus during a recent grading session with a message like, "I noticed your exceptional dedication while grading the other day. Keep up the remarkable work." These personalized notes carry significant meaning, authenticity, and surprise. By actively demonstrating that you genuinely care about the people around you, you create an enriching experience that fosters strong relationships with individuals who will reciprocate the sentiment.

You might even expand this strategy to include teachers' families. For instance, if you have teachers who consistently show up for work without taking a day off, make a point of handwriting notes to their spouses and children, expressing your gratitude (with the staff members' permission, of course). Include a heartfelt message like, "I understand that you need your parent (or partner) to be with you at home but thank you for your selflessness in allowing them to come to work each and every day." Such notes have a ripple effect, as they strengthen relationships with the individuals who matter most to your teachers.

Recognize and honor the sacrifices your team members make every day to show up and give their best. Yes, their jobs provide them with a paycheck once a month or every two weeks, but they also live in a world beyond their professional responsibilities, just like you do. Take the time to acknowledge their dedication, their commitment, and the challenges they may face outside of work. Engage in conversations that allow you to understand their aspirations, concerns, and personal lives. Show empathy and support, creating an environment where they feel valued and respected. By incorporating these actions into your context, you can cultivate meaningful relationships, strengthen your leadership abilities, and foster a workplace culture that thrives on genuine care and appreciation.

I gave teachers gift cards, acknowledged them in the school newsletter, and ensured parents were part of celebrating teachers with perfect attendance. After all, the entire group was benefiting from those teachers' steadfast dedication, so why wouldn't we celebrate with all of them as well? Those steps were fundamental building blocks to a culture of appreciation. I even went beyond giving teachers my personal recognition. Early in my tenure as a high school principal, I embarked on a mission to get President Barack Obama to acknowledge my teachers who had perfect attendance. I wanted to celebrate those teachers at the highest level possible, while also improving teacher attendance. The first year, I sent one letter and one email to the White House requesting that acknowledgment. I received no response. Undeterred by the lack of response, I doubled my efforts the next year. We emailed and mailed a letter every day during the last six weeks of the school year. The letter went as follows:

> *Dear Mr. President,*
>
> *There are few professions more honorable than that of the professional educator. Teaching requires more than just dissemination of information; it demands the skill to convey content in a relevant way, combined with the passion to reach the hearts and minds of often unmotivated and distracted students.*
>
> *Teaching is a demanding and sometimes thankless profession. It can take a toll on both the body and the mind. Teachers who selflessly refuse to use the days that they have been given to be absent so as to ensure that students never miss out on an opportunity to learn from the most qualified asset in the school, their teacher, should be recognized and celebrated. As the principal, I understand the dedication and commitment that it takes to inspire, motivate, and educate our youth. I am asking you to join me in celebrating my teachers with perfect attendance. Please consider sending an official memorandum in appreciation of their service.*

The persistence paid off. The next summer, the White House responded with letters addressed to each teacher with perfect attendance on my campus. Investing in people is about creating opportunities to show you care. When you are genuine and persistent, you build relationships on a foundation of trust. People start to understand your heart, and you start to understand theirs as well. When those teachers received a letter from the president congratulating them for perfect attendance, they were so proud, and they were excited. Teacher attendance skyrocketed the following year, and the president wrote us again.

Now, the letters were a really great motivator for our teachers to establish excellent attendance. But the investment in people didn't stop with the teachers. Since teachers were consistently showing up each and every day, students were learning. That consistency forged positive relationships between the teachers and their learners. Less time was spent having substitutes fill lessons with busywork. Less time was spent trying to make sure classrooms were covered. Students knew that every day they woke up and went to class, their teacher would be there. And that certainty meant something.

By sharing my personal journey and the challenges I faced, I hope to inspire you to persist in your own quest for recognition and appreciation. It's not always easy, and setbacks may come along the way, but with consistency and unwavering determination, anyone can achieve their goals.

Be Consistent

Consistency develops routines and builds momentum. It forms habits that become almost second nature. When you care about people, you care about what they do and what they experience. It is well-researched that people value consistency and predictability (Michigan State University, 2016). Commitment and consistency as means of behavior change have a long history in social psychology. As the research has shown, the mechanisms of commitment and consistency are important motivators that powerfully shape human behavior (Lokhorst, Werner, Staats, van Dijk, & Gale, 2013). Robert Joss, former dean of the Stanford Graduate School of Business, says:

> The minute you move from being a task-oriented professional to being a [leader], it stops being about your individual talents, your successes, and starts being all about coaching, motivating, teaching, supporting, removing roadblocks, and finding resources for your employees. Leadership is about celebrating their victories and rewarding them; helping them analyze when things don't go to plan. Their successes become your successes. Their failures are yours too. (Stanford GSB Staff, 2007)

Investing in people is paramount. Your investment in people will encourage them to come to work while you assist them along the way. The commitment and consistency highlighted in research play a crucial role here, as they form the foundation for developing and maintaining strong relationships within a team. On your first day in a leadership role, begin the process of encouraging, shaping, motivating, and developing your people into exceptional examples.

Leaders who consistently embody their core values, communicate openly, and invest in their people create a foundation of trust and loyalty. By celebrating victories, supporting setbacks, and modeling the behavior you expect, you inspire your team to excel. Establish clear routines and processes to reduce confusion and build momentum. Finally, embrace self-awareness and actively seek feedback to continuously refine your leadership style. Remember, consistency is a journey, not a destination. By committing to these practices, you unlock the true potential of your team and pave the way for lasting success.

Recognize the Consequences of Not Investing in Others

The absence of investment breaks down trust within an organization and yields far-reaching consequences that permeate the attitudes and behaviors of employees (Yu, Mai, Tsai, & Dai, 2018). Extensive research consistently reveals the detrimental impact that a lack of interpersonal trust has on various aspects of organizational dynamics. Productivity, performance, commitment, teamwork, organizational loyalty, adaptability to change, stress levels, and employee turnover all suffer in the absence of the investments that lead to high levels of trust (Bond-Barnard, Fletcher, & Steyn, 2018; Güçer & Demirdağ, 2014; Guinot & Chiva, 2019; Lumineau & Schilke, 2018; Ng, 2015; Zeffane & Melhem, 2018). In environments devoid of investment and mutual trust, employees become disengaged from decision-making processes, job satisfaction wanes, and creativity in task accomplishment diminishes (Kauffmann & Golan, 2017; Kim, Wang, & Chen, 2018). In one of my experiences, the staff filed a myriad of grievances, and people quit left and right. Worse, the culture impeded our ability to ensure student learning. The school's core rested on the shoulders of uncertainty and mistrust. Gossip prevailed. Basically, we discovered cracks in our cultural foundation.

When you invest in others, you keep your promises, no matter how small. You listen and try to understand. You are proactive and do things without being asked. You find genuine, unique, and meaningful ways to celebrate others' progress and goals. Those actions create trust and security. By investing in others, you are intentional about managing the perceptions of others. Misperception can be a base for conflict. If you perceive others as adversaries and act accordingly, you will generate responses in kind.

Effective leadership shapes employee experience, engagement, and well-being, all of which are vital to a thriving workplace culture. The leader sets the tone for what is valued. If the leader values people, then others will as well. When administration values and invests in the staff, staff will, in turn, value and invest in parents, students, and the community. As a leader, you need to make people believe they can succeed and show them what you want and expect of them. Philosopher-poet Johann Wolfgang von Goethe advised, "When we treat [people] as if they were what they should be, we improve them as far as they can be improved."

Ensure Success by Investing in Others

First and foremost, you must focus on matters within your control, rather than fixating on things you cannot change or influence. When you focus on others' responses rather than invest in them as people, your attention is arrested by assumptions and expectations. Various attitudes, emotions, situations, challenges, and circumstances will always hinder your progress. So, it is essential to concentrate on the aspects within your sphere of influence. This valuable information, had I known it when embarking on my journey as a principal, could have spared me a great deal of heartache. Nonetheless, I am immensely grateful for that leadership experience and the invaluable lessons it taught me. Keep in mind that the process is just as significant as the goal, if not more so.

In Stephen R. Covey's (2004) book *The 7 Habits of Highly Effective People*, true transformative leadership lies in habit 5: "Seek first to understand, then to be understood." The next key to success is to actively seek to understand others, fostering a transformative leadership approach rather than merely aiming to be understood. Research, such as that by Olga M. Klimecki (2019), has demonstrated that actively seeking to understand others is associated with more favorable attitudes and a higher readiness for reconciliation in various intergroup settings.

For a school leader, integrating this concept involves creating the time, space, and permission to genuinely listen to what teachers are expressing without immediately formulating a response. It's about pausing, actively listening, and embracing the valuable perspectives of those on the front lines—the ears, eyes, and heart of the school. According to researchers Avraham N. Kluger and Guy Itzchakov (2022), the act of listening can lead to a transient state of togetherness, fostering a mutual creative thought process. This process not only brings clarity but also facilitates the generation of novel plans, enhances well-being, and strengthens attachment to the conversation partner.

By purposefully seeking to understand the viewpoints of teachers, you avoid the risk of misinterpreting cultural nuances within the school as merely "other people's problems." In reality, these nuanced ripples could signify underlying leadership challenges that need your attention. Embracing a proactive approach to understanding others fosters a collaborative and supportive school environment, laying the groundwork for effective leadership and positive cultural growth.

Finally, commit to the high road. Clearly, people let us down on occasion—sometimes in a way that sends shock waves through our system. Oftentimes, the people who have been given the most are the ones who appreciate it the least.

When such an instance inevitably happens, remember it is not your fault. Your efforts are not pointless. Do not second-guess yourself for a moment. Take the high road. You will get all your efforts back in different ways with different people.

Key Points

Effectively leading others isn't just about achieving goals; it's about investing in people and fostering a positive journey. This chapter emphasized the importance of shifting from focusing on end goals to appreciating the learning process, prioritizing personal interactions, and understanding how experiences shape beliefs and actions. By listening, asking, and observing before taking action, you can build trust and empower your team. Remember, consistency breeds trust and momentum, and neglecting to invest in others can have detrimental consequences.

As we move into chapter 2, these principles become even more crucial. This next chapter will explore how transforming schools into institutions of learning, not just teaching, requires shifting the focus to student-centered learning so we empower students to unlock their potential and embrace the joy of discovery. By applying the lessons learned here about prioritizing relationships, understanding individuals, and investing in their growth, we can create truly empowering learning environments for all.

As you leave this chapter, remember the following.

- Acknowledge the sacrifice your team makes each day to show up and do their best.
- Effective leadership shapes employee experience, engagement, and well-being.
- Seek first to understand and then to be understood.
- The difference between ensuring and doing comes down to guaranteeing something is getting done versus simply getting something done.
- Don't spend time on people; invest time in people.
- The simplest gestures are sometimes the most influential.
- There is a research-practice gap where leaders fail to deploy best practices from research to their daily decision making.

Reflective Activity: Investment

When reflecting on your investment in others, consider asking the following questions and completing the final prompt.

- Are you more engaged in spending time with others or investing time in others?

- In what ways could you improve your investment in others?

- What challenges or barriers would hinder your improvement?

- How do you plan to overcome those barriers or challenges to ensure quality investment in others?

- Identify three things you want people to remember about your leadership.

EMPOWER LEARNERS

Children are likely to live up to what you believe of them.

—Lady Bird Johnson

TRADITIONAL TEACHING methods often focus on the delivery of information without considering the actual learning process (Brown, 2020). This approach can hinder student engagement and comprehension, leading to a lack of meaningful learning experiences. Additionally, students often struggle to see the relevance of classroom lessons to their everyday lives, which further hampers their motivation and overall learning outcomes (Albrecht & Karabenick, 2018; Alexander, 2018). To address these challenges, teachers need to shift their perspective and embrace their role as facilitators of learning, fostering clarity, relevance, and effective communication in the classroom (Jagtap, 2016).

The purpose of this chapter is to highlight the importance of effective communication in enhancing learning outcomes and provide practical strategies for teachers to implement in their classrooms. By emphasizing the need for clarity, relevance, and a learner-centered approach, the chapter aims to inspire teachers to rethink their instructional practices and create an environment that fosters deep understanding, engagement, and a genuine connection between classroom content and students' lives. Ultimately, we will explore what it means to ensure that teachers are successful facilitators of classroom learners. That triumph is paramount to ensuring clarity of the mission. What does such success even look like?

Clarifying What It Means to Ensure Learning

First, let's explore what we mean by the phrase *ensure learning*. There are a few acceptable definitions of the concept, but in short, it means that the teacher has determined what constitutes acceptable evidence of comprehension of the outcomes or results (assessment). When assessed for competency and comprehension, students are able to provide evidence of their understanding—the learning—at the intended level. Ensuring learning also means the instructional leader has established the systems and processes to verify that expectations are being met. There has to be continuity. Consistency, or the absence of it, can be the defining factor between failure and success. Effective educational leaders should always establish a consistent mission to prioritize the process of learning and the student experience.

Understanding what ensuring learning truly means is crucial. It shifts our focus from simply delivering content to empowering students to demonstrate their comprehension. This lays the foundation for building relevance and self-awareness, ultimately putting the learner at the center of their educational journey.

Establish Relevance

When you have a student (or even students) who does not find the instructional content worthy of their time or effort, a few questions will arise (Nagashibaevna, 2019). Students will ask themselves or their teacher, (1) "How is this information going to benefit me?" and (2) "What does this information have to do with me?"

You should not dismiss those questions as acts of insubordination or disruption. The students are simply seeking relevance. Think about your own experience as a student. Was there a subject where you thought to yourself, "When will I ever need to know this in real life?" It is human nature to question relevance, but our goal as educational leaders is to eliminate the need for that question.

While many educators often undervalue the importance of relevance as an aspect of teaching and learning, we know from research that teaching without relevance can be demotivating to students (Rone et al., 2023). Students who are demotivated find other things to capture their attention, and those things might be destructive. It should be refreshing then to realize that inattentive, unmotivated behaviors could simply be due to a lack of relevance in what is being taught. Why? Because that problem has a myriad of solutions.

Teachers can easily establish relevance by showing how the lesson can be applied in practice, demonstrating relevance to local cases, relating material to everyday applications, or finding applications in current newsworthy issues. Students deserve relevant and interesting lessons that also match their individual learning styles.

Take geometry. A student may question the relevance of the Pythagorean theorem. In what ways can a teacher establish relevance? Perhaps they can apply the theorem to a construction project involving angles. Or they can use a video game to illustrate the concept. The key is to find out what is most relevant to students and build the lesson around that relevance.

What about finding relevance in history? We all know that history often repeats itself. Are there historical concepts that share similarities with current events? The events that hold the most significance for any given person are typically those events occurring in the present. Teachers can help bridge the past to the present for students by developing a scavenger hunt. Can students spot the similarities and differences between a historical event and a present-day one? Once students establish correlations for themselves and discover historical and present-day connections, they can begin to uncover the relevance of their history lesson.

Encourage Self-Acknowledgment

Students deserve to recognize when they have learned something and feel a sense of accomplishment. This acknowledgment is pivotal, as research in the field indicates that a student's belief in their ability shapes their feelings about learning and influences their approach to education. The results of structural equation modeling suggest that this belief system, when coupled with successful experiences, triggers emotions that significantly impact learning strategies, consequently influencing overall academic performance (Hayat, Shateri, & Shokrpour, 2020).

As we contemplate the role of teachers in this process, it becomes evident that fostering an environment where students can engage in self-assessment practices is paramount. Such practices not only increase students' interest and motivation but also support them in becoming more proficient in their work. This aligns with the findings of studies by Mariëtte H. van Loon and Claudia M. Roebers (2017) and Vasu and colleagues (2020), which highlight the positive effects of self-regulated learning on students' academic success.

In essence, by instilling a culture of self-assessment in the classroom, teachers can contribute significantly to students' recognition of their own learning. This recognition, coupled with a sense of accomplishment and belief in their abilities, paves the way for a more proactive and engaged approach to learning. Therefore, the teacher's role in shaping perceptions, fostering self-assessment practices, and ultimately influencing students' academic success is undeniable (Sharma et al., 2016).

Managing Individual Expectations

Perception shapes, defines, and influences the experience of our personal reality. We believe that what we perceive to be reality is accurate. With that perception, we create our own reality. A plethora of research has been completed on how teacher perceptions shape student experiences, for better or for worse. Of the most notable is research on the Pygmalion effect, also known as the self-fulfilling prophecy.

In their research, Robert Rosenthal and Lenore Jacobson (1968) demonstrated how teacher expectations influence student performance, both positively and negatively. Researchers generally agree that teacher expectancy affects student learning. Teacher achievement expectations can thus affect child development from the first school days onward, as well as affect later educational achievements and eventual outcomes (Wang, Rubie-Davies, & Meissel, 2018). When teachers have positive expectations, they influence student performance positively. Ditto for negative expectations. That reinforcing cycle is where beliefs shape expectations. Because expectations shape actions and behaviors, those actions and behaviors affect outcomes for better and for worse. Effective leaders work to ensure a healthy, positive, unbiased, and inclusive perspective of all learners.

While managing individual expectations is crucial for any learning environment, the term *student* can unwittingly hinder this process. Its passive connotation implies external control, limiting the potential for self-directed learning. Using the term *learner* is a deliberate shift that goes beyond just language. It fosters ownership and collaboration, allowing for a more dynamic and adaptable educational experience. This empowers individual exploration and unlocks the true potential within each learner.

Limitations of the Term *Students*

When a teacher perceives their classroom as a room full of *students*, ensuring the highest degree of student achievement could potentially be a challenge. The word implies compliance and an external form. Perceiving a classroom of students places the teacher in a purely authoritarian role, dictating what to read and recall, instead of a collaborative one. They assign, instruct, and supervise, leaving students in a reactive, obedient role. But what guides these instructions? District standards? Pass/fail benchmarks? Lessons buried in binders, awaiting universal application?

Effective leaders challenge this perspective. They empower teachers to own their individual approaches, fostering student-centered environments that ignite intrinsic motivation. Notably, educational researcher Cagri Tugrul Mart (2013) emphasizes motivation as "one of the leading factors in educational achievement" and highlights its link to commitment (p. 38). When teachers embrace student-centeredness, they not only transform the classroom from static to dynamic and collaborative, but also cultivate student autonomy and responsible decision making. This fosters cooperative learning, hones problem-solving and critical-thinking skills, and encourages reflection.

Effective leaders understand that in student-centered classrooms, the teacher's role doesn't vanish. Instead, their role becomes that of facilitator, guiding and supporting learners on their educational journeys. This aligns with the understanding that effective teaching involves motivating students and nurturing an environment of active engagement. Research by Peter J. Woods and Y. Copur-Gencturk (2024) reveals that teachers who employ student-centered teaching report greater gains in their own pedagogical content knowledge than those who use direct instruction. By incorporating student-centered practices, teachers empower learners as active participants in their education, creating a dynamic and collaborative environment where both teachers and learners flourish (Hamdi, 2018).

Potential of the Term *Learners*

By approaching their classrooms as rooms full of learners, teachers aren't simply teaching; they are guiding. They are preparing for a collaborative experience, not an authoritarian approach. Teachers are showing up to ensure learning, not to ensure teaching. Being a learner implies having a limitless opportunity to obtain knowledge. Meanwhile, being a student implies being taught a limited amount of knowledge. Can you see the difference?

Learners ask questions, find answers, think critically, and work together. Learners are driven by their curiosity to never stop seeking (and owning) and developing abilities. That open investigation of knowledge also enables learners to discover their strengths and social-emotional needs without the traditional educational constraints.

By being encouraged to explore possibilities, learners can meet new ideas and areas of interest, rather than simply finding an answer to a particular question or regurgitating knowledge in the form of a test. That desire will aid learners later in their careers when they can arrive at unusual solutions to ordinary problems.

Teaching and "seeing" learners, instead of just students, implies that education is no longer just a one-way path with the teacher as a lecturer and deliverer of knowledge. Teachers become facilitators who work together with learners to accomplish results. They encourage those they teach to take ownership of their learning. This approach especially makes sense when we think about the rapidly evolving pace of change today. Teachers cannot be a source of all knowledge and distribute access to information while simultaneously providing opportunities for their learners to collaborate with them.

Re-Envisioning Classroom Success

If you would like to experience thriving classrooms within your school, team effort is required. In today's dynamic and intricate world, effective communication and collaboration are vital skills for success. Research emphasizes that students need to adeptly navigate diverse teams, and collaborative learning emerges as a potent method to hone these crucial skills (Amalia, 2018). Through collaborative learning, students engage in joint tasks and projects, fostering the development of communication and problem-solving skills. The collaborative process, enriched by discussion, clarification, and evaluation of peers' opinions, is shown to enhance learners' critical-thinking abilities (Lin, 2015).

In classrooms centered on collaborative learning, teachers evolve from being the sole sources of information to becoming guides and facilitators. This shift encourages students to actively interact, collaborate, and share their unique perspectives, steering them toward common learning goals. Teachers who step back from a more didactic role create a more engaging and less stressful atmosphere. Students, taking ownership of their learning journey, experience enhanced self-development, autonomy, and ultimately, improved achievement (Amalia, 2018).

In essence, collaboration in the educational setting fosters a sense of limitless possibility and solidifies relevance to the learners' lives. By developing an appreciation for shared input, students are more adept at navigating diverse perspectives and also are more likely to welcome a multitude of viewpoints. This collaborative mindset prepares learners to seamlessly work with others and across functional areas, aligning with the expectations of the future workforce.

Imagine a scenario where, instead of the traditional method of conducting standardized tests focused on memorization at the end of each unit, a teacher adopts a more progressive approach. In this re-envisioned model, students engage in self-assessment throughout the unit using collaboratively crafted rubrics that emphasize mastery of skills and application of knowledge.

Traditionally, feedback from teachers often consists of generic comments like, "Good job" or "Needs improvement," on assignments. However, in a reimagined educational setting, teachers provide specific, actionable feedback that guides students in understanding their strengths and areas for growth. Additionally, students actively participate in peer-review sessions, offering constructive feedback and suggestions to their peers.

Consider the conventional classroom arrangement with desks neatly aligned in rows and the teacher positioned at the front for instruction. In a re-envisioned approach, the classroom transforms into a flexible space, featuring designated areas for individual work, group collaboration, and movement. Students not only have ownership of their learning environment but also actively contribute to its creation.

Which classroom is going to be more successful in ensuring learning? Which classroom is more collaborative? Substituting learners for students is an exciting opportunity for all parties. The change in perspective provides a challenge for educators because the fact is learners can learn without us.

For many leaders, shifts in thinking like moving from seeing students to seeing learners are challenging, but leaders often say they are ready for change. However, you can't just say that you want change; you must actually have a motivational desire to make it happen. Ask yourself questions that start with *what*, *when*, *where*, *how*, and *who* with respect to your desire for change. Avoid asking *why* questions because the answers to those are judgment calls that will prevent objective progress. Examples of good questions include, "When do my beliefs contradict my actions?" "Who is affected by my beliefs?" and "What would it be like to think the opposite of my beliefs?" In asking such questions, you will yield answers that reveal the true nature of your underlying beliefs. Keep asking questions until you uncover the core belief that is driving you.

Then, identify potentially damaging consequences of holding on to the belief. For example, holding on to the belief that others are incapable of succeeding prevents you from challenging and supporting them in their pursuit of achievements.

If you need to modify your belief, you must both identify your new belief and incorporate it into daily practice. That transition may not be easy. Depending on how long you have held on to your old belief, you may have an emotional attachment to it. But remember, true change requires strength and courage to shift your thinking.

Here's where the power of visualization comes in. Conditioning yourself to your new belief involves creating the reality you desire in your mind and vividly picturing the results you want to achieve. Imagine a well-behaved, respectful, orderly, and highly successful class of learners. Close your eyes and truly see them engaged, motivated, and thriving. Research has shown that visualization activates the same brain areas as actual sight (Pearson et al., 2015). This means by visualizing your desired outcome, you're essentially training your brain to believe it's possible. Additionally, processing emotions through visualization can be even more powerful than verbally processing them (Blackwell et al., 2019). So, visualize the positive emotions you'll feel—the pride, joy, and satisfaction—from guiding such a successful classroom. By consistently incorporating visualization into your practice, you'll create anticipation for these results and pave the way for concrete success.

Ensuring Learning for Independent and Dependent Learners

One school of thought worth considering claims there are two types of learners in every classroom, and educators bear the brunt of the responsibility for ensuring the success of each.

The first type consists of independent learners (Kopzhassarova, Akbayeva, Eskazinova, Belgibayeva, & Tazhikeyeva, 2016). They are the students who can function with very little direction and equally little feedback. They catch on quickly, and if they don't know the answer, they follow their curiosity and seek out resources on their own; independent learners feel encouraged and safe to do so. These learners typically interpret instruction in a way that provides them opportunities to think critically, engage in regular self-assessments, and reflect on their learning: "How am I learning? What do I need to work on next? How should I approach this new task?" Their curiosity is rewarded, and their learning is easily ensured.

The second type is composed of dependent learners. In their case, the teacher owns the entire learning process. In fact, some dependent learners don't even know whether they are learning or not. Dependent learners show up to school each day and sit passively, awaiting instruction. They require feedback to keep them progressing. They typically receive instruction based on test taking and memorization of facts.

That approach is somewhat akin to saying, "Here! Don't worry or think too much about it. Just memorize this!" While there is nothing inherently wrong with dependent learners, the goal is to enable all learners to become more independent. Conversion invites collaboration wherein the learner also takes ownership of the learning process. Helping students understand where they are in the learning process and where they are going is what enables them to grow. That progress is far more important than "getting it right." Together, the teacher and learner can achieve great things.

Instruction enabling both dependent and independent learners is prevalent in education. It's no wonder low-performing students simply give up. Instead of helping students accelerate their learning to catch up to their grade-level peers, so-called support classes often unintentionally set students further and further behind and make them increasingly dependent. Dependent learners need more of teachers' time and guidance in order to become independent learners.

On the flip side, the skills needed for independent thinking are at the forefront of learning how to be great thinkers and great leaders. Such skills teach our learners how to make sense of the world based on personal experience and observation, which encourages them to make critical, well-informed decisions in the same way. Accordingly, learners gain confidence and the ability to learn from mistakes as they build successful and productive lives.

Effective leaders need to be able to answer two fundamental questions: (1) "How do we know if students are learning?" and (2) "When they are not, what do we do about it?"

To ensure that every classroom is occupied by independent learners, effective leaders take the time to walk the campus and monitor how well teachers' beliefs align with their actions to inspire, motivate, and ensure student success. The effective leader must ensure that each teacher develops a learning environment relevant to and reflective of their students' social, cultural, and linguistic experiences. Teachers act as guides, mediators, consultants, instructors, and advocates for their students, helping to effectively connect their culture- and community-based knowledge to classroom learning experiences.

Key Points

This chapter has equipped you with the building blocks for empowering learners in your classroom to reach their full potential. We've moved beyond simply delivering content, instead empowering students to demonstrate their comprehension and own their educational journey. By making learning relevant, fostering self-awareness, and positively managing expectations, you can create an environment where every learner thrives.

Remember, shifting from *students* to *learners* isn't just semantics. It's a deliberate choice that fosters collaboration and ownership. As you step back from a purely didactic role and become a facilitator, you'll witness the magic of student-centered learning unfold. Collaborative activities will ignite intrinsic motivation, hone critical-thinking skills, and prepare learners for the dynamic future they'll face.

But not all learners are created equal. Some, the independent spirits, require minimal guidance and eagerly seek out resources. Others, the dependent learners, need more structure and feedback to blossom. The key lies in nurturing independence in all, recognizing that diverse learning styles and needs exist within your classroom walls.

This is where effective leadership shines. By ensuring classrooms are relevant and reflect students' backgrounds, you provide the foundation for success. You empower teachers to create dynamic and collaborative spaces and act as guides and mentors on this journey of discovery.

The next chapter builds on these principles. By putting these key takeaways into action, you'll be well on your way to fostering a learning environment where every student reaches their full potential. So, let's dive in and explore how to translate these insights into impactful classroom practices.

As you leave this chapter, remember the following.

- Schools are institutions of learning, not just teaching.
- To ensure learning, teachers must ensure clarity in the classroom.
- Students crave lessons that are relevant to their everyday lives.
- Teachers need to shift their perspective and see a classroom full of learners instead of a classroom full of students.
- An effective leader is an effective communicator.

Reflective Activity: Ensuring Learning

Answer the following questions to complete this reflective activity. By pondering these questions, you can gain valuable insights into your classroom practices and identify areas for improvement. Remember, empowering learners for success is an ongoing process that requires constant reflection, adaptation, and commitment.

- Do your students have opportunities to demonstrate their understanding in different ways?

- Can you identify any topics in your curriculum that students might find irrelevant? How can you make those topics more engaging and relatable to their lives and interests?

- In what ways do you currently foster an environment for students to engage in self-assessment practices?

- What are your underlying expectations for each student? Are they based on individual potential or influenced by unconscious bias?

- Can you identify independent and dependent learners in your classroom? How are you supporting each group to reach their full potential and cultivating independent learning skills in all students?

ESTABLISH QUALITY INSTRUCTION AND LEARNING

3

The most common cause of failure in leadership is produced by treating adaptive challenges as if they were technical problems.

—Ronald Heifetz

SHIFTING OUR focus from empowering learners, we now turn our attention to ensuring learning. After all, we hire teachers not only to teach, but also to ensure students are learning. This chapter delves into the crucial shift beyond simply providing learning opportunities to verifying their genuine impact.

This chapter unpacks the key components of effective learning assessment, navigating common misconceptions and confronting a critical issue: the tendency to prioritize activity over actual learning. We'll explore the power of a growth mindset and differentiate between technical challenges (fixing skills) and adaptive challenges (transforming mindsets). Finally, we'll contrast the limitations of prescriptive and descriptive feedback with the transformative potential of reflective questioning, equipping you with tools to guide people toward reflecting, solving problems, and making new connections and insights.

The Outcomes and Assessments of Ensuring Learning

Effective teachers must find ways to monitor evidence of competency and comprehension among their learners. While grades offer a snapshot, they often fall short of telling the whole story. What does a single number truly reveal about a student's understanding of complex concepts, their ability to solve problems, or their capacity for critical thinking?

Consider this: A grade is typically assigned to a project, paper, test, or participation benchmark. It can reflect effort, adherence to instructions, or performance on a specific task. But does it necessarily assess deep understanding? Does it guarantee genuine learning has taken place?

Grades hold value, serving as communication tools and motivators. They can indicate areas for improvement and track progress over time. Yet, relying on grades as the sole measure of student learning creates a narrow and potentially misleading picture. This becomes evident when classroom grades paint a rosy picture that diverges from standardized test results. This doesn't imply dishonesty or a lack of learning, but rather highlights the limitations of grades in capturing the nuances of true understanding.

Effective educators go beyond the single data point of a grade. They employ a strategic system of diverse assessment methods to paint a rich and multifaceted portrait of student learning.

- **Performance tasks:** These open-ended, real-world applications of knowledge allow students to demonstrate their ability to think critically, solve problems, and communicate effectively.
- **Student self-evaluations:** Encouraging students to reflect on their own learning journey fosters metacognition and empowers them to take ownership of their progress.
- **Observations:** Observing students during group work, discussions, and individual tasks provides valuable insights into their thought processes, collaboration skills, and understanding.

Clear rubrics align expectations with assessments, and regular, specific feedback guides students toward improvement. This ongoing loop of monitoring, assessment, and feedback forms the foundation of effective learning. By moving beyond grades and embracing these multifaceted strategies, educators unlock the true potential within their learners.

Misconceptions About Learning Assessment

Indeed, effective instructional leaders embrace and understand eight misconceptions about grades and assessments. Those misconceptions are as follows.

Assessment and Evaluation Are the Same Exact Thing

Unfortunately, many educators, particularly those at the secondary level, continue to cling tenaciously to the traditional practices, which are counterproductive to the goals of modern education (Key Differences, 2016). All too often, we evaluate student work and tell ourselves that what we have done is assessment.

Assessment involves giving timely, detailed feedback based on clearly defined learning outcomes. Simply stated, the teacher has ensured clarity of those learning outcomes, and the assessment is feedback based. Assessments are not pass/fail. Rather, they are strength and improvement based. Assessments are timely; you can't have an honest dialogue with a learner while only assessing learning outcomes from an entire quarter.

Evaluation is giving a grade to a piece of work, usually based on normative criteria. If the whole class doesn't do well, the teacher might be motivated to instill a grading curve, thus benchmarking evaluation on the student with the highest evaluation. That option is not a true assessment of learning. But assessment and evaluation can be formative (undertaken while an educational process is ongoing) or summative (undertaken at the conclusion of an educational process).

Rule for success: It is crucial to communicate to everyone whether you are conducting an assessment or an evaluation.

Data Inform Best Decisions

Data are good; information is better. Data and information are similar concepts, but they are not the same thing (Schildkamp, Karbautzki, & Vanhoof, 2014). The most noticeable difference between data and information is that information provides context through interpretation, processing, and organization. Data are raw material. This raw material needs interpretation and relies on actions performed by different actors in order to become evidence (Prøitz, Mausethagen, & Skedsmo, 2017). Data are a part, a segment, a snippet. The translation of raw data to information has a significant impact since information may affect decisions. Information represents the whole, offering a comprehensive view that enables meaningful insights and informed choices. Consider this: knowing you stand at the 80th percentile is informative, but without context (age group, test type, and so on), it offers little actionable guidance. Similarly, scores like "fourth quintile" or "RIT 280" become truly meaningful only when interpreted within a relevant framework of information. Why do leaders trust that district and state (or provincial) decisions based on data are more relevant than teachers' insights and information?

Assessments that are relevant, mutual, engaging, and instructive have proven to be useful, powerful tools for improving learning and raising achievement (Paulo, 2014). Data inform some decisions, but information is much more comprehensive.

Rule for success: To ensure the right decision, ask yourself, "How am I converting data to information to better understand the reason for the differences in results?" Also ask yourself, "How am I using the information to make good decisions when addressing challenges?"

Most Assessments Are Summative

Many teachers wrongfully assume assessments are summative, meaning the focus is on the outcome of a specific program or class (Aboulsoud, 2011; Dolin, Black, Harlen, & Tiberghien, 2017). There are three types of assessments: (1) diagnostic, (2) formative, and (3) summative (Connors, 2021). Diagnostic assessments are administered at the beginning of a unit or lesson. They check students for prior knowledge. Formative assessments are meant to guide adjustments, as they are administered during the learning process. Finally, summative assessments measure overall learning gained at the end of the unit or lesson.

We need to continually assess both student work and the quality of teaching throughout the semester. By the time we get to the end of a unit or the end of a lesson, learners should have had multiple opportunities to rethink and redo their work. Learning is the journey, not the destination. Assessing ourselves at the end of a journey with one summative assessment will not measure learning.

Remember, teachers can learn as much from their learners as those learners can learn from their teachers. (That fact will bring us to our next misconception.)

Rule for success: Establish assessment checkpoints along the way.

Assessment Is One-Way Communication

It is a common misconception that only the teacher gives feedback on the learner's work (Sah, 2013). In traditional assessment and evaluation models, the learner completes a task; then the teacher assesses the work and tells the learner how they did and what they could have done to improve.

The question is, "How do teachers assess the success of their instruction?" Is there any measuring instrument? Teachers do have a way to determine how well a lesson is going—that is, whether the pupils are motivated to improve their learning. To gain feedback on their own teaching, teachers might continually use assessments that provide them with vital information from students about their learning. These assessments might look like questioning students, having them repeat lines or words more and more accurately, asking them to think and discover the right information, interacting with students to reach a logical conclusion, assigning classwork and homework, or administering a class test (Sah, 2013).

Rule for success: Establish opportunities for students to dialogue about their learning.

Assessments Are for Grading Purposes

Traditionally, an assessment earns a grade in the classroom. That custom is the most pervasive and damaging holdover from traditional teaching. Yes, grades should reflect what has gone on between the learner and the teacher. Grades are necessary! But grades are not tally marks you collect to arrive at a final grade.

Take homework, for example. Homework reinforces a lesson and gives learners the opportunity to practice the concepts that are taught and shared in the classroom. Then, students are graded on their homework, which means that they are graded on their practice.

During a basketball team or football team practice, often the scoreboard will not display the score as it would in a real game. Practice is designed to help build the skills necessary to compete. It is a time to build each skill set that is important for a sport or any type of competitive performance. For example, a quarterback needs to break down the mechanics of a pass. He needs to know how to grip the football, how to position his final drop back–plant step, and how to lean his torso forward with his shoulders turned perpendicular to the passing target.

The purpose of practice is to figure out how to correct any mistakes. It is how you grow and get better and stronger. You get the opportunity to think about what you are doing, what you are not doing, and what you need to do differently.

Why should homework be any different? Why should we be grading learners on their practice, on their work that they do before they have mastered the material?

Assessments should be used to monitor learning—that is, to establish and understand where learners are in their long-term learning progress; to evaluate growth over time; and to provide teachers, students, parents, and school leaders with quality information to promote further learning. Shifting the focus from judging and grading to monitoring would be a significant change in assessment practice with the potential to better support successful learning (Masters, 2022).

When a learner sees a failing grade, it damages their confidence. They feel as if they're not smart, they're not good enough, and their efforts are pointless. They feel as if they are falling behind and that school is not a good investment of their time. Such an effect is not to say that a teacher can never give a student an F if that is what the student earned, but remember that assessment is not the grade.

In a sense, grading is one by-product of assessment. Teachers periodically assign each student a grade throughout the year to reflect all of the student's performance up to that point in one collective sum. It is not a simple task! But the task should be to construct a grading system that best reflects learning in a way that informs students of their learning. Students should know where their grade is coming from. They should know what is valued and should have ways to participate in the process.

Rule for success: Allow for mistakes in the learning process and provide quality and timely feedback.

Everything a Learner Does Needs a Grade

In summative situations where grades are necessary, that may be true. Yet, too often, teachers put a grade on everything, hoping to use the work formatively. Learners are graded on participation, homework completion, tests, attendance, projects, teamwork, and the list goes on. As soon as a learner sees a grade on a piece of work, they are going to think the learning is done: "I got a C? Well, then that's as good as it is going to get." That impression couldn't be further from the truth. No matter what the teacher's intention, grades imply finality. That inference contributes to a dependent-learner mentality, so be judicious about what you assign a grade to and what you do not. Note that we are more interested in student learning (Schwab, Moseley, & Dustin, 2018).

Rule for success: Value the learning by providing quality feedback rather than only a grade.

Grades and Test Scores Maximize Student Motivation and Learning

A teacher's demands, grades, and promises of additional opportunities are entirely external rewards. Decades of research, about both educational best practices and the way the human mind works, suggests that those types of motivators are dangerous. There is no evidence that they improve exam performance for those students who stand to gain the most from additional study (Grant & Green, 2012). In fact, research indicates grades have an undesirable impact on students' motivation and sustained performance (Qasserras, Asmae, Qasserras, & Anasse, 2023). Offering students a reward for learning will create reliance on the reward, even a fixation. Students will strive for the best grade but only to achieve that letter or number, not to learn the material. Then, if the reward becomes less interesting to the student or disappears entirely, the student's motivation will do the same.

Inspiring students' intrinsic motivation to learn isn't just about keeping them interested; it's about unlocking their natural love of learning. Research guided by self-determination theory (Ryan & Deci, 2017) shows that intrinsically motivated students put in more effort and tackle tougher challenges, and also learn, retain, and understand information more deeply. When fueled by curiosity and enjoyment, rather than external rewards, students become active participants in their own education, taking ownership of their learning journey. There's a shift from "have to" to "get to," fostering a lifelong love of knowledge and exploration.

Rule for success: Frame learning as the reward by asking, "What were you excited to learn about today?"

An Assignment Turned in Late Should Not Count for Full Credit

Decisions always have consequences, but consider this: If the focus of school is truly on learning and ensuring learning, does it matter if a learner turns in an assignment a few days late? Yes, life is full of deadlines, and turning in your rent or your work project late will come with consequences, but teachers are in the business of ensuring learning, right? If the teacher says everyone is expected to learn material by Monday, and a learner demonstrates that learning by Wednesday instead, should they be penalized because they have not learned the material in the time the teacher has dictated?

There is nothing wrong with having a consequence for late work, but the assignment of grades should always reflect the learner's learning. If a learner hands in work worthy of an A one day late, is the worth of that work any different (say, a B)? When teachers rethink and reform their views on what assessments are all about, they can see how assessments properly done can ensure learning and how grading haphazardly impedes learning. They should remember that short and single assessment instruments alone cannot capture the full complexity of a competency (Rahman & Majumder, 2015).

Rule for success: Frame consequences as a necessary step toward improvement and an important part of the journey.

A Common Issue: Focusing on Action Over Learning

Too often, teachers grade students on what they do, not what they learn. This is like measuring how well students can borrow information and return it. We don't want our learners to borrow information. We want our learners to buy information. Teachers want buy-in. If you have any doubts, ask any one of your students what they learned in class on a given day. I bet they will tell you what they did, not what they learned. For example, let's say you ask your student, Sasha, what she learned during yesterday's geography class.

"We went over the map of Europe and talked about the different countries that make up the European Union," Sasha replies. Sasha is correct. That is exactly what the class did. But what did Sasha learn? Education is so focused on teaching that learning feels secondary. But learning isn't an activity. Learning is the result of an activity.

Teachers need to ask the question, "What type of experience do I need to create to allow my learners to demonstrate what they're absorbing?" Effective educators need to know what stages it will take to get learners to that learning experience and to close learning gaps. They cannot understand at what stage the learner is without understanding the person who is learning. People all have different styles of learning. If we don't understand that, we can't assess learning. That knowledge is hard to obtain with a huge class, but without it, so many educators and educational institutions are struggling.

We have potentially derailed students from developing critical skills because we have diminished creative expression and innovative thinking. Research suggests this approach is detrimental, as these constraints can stifle spontaneous encounters and idea sharing, which are key ingredients for sparking creative insights (Acar,

Tarakci, & van Knippenberg, 2019). Furthermore, excessive constraints on innovative and expressive thinking can dampen intrinsic motivation, creative self-efficacy, and prosocial motivation, hindering deeper learning (Liu, Jiang, Shalley, Keem, & Zhou, 2016). Additionally, risk taking and experimentation, crucial for innovation, are often discouraged by rigid constraints (Mehta & Zhu, 2016). This dependence on prescribed methods fosters a culture where students become reliant on "doing things our way" rather than developing their own critical-thinking and problem-solving abilities.

We make students dependent on how we want them to do things. Then, thinking our students have "done" something, we assume they have learned it. That assumption is why there is such a discrepancy between what a teacher says a student has learned and the true amount of learning the student shows at the end of the year. Effective leaders who empower teachers to use assessments in more productive ways can bridge this gap. By fostering creativity and innovation through open-ended explorations and allowing for experimentation, assessments become more fruitful, more meaningful, and less focused on mere grading.

Avoid shortcuts whenever possible. When it comes to ensuring learning, there are some things that should be nonnegotiable but have become negotiable because of time, other foci, other priorities, and other distractions. Examples of these shortcuts could include not ensuring lessons or assessments are on grade level, misaligning the unit being taught or assessed in relation to the expected standard, and neglecting to have students demonstrate proficiency in the manner in which they will be assessed at the state or provincial level. For schools to be truly educational institutions of learning, everything we do should focus on the impact of learning.

Rule for success: Ask yourself, "How did I have students demonstrate their learning in order to prove their mastery?"

A Tale of Two Mindsets

My hope is that, by now, this chapter has slightly shifted your perception. This section will address another key component that will aid you in your quest to ensure learning and quality instruction: mindset.

In her book titled *Mindset*, Stanford University psychologist Carol S. Dweck (2016) outlines how people's success in school, work, sports, the arts, and almost every area of human achievement can be dramatically influenced by how they perceive their talents and abilities. In education, we endeavor to work with individuals in such a way that we both exemplify and support improvement in mindset. To do this effectively, we must understand two mindset types we encounter.

Fixed Mindset

Some people have a fixed mindset. Individuals in this category are less likely to embrace change; they feel that whatever skills they have are all they will have. They are less likely to be flexible as well, always clinging to the status quo. A fixed mindset is a performance-focused mindset. Such individuals may even ask, "How will this situation make me look?" Challenges are roadblocks to them, and they take feedback personally. Individuals with a fixed mindset hate making mistakes because they think that making a mistake is a poor reflection on them.

Teachers who have a fixed mindset rarely take risks. They play it safe in and out of the classroom. They may even have a passive-aggressive attitude with an air of "it is what it is." They're defeated before they put their lunch in the break room fridge.

Students with a fixed mindset feel like they're never going to learn. They give up before they enter your classroom. They allow self-fulfilling prophecies to dictate their lives and future ambitions. "Well, I'm not good at math," one might say, and they will believe that statement to their core. They will believe it so much that they will do anything to make it true, even without meaning to do so. It is almost as if they put up blockers preventing learning from happening, thanks to their fixed mindset.

Growth Mindset

We must strive for everyone to develop and embrace a growth mindset. Those with a growth mindset seize opportunities and recognize the transformational power of change. They are the individuals who feel that skills and intelligence can grow and develop over time. A growth mindset is always focused on process and improvement; challenges are learning opportunities. Individuals who possess a growth mindset love feedback and use it for the greater good. When such individuals look in a mirror, they see everyone standing behind them before they notice their own reflection.

Teachers in this category are flexible and understand they may learn from their learners. A growth mindset in a teacher makes them willing to try new things, such as making a rap of the U.S. Constitution or using references to the video game *Fortnite* in mathematics class. These are the teachers who take feedback to heart, but not on the defensive. They use that feedback to improve, to grow, to learn, and to be even better and more effective.

What does a growth mindset look like in students? Well, students who have a growth mindset aren't afraid to fail. They will ask questions and try different ways of learning and growing. Such students trust their instructor and feel safe to ask questions related to their individual learning. There are no self-fulfilling prophecies holding them back.

Based on the two descriptions alone, it is clear which mindset is more effective, desirable, and powerful for educational leaders and teachers alike. Yet, adopting such a mindset comes with challenges.

Two Types of Challenges

Educational leaders and teachers face two different types of challenges every day: (1) technical challenges and (2) adaptive challenges.

Technical Challenges

In education, what type of mindset are we cultivating? When teachers meet, they talk about data, alignment of the curriculum, pacing of lessons, and so on. Simply put, teachers and leaders spend a lot of time talking and thinking about technical challenges. Technical challenges are problems that are easy to identify. They are easy to solve with existing resources. Technical challenges in education are related to data, strategies, interventions, pacing, activities, and so on. They typically can be solved swiftly by an expert or authority.

Why is this focus on technical challenges problematic? Well, what you feed grows, what you focus on becomes a priority, and what you monitor becomes a cultural norm. So, if all you focus on are technical solutions to seemingly adaptive challenges, your adaptive challenges will not be addressed and will continue to grow, as will the mindset that nearly all problems in education are technical. That idea couldn't be further from the truth.

Commonly, during teacher development meetings, an educational leader will stand up in front and say, "We're going to discuss how to ensure learning and unleash the potential of our students today." Then the leader proceeds to talk about data, pacing, and interventions. One teacher brings up lesson-planning hacks. Another teacher tells a story involving strategies she uses for behavior management. Although alignment and best practice in each of those areas are vital, they are often discussed in isolation of their impact on student learning. What about the relationships? What about the empowerment of students? What about the creation of a culture of learning? What about teacher-student empathy? Where do those aspects come up in the meeting? They don't. But they should because they're adaptive challenges. They are part of what is called the *art of teaching*.

What we're struggling with most in education is not data, alignment, or pacing. It is that students are not inspired to learn. Across the United States, we are lacking a culture where students are excited about learning. We're struggling with teachers' and students' belief that they can achieve greatness.

We're struggling with a lack of relationships between students and their classrooms. No data plan or activity assessment is going to solve that problem. We can spend all day on technical aspects, but if students aren't inspired and they have no motivation to learn, we will not ensure learning. Once we cultivate an awareness of adaptive challenges, learning can take place.

Adaptive Challenges

Adaptive challenges are fluid and change with circumstances; they are unpredictable, volatile, and complex. They are hard to identify, and therefore easy to deny. And if identified, these types of challenges are difficult to solve because their solutions usually require people to learn new ways of doing things; change their attitudes, values, and norms; and adopt an experimental mindset. Adaptive challenges deal with relationships, emotional intelligence, empathy, culture, inspiration, and self-awareness. Most importantly, adaptive challenges have to be solved by the people with the problem. You can't call in a quick-fix expert to solve an adaptive challenge. In fact, adaptive challenges require constant experimentation.

This is where the growth mindset is of additional value, beyond just ensuring learning. It can help you tackle both technical and adaptive problems head-on.

When you're dealing with people, emotions, relationships, cultures, expectations, and personalities, you are going to encounter adaptive challenges. Is a school made up of these things? Absolutely. But for years, traditionally, we have tried to implement technical solutions to adaptive challenges in everything we do in education. Why is that the case?

Well, leaders are always on a timeline. Technical problems are easy to identify. Sometimes, we feel we need to check the boxes. An expert can surely solve the problems, right? Although such excuses are valid, they will prevent all the key players in educational institutions from ensuring learning in the long run. Treating adaptive problems like technical ones is like putting a small bandage on a gaping wound that requires fifty stitches. It simply is not sustainable.

Technical and Adaptive Challenges in Schools

In classrooms, we've been laser focused on technical challenges, easily solvable problems like data analysis and lesson pacing. But these quick fixes neglect the deeper issues that truly hinder learning: adaptive challenges. These are the messy, complex problems like student motivation, teacher-student relationships, and development of a culture of learning. They require not just technical solutions, but a complete cultural shift.

Think about it: no amount of data analysis can fix a student's lack of motivation, and prepackaged interventions rarely address the unique dynamics of each classroom. Adaptive challenges demand a different approach: experimentation, collaboration, and a growth mindset. Educators need opportunities to reflect, share, and learn from each other, constantly adapting their methods to the ever-evolving needs of their students.

So, how do we shift the tide? Start by reframing the conversation. Move beyond technical jargon and delve into the real challenges: student engagement, social-emotional learning, and the formation of positive relationships. Empower educators to experiment, celebrate their efforts, and learn from each other's successes and failures. Remember, a school is a tapestry woven from relationships, emotions, and shared experiences. Let's focus on these threads and watch as the true magic of learning unfolds.

Feedback

Feedback is one of the most powerful influences on learning and achievement—if you get it right. It is no secret that feedback should be actionable, timely, and related to agreed-on learning outcomes.

Too often, feedback provided supports the old notion that "the only good teacher is a busy teacher." That premise can't be correct. Simply being busy with feedback isn't enough. Effective feedback hinges on facilitating a dialogue about learning itself: Does the feedback clarify misconceptions, reinforce understanding, and guide the next steps? Only by asking these crucial questions of "how" and "why" can teachers ensure their feedback truly empowers students—and avoid perpetuating the tired adage that equates busyness with effectiveness. This shift in focus allows teachers to move beyond "doing" feedback to cultivating a learning culture where both students and educators actively engage in understanding the *why* and *how* of their progress.

The popular walkthrough model, where the administrator unobtrusively visits the classroom for two to fifteen minutes and then provides written or oral feedback on look-fors, is an inefficient feedback method. It does little to ensure a growth-minded culture to support teacher development and ensure student learning. Such advice doesn't provide true attention and time, which administrators must take to engage with teachers regarding the feedback in a purposeful manner.

Although it might feel counterintuitive to administrators, the first thing they should say during an in-person debriefing session is nothing. You should give your full attention to the teacher as you listen. Then, instead of advice, the first words out of your mouth should be a question to which you do not know the answer. Only interrupt in order to keep the discussion focused on student learning—for example, "When did deep learning occur? What evidence leads you to that conclusion?"

Unfortunately, most feedback provided to teachers is relegated to a *one-way written analysis*, usually prescriptive or descriptive in nature. That method lacks follow-up or a reflective question that probes the teacher to think about evidence of student learning. Prescriptive feedback provides specific directions on what to do differently. Think of prescriptive feedback as a road map to improvement. It offers clear directions and concrete steps to help you reach your desired outcome. Whether it's a teacher suggesting problem-solving strategies or a coach advising on technique, prescriptive feedback is especially valuable when others need guidance to overcome challenges or learn new skills. However, relying solely on this type of feedback can hinder their ability to think critically and independently. Imagine always having someone tell you exactly what to do—you might never develop your own problem-solving muscles.

Descriptive feedback takes a different approach. It acts like a mirror, reflecting your performance in detail, highlighting both strengths and areas for improvement. Instead of telling you what to do, it paints a picture of what worked and what didn't. For example, an administrator might analyze a teacher's instructional delivery, praising successful strategies while pinpointing areas needing refinement. This feedback encourages self-assessment and reflection, helping the teacher understand their strengths and weaknesses on a deeper level. But remember, the mirror doesn't offer solutions. While you gain valuable insights, translating them into action might require additional support.

Neither prescriptive nor descriptive feedback is inherently better. The most effective approach often lies in the middle ground. By strategically combining both, you gain the benefits of both worlds: clear guidance when needed and the self-awareness to learn and grow independently. This balanced approach equips others with the skills to reflect critically, solve problems effectively, and continue on their learning journey with confidence.

Curious as to the impact of feedback from administrators to their teachers, I analyzed feedback across multiple districts in various locations, including more than one hundred administrators. I gathered local data from four urban school districts with student populations ranging from 8,564 to 63,451 students. The schools' economically disadvantaged populations ranged from 43.7 percent to 89.2 percent of their total populations. The average professional experience of the schools' principals ranged from 3.4 years to 6.6 years. In each district, administrators are expected to conduct walkthroughs in all their teachers' classrooms and provide feedback. I collected the feedback and completed a comprehensive analysis, sorting the feedback into the four categories featured in figure 3.1: (1) technical teaching, (2) technical learning, (3) adaptive teaching, and (4) adaptive learning.

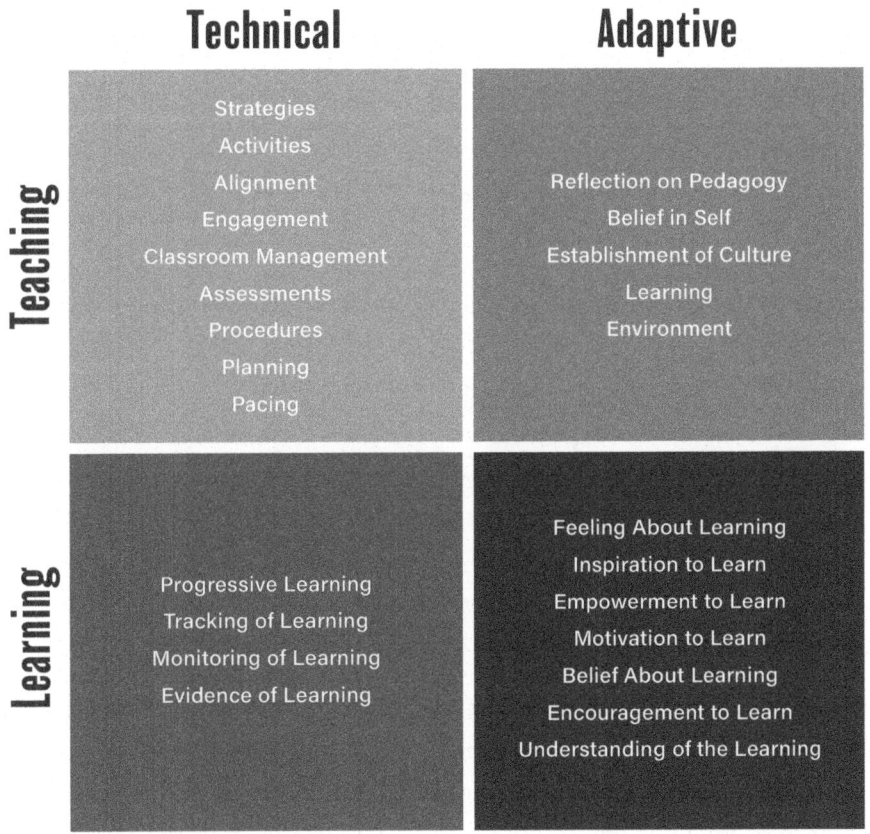

FIGURE 3.1: Feedback quadrants.

Technical Teaching

Technical teaching feedback is categorized as anything related to teaching strategies, activities, curriculum alignment, classroom management, procedures, planning, and lesson pacing. Those elements are the areas that hinder a teacher's ability to provide quality, efficient, aligned instruction. The absence or ineffectiveness of such practices continually impedes student progress; however, such feedback is focused on technical aspects of teacher actions and outcomes and offers no reflective opportunities for student learning. See figure 3.2 for samples of technical teaching feedback.

Example of Feedback	Feedback Quadrant	Rationale
How will the goals for learning be communicated to students?	Technical teaching	The focus of this reflective question is on goals and how they will be communicated to students. Goals are technical, and the action of communicating the goals to students is a teacher action. Although the word *learning* appears in this question, there is no actual focus on the teacher providing evidence of student learning or even reflecting on student learning.
How do you use differentiated instructional methods within your lesson?	Technical teaching	The focus of this reflective question is on how the teacher uses differentiated instructional methods. Each of these is a technical approach to the lesson. In addition, the focus is on the teacher's action, void of any reflection on evidence of student learning.

FIGURE 3.2: Technical teaching feedback.

Technical Learning

This type of feedback is focused on technical aspects of the learning process such as progressive learning (showing learning over time), tracking of learning (evaluating learning along the way), monitoring of learning (setting benchmarks), and evidence of learning (gaining clear demonstrations of student learning). This feedback concentrates on both teacher actions and student outcomes. Learning is the focus as the result of teacher actions, which means that the learning aspects are data driven and can be addressed quickly with clearly identifiable solutions. See figure 3.3 for samples of technical learning feedback.

Example of Feedback	Feedback Quadrant	Rationale
How are students expected to communicate what they have learned?	Technical learning	The focus of this reflective question is on how students will communicate. This strategy or activity is technical. However, *what* they are expected to communicate is focused on evidence of their learning.
What strategies do you use to gather input from students during instruction? What evidence can you share that the strategies ensure all students are learning at the level of the standard?	Technical learning	The focus of these reflective questions is on strategies. However, the teacher is asked to reflect on and produce evidence of the strategies' impact on student learning.

FIGURE 3.3: Technical learning feedback.

On your own, practice turning a technical teaching reflective question into a technical learning reflective question using figure 3.4 and the corresponding reflection box.

Example of Feedback	Feedback Quadrant	Rationale
What are some strategies you use to provoke and guide discussions with students?	Technical teaching	This reflective question is focused on strategies and teacher actions.
How would you turn the preceding question into a technical learning reflective question?		

FIGURE 3.4: Sample technical teaching feedback.

*Visit **go.SolutionTree.com/leadership** for a free reproducible version of this figure.*

Adaptive Teaching

On the other end of the spectrum, there is feedback that falls into the adaptive teaching quadrant. This quadrant is reserved for feedback that focuses on the adaptive nature of pedagogy (the method or practice of teaching), yet is still teacher centered. Adaptive aspects such as belief in self, establishment of culture, learning environment, and even engagement in reflection of best practice are not easy to identify or fix. However, feedback that falls into this quadrant is absent of reflection or discussion of the eventual or immediate impact that these adaptive aspects have on student learning. The challenges that arise in each area of feedback are often ambiguous and subject to change. See figure 3.5 for samples of adaptive teaching feedback.

Example of Feedback	Feedback Quadrant	Rationale
How do you keep your students motivated when they have repetitive tasks?	Adaptive teaching	The focus of this reflective question is on teacher activity. However, asking the teacher to reflect on their impact on student motivation is adaptive by nature. This question does not focus on evidence of student learning.
Think about challenges that occur when preparing the learning environment for students; how do you address obstacles?	Adaptive teaching	The focus of this reflective question is on challenges and obstacles, both of which are adaptive. Even though students are mentioned, the focus is on the teacher actions.

FIGURE 3.5: Adaptive teaching feedback.

Adaptive Learning

The fourth quadrant is adaptive learning. Much like the elements of adaptive teaching, these elements of feedback are related to people, not processes. They involve adaptive aspects such as emotion, relationship building, and complex human concepts. This quadrant includes a focus on student learning to determine how students felt about learning, whether students were inspired and motivated to learn, and what their beliefs about learning were. See figure 3.6 (page 55) for samples of adaptive learning feedback.

Example of Feedback	Feedback Quadrant	Rationale
How are students encouraged to establish a culture of positive persistence, and what evidence will you be able to share that it has a positive impact on student achievement?	Adaptive learning	The focus of this reflective question is on student culture and persistence, which are adaptive aspects. This question requires the teacher to reflect on evidence of student learning.
How does knowledge of your students help you ensure high levels of learning, social and emotional development, and achievement for all your students? What evidence supports your statement?	Adaptive learning	The focus of this reflective question is on an adaptive aspect of knowing and understanding the students. This question is followed up by a reflection on evidence of this knowledge's impact on learning.

FIGURE 3.6: Adaptive learning feedback.

Feedback in Action

After I reviewed hundreds of feedback evaluations based on these walkthroughs and categorized the feedback into one of these four types, I made a startling discovery. Nearly all the feedback was focused on teaching, both technical and adaptive, but mostly technical. It turned out that over 50 percent of all feedback for teachers was about technical teaching, while only 2 percent was about adaptive learning. Moreover, 12 percent of the time, teachers received no feedback at all. By overemphasizing technical teaching feedback, too few were talking about the adaptive aspects of learning. Schools are institutions of learning, and our goal as leaders is to ensure learning, but that wasn't happening here. How can we ensure learning when the majority of feedback is focused on teaching? We can't, because without proper and timely feedback about learning, teachers can't ensure learning. Yet, administrators have no problem with providing abundant feedback on teaching.

Why? Well, it is easier to tell teachers to plan faster, collaborate harder, and run their lessons more efficiently. However, it is possible to have the greatest lesson plan, complete alignment, and unparalleled pacing and for students to still not learn.

Teachers need to be empowered to meet with their administrators and request feedback on learning. Leaders need to realize that while technical feedback is easy, it is not always the most beneficial challenge to tackle when you want to ensure learning throughout your institution. Remember, what you spend time on grows. So, if administrators are spending all their time providing feedback on technical issues . . . well, technical issues are going to grow.

Feedback should not tell teachers what to do. Feedback should guide teachers to come up with solutions and help them in the thinking process. After all, adaptive challenges are the hardest to pinpoint and the easiest to deny, yet the people involved in the challenges are tasked with finding solutions.

A building full of people who process feedback well will always outperform a building full of people who have to have the answers, just like a classroom full of learners will always outperform a classroom of students.

Key Points

This chapter emphasized the need for administrators to prioritize feedback on learning over technical issues, and thereby empower teachers to address adaptive challenges and foster a culture of continuous improvement. Ultimately, effective feedback should not dictate solutions but rather guide teachers in their reflective journey toward finding solutions to complex educational challenges, thus ensuring a more impactful and student-centered learning environment.

In the next chapter, you will be introduced to the leadership cycle, a powerful framework that empowers you to turn your knowledge into action and achieve your educational goals. Think of this chapter as laying the groundwork for a magnificent building. You've gathered the finest materials (quality instruction), chosen the right tools (assessments and feedback), and even identified potential obstacles (challenges). But to truly see your vision come to life, you need a structured blueprint: the leadership cycle. It's not just about knowing what to do; it's about knowing how to do it effectively and sustainably.

As you leave this chapter, remember the following.

- Assessment and evaluation are not the same. Assessment involves giving timely, detailed feedback based on clearly defined learning outcomes. Evaluation is giving a grade to a piece of work, usually based on normative criteria but too often compared to the work of other students.

- There are two types of mindsets: (1) fixed and (2) growth. The growth mindset is where we should strive to be. It embraces flexibility and change.
- There are two types of challenges: (1) technical and (2) adaptive. Technical challenges have quick, obvious solutions and can be solved by an expert or authority. Adaptive challenges have ambiguous, ever-changing, complex solutions and must be solved by the people who have the challenge.
- In education, most administrators give feedback on technical teaching and adaptive teaching, while failing to provide quality constructive feedback on learning. For schools to ensure learning, teachers need to receive feedback and guidance to ensure learning. Less focus needs to be put on the teacher, and more focus needs to illuminate learning.
- Feedback should always conclude by providing teachers an opportunity to reflect on evidence of student learning.

Reflective Activity: Adaptive Teaching

Review the following examples of how to turn adaptive teaching reflective questions into adaptive learning reflective questions. Complete this activity by filling out example 3.

Example 1

Example of Feedback	Feedback Quadrant	Rationale
How do you keep your students motivated when they have repetitive tasks?	Adaptive teaching	The focus of this reflective question is on teacher activity. However, asking the teacher to reflect on their impact on student motivation is adaptive by nature. This question does not focus on evidence of student learning.
Consideration for Improvement		
How are you motivating students to stay engaged, and what impact is such motivation having on their learning? What evidence supports this?	Adaptive learning	The focus of this reflective question is on evidence of student learning while still requiring the teacher to reflect on their ability to motivate students.

Example 2

Example of Feedback	Feedback Quadrant	Rationale
Think about challenges that occur when preparing the learning environment for students; how do you address obstacles?	Adaptive teaching	The focus of this reflective question is on challenges and obstacles, both of which are adaptive. Even though students are mentioned, the focus is on the teacher actions.

Example of Feedback	Feedback Quadrant	Rationale
Consideration for Improvement		
How did the learning environment engage, challenge, and encourage student learning? What evidence of student learning supports this?	Adaptive learning	The focus of this reflective question is on adaptive aspects of the learning environment that affect student learning. Asking for evidence of impact keeps the reflection grounded in student achievement.

Example 3

Example of Feedback	Feedback Quadrant	Rationale
In what ways are students expected to take initiative for their own learning? What role do you play in this?	Adaptive teaching	The focus of this reflective question is on the teacher's role of communicating expectations for students taking initiative for their own learning. The question does not focus on evidence of student learning.
How would you turn the preceding question into an adaptive learning reflective question?		

Reflective Activity: Where Is Your Focus?

Reflect on which of the following ideas, organized by teaching and learning, you hold true to.

Focused on Teaching	Focused on Learning
Respect is earned.	Respect is given, regardless of how it is received.
Student work must be submitted on time in order to obtain full credit.	Student demonstration of mastery should be awarded full credit regardless of how long it takes.
It is my responsibility to provide the information. It is students' responsibility to learn it.	It is my responsibility to ensure learning.
My students need to understand me.	I need to understand my students.
Start with the *what*.	Start with the *why*.
I rarely, if ever, engage in discussion pertaining to evidence of student learning.	I always engage in discussion pertaining to evidence of student learning.
Topics, lessons, and discussions should be teacher driven.	Topics, lessons, and discussions should be student driven.
Assessments should be used to monitor learning.	Assessments should be used to promote and diagnose learning.
I answer questions and offer advice.	I probe reflective thinking in others.
I establish a culture of competitiveness.	I establish a culture of collaboration and support.
I emphasize giving correct answers.	I emphasize generating better questions and learning from mistakes.

LEARN THE LEADERSHIP CYCLE

A system is never the sum of its parts; it's the product of their interaction.

—Russell Ackoff

FOR YEARS, I observed principals who had remarkable intelligence, determination, and commitment to improvement. However, they often lacked a structured framework for strategic thinking—a process that was intentional, comprehensive, and systematic. Busy with daily tasks, they found it challenging to step back and consider the bigger picture of how their work impacted the entire organization, from planning to execution to measurable impact.

Recognizing the imperative for a more methodical approach, I sought to integrate the principles of decision theory into my leadership development program. Decision theory describes the steps involved in making any decision, including recognizing that a decision must be made, understanding the goals that one hopes to attain, making a list of options, determining the consequences—both positive and negative—of each option, determining the desirability of each consequence, evaluating the likelihood of each consequence, and integrating all the information.

Inspired by this need and armed with decision theory principles, I developed the leadership cycle (see figure 4.1, page 62). Training principals on this strategic thought

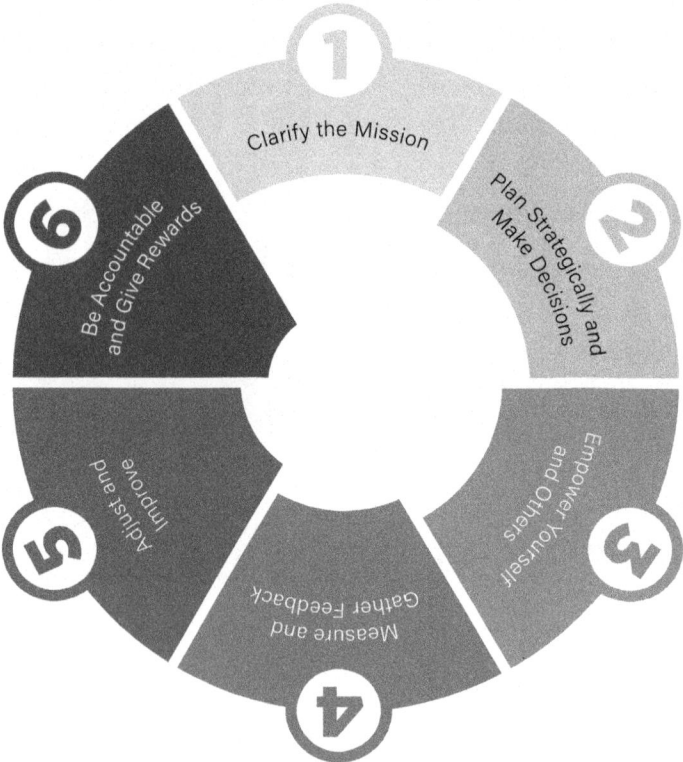

FIGURE 4.1: The leadership cycle.

process saw immediate results. Both the quality of each initiative and the success rate improved, as measured by key performance indicators. This demonstrated the power of intentional and systematic thinking in driving impactful leadership.

To be a good leader, you need to follow certain steps that fit together like pieces of a puzzle. If you don't follow these steps, it can throw things into disarray; deviating from this systematic path carries repercussions.

Before we learn about these steps, let's talk about how someone becomes a leader. Becoming a leader is a transformative journey, one that requires a delicate balance between past accomplishments and continuous growth. For example, if someone was really good at teaching social studies, they might leverage their experience as a proficient social studies teacher to uplift the social studies department as an assistant principal and ultimately enhance student achievement. But being a leader isn't just about what you've done before—it's about always learning and changing.

Now, imagine this assistant principal becoming a principal and gaining the realization that leadership is not about having all the answers, but about knowing where to find them and having the humility to learn. Before, they were comfortable with what they knew, but now they need to learn new ways of doing things. In other words, they need to break out of a cozy shell and face new challenges.

As the principal, they find out that using research-based ideas is more important than they previously thought because they relied on their talent and innate ability to perform well. This means they have to learn about strategies that are proven to work. They have to admit that they don't know everything, and they have to be open to learning from others. Using research-based ideas isn't just about replicating what has worked before; it is about adapting and evolving, ensuring that every decision is grounded in evidence and tailored to the unique dynamics of the school. Equally vital is the journey to empower the instructional leaders, amplifying the principal's influence and fostering a culture where learning thrives organically.

Becoming a better leader isn't instant for this principal. It takes time and learning from mistakes. The principal learns that being a leader means always wanting to learn and grow, and also helping others do the same. In the end, leadership is about not just what you know, but how you keep learning and making things better for everyone in the school.

In this chapter, you will learn all six steps of the leadership cycle, how to apply them to your work as a leader, and methods to use research and data effectively. This chapter will finish with a reflective exercise so you can gauge just how much of your work already encompasses components of the cycle.

Processing as Part of Leadership

Principals and other educational leaders are entrusted with a myriad of responsibilities, and the ability to make timely and effective decisions is paramount. However, concerningly, most individuals never formally learn how to be proficient decision makers (Keeney, 2020). Furthermore, research indicates that many people are unaware of the extent to which their decision making is influenced by biases (Scopelliti, Morewedge, McCormick, Min, Lebrecht, & Kassam, 2015) and deviates from principles of decision quality (Spetzler, Winter, & Meyer, 2016). This lack of formal training, coupled with the inefficiency of relying solely on experience, underscores a crucial gap in our educational systems.

The consequences of poor decision making by principals resonate throughout the entire organization. Inefficiencies at the top cascade downstream, affecting assistant principals, teachers, and ultimately, students. This perpetuates the cycle that creates the research-practice gap (described in chapter 1, page 9), where leaders may default to familiar practices rather than embracing more effective strategies.

Today's educational leaders face the challenge of thinking in the same patterns they always have, often overlooking evidence-based best practices. Leaning on what is comfortable leads them to rely on what has worked in the past, even if those methods are outdated or suboptimal. This reactive approach, driven by a sense of urgency and environmental pressures, limits their ability to engage in strategic decision-making processes.

Research finds that more careful decision making usually increases the odds of achieving the desired decision outcomes (Spetzler et al., 2016). Moreover, results from studies of individuals who utilize effective decision-making frameworks substantiate the assumption that decision-making training is of practical relevance. Decision-making training increases participants' knowledge about effective decision making, self- and peer-reported proactive decision-making behavior, and general satisfaction with their decision making (Siebert, Kunz, & Rolf, 2021). This highlights the importance of equipping educational leaders with the necessary tools and skills to make informed decisions that positively impact their schools and communities.

To bridge the research-practice gap and cultivate conscious, analytic decision-making skills, leaders at all levels—whether novice or veteran—must aspire for greater heights. They must strive to break free from the constraints of past experiences and embrace a sky-bound mindset. This entails seeking out opportunities for professional development, staying abreast of the latest research findings, and fostering a culture of continuous learning within their organizations. By doing so, educational leaders can empower themselves and others to make informed decisions that drive positive outcomes for their schools and communities.

Learning the Leadership Cycle

The aeronautical decision-making thought process is a strategic process with concrete steps, each step informing the next. Today, it is widely practiced and contributes to aeronautical safety. Research conducted on aeronautical decision making proved that pilot behavior not only is learned but also can be developed over time through structured training and strategic thought processes (Adams & Ericsson, 1992). When the aeronautical decision-making thought process was implemented and studied, a 48.2 percent reduction in accidents from human performance errors occurred in the United States. A 72.3 percent reduction in accidents from weather-related decisions also occurred.

Effective principals may not be piloting aircrafts, but they are certainly piloting their schools. The educational training principles from aeronautical decision making that we as educators can adopt are found in the leadership cycle. This six-step process of thinking and implementation is similar to the process pilots now rely on.

Like any cycle, the steps must be completed in order so that positive results and alignment among teachers and faculty are achieved. Go out of order, and you will face negative consequences. The leadership cycle is incredibly simple. Yes, it takes time, but it is worth the investment. By engaging in each step, leaders will make strategic and conscious decisions every single time. The following six chapters (chapters 5–10) elaborate on the six steps. But to get started, here is a brief introduction to what we'll be covering.

1. Clarify the Mission

The first step in the leadership cycle is to clarify the mission. When I say *clarify*, I do not mean *tell*, *share*, or *give*. I do not mean send an email or drop off a memo. There is a big difference between clarifying and sharing. To clarify means to ensure understanding. It means you have taken time to garner that understanding and ensure that the person to whom you have delivered the message has comprehended what you are trying to communicate. High clarity leads to high comprehension and achievement (Cakir, 2015).

For example, a principal looking to clarify the initiation of a new intervention program for the campus convenes a staff meeting dedicated to introducing the idea of the program. During the meeting, the principal clearly presents the program's mission, objectives, and rationale, while also providing opportunities for staff members to ask questions and express concerns. Engaging in open discussion and soliciting feedback help gauge staff members' comprehension and address any areas of confusion. The principal follows up with a summary communication to ensure that all staff members have a clear understanding of the program's mission and goals, fostering a shared commitment to its success. This emphasis on clarity not only ensures comprehension but also enhances the likelihood of achieving the intended outcomes of the initiative.

This step lays the foundation for everything else. A clear mission provides direction, purpose, and motivation for both the leader and the team. It also helps attract and retain talent who share the same vision.

2. Plan Strategically and Make Decisions

Once the mission is clear, it's time to develop a road map for achieving it. This involves setting goals, analyzing options, and making informed choices. This step translates the *why* into actionable *how*s.

People often ask, "What's the difference between planning and strategic planning?" The key lies in the depth and intentionality of the decision-making process. Strategic planning goes beyond a high-level overview and delves into conscious, analytic thinking. It's detailed, calculated, and clearly defined, drawing on robust frameworks that enable managers to prioritize complex issues and accelerate decision making (Dlamini, Mazenda, Masiya, & Nhede, 2020).

Think of it this way: planning might be like sketching a rough outline of your destination, while strategic planning is meticulously crafting a road map with detours, milestones, and potential roadblocks identified. This systematic approach ensures you're not just winging it but making informed choices based on available information and potential outcomes (Sahay, 2019; Zhu, Wolfson, Dalal, & Mathieu, 2021).

While both planning and strategic planning are crucial, the latter empowers you to navigate uncertainty with greater vigilance and organization (Zhu et al., 2021). This translates to more effective and sustainable results, ultimately leading you to your desired destination with greater confidence and efficiency.

A principal strategically planning the implementation of a new intervention program works with department leaders to map out challenges, define goals, analyze resources, and research options. Together, they consider evidence, cost, impact, and stakeholder feedback. They outline steps, timelines, and evaluation methods.

3. Empower Yourself and Others

The third step in the leadership cycle is to empower yourself and others. Now that you have a clear direction and plan, it's time to equip the team with the tools, resources, authority, and support they need to execute the plan, make decisions, and take action. This involves delegating tasks, providing training, and fostering a culture of ownership and accountability. As John C. Maxwell states, "Leaders become great not because of their power, but because of their ability to empower others" (Maxwell Leadership, 2018). This principle goes beyond simply giving someone a task. True empowerment rests on a foundation of self-empowerment, which research has shown is linked to stronger job performance, increased satisfaction, and deeper commitment within organizations (Siebert et al., 2011).

But what does self-empowerment truly mean? It's not just about thinking positively; it's about cultivating skills and knowledge that allow you to influence outcomes and produce tangible results. This involves understanding your strengths and weaknesses, as well as the situations you navigate. With this self-awareness, you can proactively take steps for your own growth and, ultimately, empower others to do the same.

If you're constantly playing catch-up and reacting to your environment, it's difficult to empower others. By actively seeking information, growing your skill set, and understanding yourself, you will become the grounded leader who can lift others up and guide them toward achieving their full potential.

The principal in the preceding intervention program scenario reads books, attends workshops, and seeks out mentors to continuously expand their knowledge and skill set. They provide resources, experiences, and support to others in areas where they may not be as knowledgeable or skilled.

4. Measure and Gather Feedback

Once empowered individuals have their initiative underway, it's crucial that leaders measure progress and gather feedback to assess performance and identify areas for improvement. This step allows leaders to track key performance indicators, evaluate the effectiveness of their strategies, and make data-driven decisions (Walston & Conley, 2022).

Effective measurement is indeed the backbone of any successful change initiative, but it's only half the story. It allows you to understand what's working and what's not, and it guides you toward achieving your goals. However, what truly fuels improvement is high-quality feedback (Levine, Roberts, & Cohen, 2020), the kind that goes beyond simply identifying mistakes to explaining why they happened and how to avoid them in the future (Wisniewski, Zierer, & Hattie, 2020).

Oftentimes, leaders excel at clarifying the mission, strategizing, and empowering their teams, but fall short in establishing systems for measurement, monitoring, and providing such insightful feedback. This is where I frequently encounter a gap when counseling leaders who are facing initiative challenges.

These measures should be straightforward and resource-light in terms of data collection and analysis, avoiding complexity that consumes time and effort. And remember, the data are only as valuable as their interpretability for the team. The data should offer clear insights to track progress, pinpoint areas for improvement, and most importantly, inform high-information feedback that empowers individuals to self-regulate and continuously improve.

Continuing our example of effectively implementing a new intervention program, the principal establishes clear goals, selects appropriate assessment measures, and conducts a baseline assessment to measure initial performance. Throughout implementation, the principal monitors progress and fidelity of program delivery, using collected data to analyze impact and provide constructive feedback to stakeholders. Adjustments to the program are made based on data analysis, and regular communication of progress to stakeholders ensures transparency and support for the intervention's goals.

5. Adjust and Improve

Based on the feedback and insights gained from measurement, leaders can adjust their strategies and processes as needed to improve performance and overcome challenges. Once you monitor and provide feedback, what action steps are you taking based on that monitoring and feedback? Remember, the main aspect of adjustment is changing behaviors rather than changing goals, wants, or circumstances (Hepler, 2023). You do not want to remain stagnant, and you surely do not want to go through all the steps of the leadership cycle to foster no change or progress. That ending would be a waste of investment in your and others' time.

Adjustment is the process of finding and adapting modes of behavior appropriate to the setting or the environment (Vyas, 2021). When you adjust and improve based on your system for providing and monitoring feedback, you will start to notice a huge, progressive push forward. That forward movement goes for everything you, as a leader, do—school budgets, lesson plans, professional development, you name it. Everything can be adjusted and improved accordingly with the right feedback in place.

Research shows that mindset plays a significant role in determining outcomes. By understanding, adapting, and shifting your mindset, you can better position yourself to overcome challenges (Primeau, 2021). Much like leadership itself, adjustment and improvement are a way of thinking. They can be learned, and they can be celebrated. So embrace the process of adjustment and improvement, for it is the pathway to growth and success in leadership.

In our ongoing example, the principal measures the progress of the implementation of the intervention plan. This involves analyzing data; gathering feedback from students, teachers, and leaders; and assessing key performance indicators.

Recognizing the initiative isn't meeting its timeline goals, the principal collaborates with the empowered leaders. Together, they identify specific, actionable adjustments with clear timelines. To ensure clarity, they collaboratively implement the changes and continue monitoring progress against the key performance indicators.

6. Be Accountable and Give Rewards

In the final step of the leadership cycle, accountability and reward play crucial roles, as supported by research. Yousueng Han and Sounman Hong (2019) emphasize that accountability directly and positively impacts organizational performance. This means that the level of support provided by leaders should increase the level of accountability or celebration of success that individuals within the organization can expect. With the incorporation of findings from Shehnaz Tehseen and Noor Ul Hadi (2015), we understand that workers are more motivated to accomplish their tasks when they receive recognition from management. Intrinsic rewards, such as employee development and recognition, highlighted in the research by Allison S. Gabriel, Arik Cheshin, Christina M. Moran, and Gerben A. van Kleef (2016), significantly influence employee performance.

To foster a culture of accountability within your school, it's essential to ensure that everyone understands what is expected of them, as clarified by the mission. This clarity enables individuals to take ownership of their responsibilities, receive quality feedback for their development and growth, and have the opportunity to make necessary adjustments to improve and meet expectations. Remember, as emphasized in the adage, "You get what you tolerate," the behaviors and actions that leaders choose to celebrate will be replicated throughout the organization. Therefore, by establishing a culture of accountability and recognizing achievements, leaders can reinforce a culture of high performance and continuous improvement.

Concluding our running example of implementing an intervention program, staff members who have excelled in implementing the new intervention process receive recognition and praise from the principal, other school leaders, and peers. This recognition takes various forms, such as public acknowledgment during staff meetings, inclusion in the school newsletter, and a personalized note of appreciation from the principal. Concurrently, the principal holds individuals or teams accountable for underperformance in implementing the intervention process; this involves constructive feedback, additional support and resources, and targeted professional development to address areas of needed improvement. Ultimately, the success of the initiative is reflected in improved student outcomes, such as academic achievement, behavior, and overall well-being. The principal's emphasis on clarity and accountability contributes to the effectiveness of the intervention process, which leads to positive changes in the school's performance metrics.

Creating a Sustainable Environment for Success

The beauty of the leadership cycle is that it is just that, a cycle. As you practice and deploy these steps, you'll begin to see how they all are interconnected. In time, the leadership cycle will become second nature, with each step guiding you to the next. While it may challenge your patience and thinking at first, it is a surefire way to foster growth and change in your school.

Because the leadership cycle is based on the framework of decision theory, its effectiveness is concurrent with research findings of effectiveness (Spetzler et al., 2016). The leadership cycle is not itself inherently impressive, but it ignites brilliant results when used as part of a comprehensive thought process.

The key is to create a sustainable environment for success by setting the tone. You must embody the values and behaviors you expect from others and demonstrate your commitment to sustainability through your consistent actions. You don't want to employ one-off solutions, which are like putting small bandages on wounds that require stitches. You want to go all in and really complete the transformational thinking process to solidify lasting and sustainable change within your organization. You want to make decisions that stick in the best possible way, and the leadership cycle is a proven way to make that happen. After all, how much is a decision worth? Decisions can cost you everything or nothing, but indecision can be even costlier. When we choose to not make the right decision, not reflect, or not employ best practices, it will cost us more than we are willing to pay.

Over the next few chapters, we're going to dive a little deeper into each step of the leadership cycle. My hope is that by the completion of this book, you will firmly believe that everything you need to foster change within your school is written in these pages—and ultimately within you, too.

Skipping Steps in the Leadership Cycle

What happens if you skip a step in the leadership cycle? If one of these steps is missing, the probability of your being successful diminishes. Let's explore why with the following explanation.

The first step, clarifying the mission, must precede the rest of the leadership cycle. Without understanding what must be done, how can you and your team possibly know how to proceed? The second step, planning strategically and making decisions, can only be successful if, first, the mission is clarified. You cannot lay out a blueprint if it is unclear what you are building. The third step, empowering yourself and others, can only be achieved once the mission is understood and the strategy is outlined. Otherwise, you cannot possibly know what you need to do in order to empower all the relevant players. The fourth step, measuring and gathering feedback, comes after everyone is aligned with the mission and is empowered in their role. Now that everyone is on the same page and begins to work toward the goal, they should receive feedback so they can make the appropriate adjustments. The cycle then brings us to the fifth step, adjusting and improving, which can only come once people integrate feedback into their actions. Adjusting needs to be done with a purpose, rather than on a whim. The final step, being accountable and giving rewards, makes no sense unless it comes after the previous steps. A leader cannot hold their subordinates accountable if the mission is not clear, if feedback is not given, and if the subordinates do not feel empowered. However, if everyone is working toward the mission and they know what must be done, accountability is appreciated by all parties.

Let's say you ensured clarity with the mission, strategically planned, and empowered yourself and others. Then, you provided professional development, gave reminders of the purpose to ensure student learning, and established a highly effective professional learning community (PLC). Despite those efforts, a teacher continues to struggle with classroom management.

It may seem justified to document that teacher's inability to improve. After all, you cannot have a poorly engaged group of students, right? The failure is not aligned with the mission. Your teacher is not empowering the students. Clearly, something has to be done. And sure, this documentation would hold the teacher accountable, but how would such haphazard decision making eventually affect your culture?

Did you already deploy the proper systems to engage in timely, quality feedback? Or are you just now addressing a behavior that has been happening for months on end? Have you had prior conversations with the teacher to find ways to foster improvement and development? Or did you just assume the teacher knew the expectations set forth on the first day of school and they have clearly failed to meet them? Proper monitoring, targeted support, and quality feedback on the part of leadership are crucial. If you skip past steps 4 and 5, heading down the fast lane to step 6, you will not get the results you intend.

As you can see, the leadership cycle, when not followed in order, is full of holes and confusion. Had you proceeded through each step in order, you would have discovered an opportunity to provide timely and relevant feedback to that teacher and set up a system to monitor that feedback, and adjusted accordingly. Sometimes corrective actions are necessary, but that method of management is rarely the "easy button" it seems to be. It is reactive, sometimes downright impulsive. Not only that, but the quick-hit method of reprimand will not create a sustainable environment for success.

Key Points

This chapter introduced the leadership cycle, a six-step framework for success in the decision-making process. It emphasizes the importance of clarity, starting with a well-defined mission and clear communication. Strategically planning, empowering your team with resources and support, and measuring progress with feedback are crucial steps. Embrace continuous improvement by adapting strategies, establishing a culture of accountability, and recognizing achievements. By internalizing these steps and viewing leadership as a cyclical thinking process, you can guide your team toward positive outcomes and become a more effective leader. As we proceed to explore each step in greater detail in the following chapters, let us remember that effective leadership is not a destination but a journey—one that requires dedication, strategic thinking, and a commitment to growth and excellence.

As you leave this chapter, remember the following.

- The pressure and responsibility placed on principals are huge and contribute to the perception that there is a sense of urgency with everything, dissuading principals from engaging in analytic thought processes.
- The leadership cycle is a proven thought process made of six steps.
    a. Clarify the mission.
    b. Plan strategically and make decisions.
    c. Empower yourself and others.
    d. Measure and gather feedback.
    e. Adjust and improve.
    f. Be accountable and give rewards.

Reflective Activity: Leadership Cycle Analysis

This activity offers example statements that correspond to different steps of the leadership cycle. For each statement, rate your school's performance as honestly and accurately as possible, with 1 indicating rarely (or never) practiced and 5 indicating consistently practiced. Draw a checkmark in the column of your chosen rating. Then, tally your total score.

Leadership Cycle Statements	1	2	3	4	5	Comments
Clarify the Mission						
Our leadership team makes a clear distinction between providing information and ensuring clarity of provided information.						
We provide frequent opportunities for people to demonstrate their understanding of provided information.						
Impacted personnel are consistently clear about the what, why, when, and how.						

Leadership Cycle Statements	1	2	3	4	5	Comments
Plan Strategically and Make Decisions						
We are strategic when planning and are prepared for multiple scenarios.						
We consistently involve the people impacted by the decisions in the planning process.						
We consistently make informed decisions that lead to clearly defined action steps.						
Planning meetings are consistently purposeful, effective, and efficient.						

Leadership Cycle Statements	1	2	3	4	5	Comments
Empower Yourself and Others						
We consistently provide people with an opportunity to engage with information in relation to the desired impact of the mission.						
We consistently read, research, and implement best practices.						
Our leadership team consistently models a growth mindset.						
We value improvement in others and prioritize their success.						

Leadership Cycle Statements	1	2	3	4	5	Comments
Measure and Gather Feedback						
We regularly monitor the quality of feedback being provided.						
Quality feedback is frequently provided to inform improvement.						
We consistently measure what is expected and make proper adjustments in a timely manner.						
Everyone is clear about monitoring and measurement metrics, including timelines for improvement.						
We regularly review feedback provided to measure its impact.						

Leadership Cycle Statements	1	2	3	4	5	Comments
Adjust and Improve						
We regularly make timely adjustments when we see a lack of improvement.						
We regularly identify root causes that impede improvement.						
Our organization consistently buys in when we need to make adjustments.						

Leadership Cycle Statements	1	2	3	4	5	Comments
Be Accountable and Give Rewards						
People at all levels have a clear sense of direction, purpose, and priorities rather than dealing with fragmented, competing, or overwhelming priorities.						
Everyone in the organization takes ownership of mistakes.						
Poor performers are addressed, coached, supported, or removed instead of ignored, transferred, or promoted.						
We regularly acknowledge and recognize people for their value and contributions, as opposed to relying on formal, structured recognitions or awards.						

- **High scores (89 and higher):** This range indicates you're exhibiting strong leadership qualities and making high-quality decisions that benefit your organization. While you're likely on the right track, don't become complacent. Use this score to identify areas for further improvement, perhaps by soliciting feedback from trusted colleagues or seeking new challenges to stretch your leadership skills.

- **Average scores (44–88):** This range indicates you have room for improvement in your decision-making process. While this is not a cause for alarm, it's important to address the areas highlighted in the rubric. Consider how you can improve communication clarity, transparency, and active listening. Explore ways to empower your team by delegating tasks, providing resources, and encouraging their input. Review your current planning process, and see if it can be made more comprehensive and focused. Develop stronger tracking systems to monitor progress and ensure goals are being met. Focus on specific areas to work on, and actively seek feedback to track your progress.

- **Low scores (43 and lower):** This range indicates there are significant challenges in your decision-making approach. It's crucial to take immediate action to address communication issues, empower your team, develop a clear strategic plan, and implement robust follow-up and progress-monitoring systems. Additionally, fostering a culture of accountability is essential for long-term success. Seeking professional development opportunities or mentoring from experienced leaders can significantly accelerate your growth.

Score	Results
89 and Higher	These high results indicate lots of quality leadership decisions. Scores in this range indicate real, influential leadership and organizational strengths as well as areas that may need some focused improvement. You have a high probability of ensuring success.
44–88	These average results indicate ineffectiveness in decision making. You have a lower probability of ensuring success.
43 and Lower	These low results indicate you have a clear issue with ensuring success.

Remember, your score is just a snapshot. Use it as a starting point for self-reflection and continuous improvement. Track your progress over time and celebrate your achievements as you develop your leadership skills. By taking action and embracing feedback, you can unlock your full potential as a leader and drive success for yourself and your organization.

STEP 1: CLARIFY THE MISSION

There is no failure except failure to serve one's purpose.

—Henry Ford

WELCOME TO the pivotal arena of educational leadership dynamics, where our compass points to the core of effective transformation. As leaders, we kick-start this journey by unearthing the bedrock principle: mission clarity. The first step doesn't merely involve stating objectives; it demands a resolute commitment to eradicating ambiguity and championing precision.

In this chapter, we are reminded that the burden of clarity rests squarely on leaders' shoulders; every word, every phrase, demands unwavering singularity of meaning. We explore the art of inviting dialogue that ensures shared comprehension. This chapter highlights the potency of prompting listeners to encapsulate the essence of discourse, spotlighting any gaps, and fostering mutual understanding.

Let us explore the first step of the leadership cycle and how effective educational leaders put it in place. I touched on that aspect briefly in the overview of the leadership cycle (page 61). This chapter underscores the significance of clarity in effectively formulating an organization's vision and mission. These two elements, the vision and the mission, stand as cornerstones for an organization's success.

The vision serves as a guiding light, encompassing the organization's future aspirations. It paints a vivid picture of what the organization aims to achieve in the long run, providing a clear direction for growth and development. However, without translating this lofty vision into clear, actionable steps, the organization's path forward can become muddled.

This is where the mission comes in—it homes in on the present actions required to materialize the vision. The mission encapsulates the strategies, structure, and plans that will transform abstract aspirations into tangible outcomes. It is through the mission that the grand vision becomes a series of achievable goals and milestones, providing a road map for the organization's journey.

In this chapter, you will learn how to align a vision and a mission by ensuring your team shares the same objectives, how to secure buy-in from stakeholders using transparent discussions and attuned listening, and how to remain consistent as a leader to project an image of trustworthiness and clear resolve.

Defining Clarity

Before we clarify the mission, we must first understand what it means to clarify. Everyone is on the same page. Everyone understands what is expected. Everyone is clear about the commitment to support as well as the levels of accountability when expectations are not met. Everyone is inspired by the forward-thinking goals that you, as the leader, have brought to light. A clear vision empowers the formulation of a purposeful mission, while a clear mission in turn empowers the realization of the grand vision. Clarity acts as a driving force, ensuring that each step taken aligns with the organization's long-term aspirations and immediate goals. When you clarify the mission, you make sure everyone shares a common sense of direction born from a unified purpose. The leader establishes the vision, which then guides the mission. As a leader, you ensure clarity by ensuring understanding of the expectations of your teams throughout your school.

As leaders, we have to recognize that the burden of clarity always rests on the communicator. Effective leaders are master communicators and must be committed to ensuring a mutual understanding. We can use the following list of steps to ensure a clear school vision.

1. **Establish a vision:** Consider a combination of personal reflection, staff feedback, and key stakeholder needs while developing your own vision for the institution's future. What changes are you aspiring to see in

your school? What impact do you want these changes to have on your community of educators and learners and the broader community?

2. **Be specific:** Assess the institution's current state. Review academic performance, teacher qualifications, student demographics, resource access, and any existing challenges or opportunities. Ensure these specifics align with your team's current or aspiring values; for example, are you hoping to improve systems of mutual support? Is ethical decision making an important tenet of your school philosophy? How will the vision address upholding these values?

3. **Share your vision:** Encourage questions and discussion to foster a deeper understanding. Share the purpose and values behind the vision to connect with individual goals, and consistently revisit the vision while leading by example to inspire commitment. How will you motivate the organization toward achieving the vision? What impact will the vision have once embodied by the organization?

4. **Hold your team accountable:** Define specific, measurable, achievable, relevant, and time-bound goals for individuals and the team. Everyone should understand what success looks like. Do all the team members understand their roles, their tasks, and how they contribute to the overall objective? Do you hold everyone accountable for the same standards?

5. **Be consistent:** Be reliable and transparent. Keep promises, explain changes, and live by your values. Lead by example, aligning your actions with your words. Maintain consistent communication across all channels for clarity and impact. Do you clearly communicate expectations to your team and provide consistent and constructive feedback?

To ensure clarity and mutual understanding, you must be specific, which means refraining from using ambiguous and extraneous vocabulary. This is crucial because, as research suggests, language significantly impacts not only how we communicate (external processes) but also internal cognitive processes like decision making, emotional processing, and even cognitive development (Altarriba & Basnight-Brown, 2022). Take the word *check*, for example. How many different meanings exist for this word? It can mean to look after a person, place, or thing. It can be a form of payment. It can even be the bill paid after dining at a restaurant.

It can refer to the symbol in a box on a piece of paper. One tiny word has many different meanings, and each meaning is based on the experiences of the person with whom you are communicating. Those individual experiences, filtered through the unique lens of language, have shaped the listener's perception and understanding of words. Remember, language isn't just a tool for communication; it shapes how we think and feel (Hodel, Formanowicz, Sczesny, Valdrová, & von Stockhausen, 2017). This means even seemingly simple, unambiguous words can carry diverse meanings based on individual experiences and cultural contexts. Recognizing this linguistic diversity is crucial for communicating effectively and building empathy.

In the educational realm, one word that has a myriad of meanings, and that teachers tend to use a lot, is *respect*. Teachers have a habit of saying, "The student did not respect me," but what is respect? If we lined up in a room full of teachers and asked that question, I assure you we would get a variety of answers. Each individual would pull from their unique experiences and exposures and provide a definition in concert with those encounters. Thus, the teachers' experiences would shape their perspectives of what it means to be respectful.

A practical, high-level scenario of defining a word could look like the following: As a principal, you're sending an email to all staff about the importance of innovation in education. However, *innovation* can be a vague term open to interpretation. Some might think it means adopting the latest technology, while others might focus on creative teaching methods. This ambiguity could lead to confusion and hinder your call to action.

To prevent this, you clearly define innovation within the context of your district's goals and values. This definition sets expectations, eliminates confusion, and rallies everyone behind a shared understanding. The following is a sample email for sharing your definition:

> *Subject: Fostering Innovation in Our Schools!*
>
> *In today's rapidly changing world, innovation is more critical than ever in education. But what does "innovation" truly mean for our campus?*
>
> *For us, innovation is not just about adopting the latest gadgets or trends. It's about fostering a culture of creativity, critical thinking, and problem solving within our schools. It's about empowering educators to experiment with new approaches that engage students and improve learning outcomes.*
>
> *Whether it's developing student-centered projects, integrating technology in meaningful ways, or rethinking traditional assessment practices, innovation takes*

many forms, driven by the shared goal of preparing our students for success in the 21st century.

By defining innovation in this way, you provide a clear direction for staff, encouraging them to contribute their unique ideas and expertise while staying aligned with the district's vision.

Ensuring Clarity

The foundation of clarity is to establish mutual understanding. One way to ensure this is to simply ask a question at the conclusion of your clarifying statement, such as, "Would you mind sharing with me what you're taking away from our conversation?"

The person with whom you are communicating will then share with you what was important to them—the information that sticks in their memory. The revelation will provide you with all you need to know about what information they found important. Now, it is your turn to listen closely. Are they sharing things you didn't intend to be a priority? If so, you will need to ensure clarity once more. This layer of verification goes far beyond asking, "Do you understand?" A question prompting a yes or no answer does not ensure clarity, but it might ensure compliance. Consider the following scenario.

- **Scenario:** You've just had a conversation with your colleague John about the timeline for an upcoming project. You explained the key deadlines and deliverables, but you want to ensure he understood everything clearly.
- **Clarifying statement:** "So, John, to recap, we need the first draft of the report by next Monday, followed by feedback and revisions by Friday. Then, the final presentation is due on the following Wednesday."
- **Question for clarification:** "What are your key takeaways from this discussion regarding the project timeline? Are there any aspects you need further clarification on, or adjustments you think we should make?"

Compared to simply confirming understanding, actively engaging John in recalling and sharing his interpretation offers several advantages. First, it helps avoid *yes, but* situations. By prompting John to articulate his understanding, you uncover any potential discrepancies early on, preventing them from snowballing into misunderstandings later. Second, this approach can reveal differing priorities. You might learn that John prioritized a different task within the timeline, allowing you to address misaligned expectations before they cause friction. Finally, actively seeking John's input demonstrates your commitment to clarity and respect for his perspective. This fosters a more collaborative and trusting work environment, where everyone feels comfortable sharing their understanding and working toward shared goals.

Asking your listener to share their takeaways from your conversation is very simple but produces powerful results. This manner of questioning is not defensive. It is nonintrusive. There is an undercurrent that says, "I care enough about you to ensure clarity." It is empowering for both parties. Like most skills in life, the more you practice that method of communicating, the easier it will get, and the more expected it will become.

As leaders, we all have different tools for communicating. In today's fast-paced, technologically savvy world, we rely heavily on email and text messages. While these methods of communication are convenient in a pinch, the problem is you can never really detect a person's tone through the text presented. You miss out on your listener's body language. A huge percentage of our communication is nonverbal; therefore, as listeners, we miss a lot of good information when we choose to communicate through email and text messages.

Moreover, researchers have long noted that far less information about the social context is available in the digital setting than the face-to-face setting, such as cues about the personalities and social statuses of the communication partners (Stieger et al., 2023). Research conducted by Mahdi Roghanizad of Western University found that people tend to overestimate their persuasiveness via text-based communication, and underestimate their persuasiveness via face-to-face communication (Roghanizad & Bohns, 2017).

This underscores the importance of face-to-face interactions, allowing for a richer exchange of information and a deeper understanding between parties. While digital communication has its advantages, leaders must recognize its limitations and strive to incorporate more face-to-face interactions when feasible, to ensure effective and nuanced communication in all contexts.

The following are several reflective questions you can use in your electronic communications to ensure clarity.

- How many times and in how many ways should you communicate this message?
- Is the context of this communication appropriate, relevant, and in alignment with your intended message?
- What feedback will you seek for acknowledgment, clarification, and understanding?
- What possible misconceptions could this message generate, and how can you avoid those misconceptions?
- Are you in an emotionally intelligent state to share this message at the moment? Are your tone and mood appropriate to share this message electronically at this time?

Remember, the focus of communication is not what is being said, texted, or emailed. It is what is being understood. Take the time to reflect. Ending with a request to summarize understanding is how you ensure clarity. The following is a scale to quickly gauge your level of effectiveness by clarifying the mission.

1. The mission is poorly defined, it lacks clear goals and objectives, and there is no check for understanding.
2. The mission has some clarity, but goals and objectives are not fully defined or communicated effectively. There are few to no checks for understanding.
3. The mission has a basic level of clarity, with goals and objectives outlined, but there is room for improvement in communication. Checking for understanding is surface level.
4. The mission is well-defined, with clear goals and objectives and a communication plan in place. Checking for understanding is evident with the majority of individuals.
5. The mission is exceptionally clear, with all stakeholders having a strong understanding of the goals, objectives, and expectations. There is evidence of understanding among all stakeholders involved.

Review the items in the list. Which one sounds applicable to your situation? If you are feeling a lack of organization, it might be time to revisit your vision.

Beginning With Vision

In order to clarify the mission, you first need a vision. A vision is a manifestation of a future direction, a way to picture the future using one's imagination and wisdom. It is never what is, but rather what could be. A vision points you in a direction but doesn't tell you exactly what to do to get there. Despite that vagueness, the vision cannot be nebulous. The vision cannot be a three-hundred-page dissertation.

Educational leaders are tasked with the never-ending responsibility to innovate and transform the educational experience. Sometimes, that commitment requires some big ideas and out-of-the-box thinking, dreaming, and imagination to create the future and change the world. Who better to lay the groundwork for the vision than the leader?

Most leadership development books (Hyatt, 2020; Shallenberger & Shallenberger, 2020) will tell you something different. They will say it is up to the team to establish the vision with the leader and then carry that vision out through the collaboratively established mission statement. Collaborative vision development will foster a sense of ownership and buy-in; therefore, everyone should have a say.

I respectfully disagree.

Positive leaders tap into the power of a vision. They use this power to determine a way forward. In order to inspire, motivate, and rally others to follow your lead, you must be able to articulate your vision in a clear and compelling manner. You must ensure clarity and inspire others.

Effective leaders know that inspiration is a valuable leadership tool, but inspiration itself must be organized and targeted. A leader has the capacity to help people bypass the present, catch a vision of the future, and obtain the ticket and ride to get there.

When Martin Luther King Jr., at a young age, assumed the responsibility to lead what we now call the Civil Rights Movement, he was incredibly inspired by Mahatma Gandhi's vision for nonviolent social change (Carson, Armstrong, Carson, Clay, & Taylor, 2005). King would go on to inspire a burdened, abused, disenfranchised, beaten generation to achieve justice and equality through nonviolence and hope. The entire movement was completely reliant on King's ability to motivate, inspire, encourage, and elicit that hope when there was no hope to be found.

King had a vision of what could be. He did not meet with the delegates of the National Association for the Advancement of Colored People (NAACP) and ask them to collaborate on his vision, his dream, his passion for his children and the plight of African Americans under constant oppression. King had a dream, and he shared it. He shared it in front of 260,000 people at the March on Washington, in what is widely considered the greatest speech of the 20th century (NAACP, n.d.).

That action is the difference between sharing a vision and seeking collaboration on a vision. King articulated that dream even knowing he might never witness its realization. He said so himself, in another inspiring speech that he made the day before he was assassinated: "I may not get there with you" (American Federation of State, County and Municipal Employees, n.d.). Still, he used his words and his hope to ignite a passionate fire throughout a divided nation. He lived each day with passion, conviction, and commitment, and he inspired people to catch his vision. Today, we're still trying to catch that vision.

Picture an African American man sitting at the dinner table with his wife and two young children. His family has witnessed nothing but division, segregation, and experiences of being "less than." After being inspired and motivated by King's vision, the man turns to his wife and says, "I am aware of the present laws of segregation, but I'm going to sit in a restaurant tomorrow. I am uncertain of what this will mean for me personally, and I do not know if I will be back. I don't know if I will be harassed, beaten, or arrested. I do know that there will be a heavy price to pay for what I plan to do. But I'm going there, not because I am allowed. I'm going so they will be allowed." He glances at his children. "I want to endure this so they don't have to."

It takes extraordinary vision to encourage people to walk right into the mouths of biting dogs, which is exactly what King did. With his only weapon being a heart of hope, King spread a message of what life could be.

Winston Churchill, Nelson Mandela, Barack Obama, and Rosa Parks are just a few other extraordinary individuals who have shared their visions and inspired millions. Messages of hope are contagious. The first commitment of leadership should be to inspire people toward the vision. A leader is always considering what could be, while everyone else considers what is. Leaders are always going to pull people with them to understand, to catch, to buy into, and to see the vision they have.

An example of a visionary in educational leadership is Jaime Escalante, a high school teacher known for his work at Garfield High School in East Los Angeles, California. Escalante had a vision of transforming the educational outcomes for his predominantly low-income and minority students, particularly in the field of advanced mathematics.

Rather than accepting the prevailing belief that his students were incapable of succeeding in Advanced Placement (AP) Calculus, Escalante challenged this notion and set out to prove that with proper support and high expectations, they could excel. He implemented rigorous teaching methods, provided extra tutoring sessions, and fostered a culture of hard work and dedication among his students.

Escalante's vision was clear: he aimed to empower his students to achieve academic excellence and break the cycle of low expectations. He articulated this vision to his students, his colleagues, and the broader community, inspiring them to believe in the potential of every student regardless of their background.

Through his leadership and unwavering commitment to his vision, Escalante transformed Garfield High School into a beacon of academic achievement. His students not only passed the AP Calculus exam but also earned some of the highest scores in the United States, defying the odds and shattering stereotypes along the way.

Escalante's story serves as a powerful example of how visionary leadership can drive positive change in education. By daring to dream big and refusing to accept mediocrity, he demonstrated the transformative impact that a clear vision coupled with passion and determination can have on students' lives. His legacy continues to inspire educators around the world to set ambitious goals for their students and never underestimate their potential.

Sustaining the Vision

From policies and procedures to funding to different personalities to regional and state or provincial accreditations, the list of challenges facing schools goes on and on. But all it takes is one effective leader with a heartfelt, bold, and transformational passion to radiate possibility and change with every conversation. That ability is what our extraordinary leaders of history have in common with our effective leaders today. Vision starts with the leader.

Too often, when leaders come into schools, they try to establish a vision with the people. They say, "OK, what is important to the collective *us*, and how are we going to get there?" Everyone in the school chimes in. They seem to be on the same page as to what the vision is and how missions will carry that vision out.

But what happens when there is a change of leadership, or a change of staff? What happens when four teachers retire, and three new teachers are hired straight out of college? Do you gather everyone together and reestablish a vision with the new parties present? Do you continue with the previously defined vision and hope the new additions buy into something constructed before their arrival? That choice can get messy and take a lot of time. Also, it brings the vision into the present moment instead of the future.

Leaders do not establish a vision with the people. Leaders are catalysts for establishing missions with people. The vision is where you are going. When people leave, that vision doesn't change, the goal doesn't change, and the audacity of hope doesn't change. Keeping that continuity isn't to say that leaders know more. That resolution is not about ego. It is about being passionate and purposeful and taking something from where it is to where it can be.

As you address your teachers and staff, you should share your vision. Then ask the question, "What does this vision mean to you?" You must take the time to ask that question and really listen to the answers. Remember the cornerstones of ensuring clarity. First, as I mentioned before, you will be able to identify what is important to each individual based on their response. Second, for the vision to come to life, it must have meaning for each person.

With that understanding established, ask your teachers and staff about their personal visions and how they can contribute to the bigger vision of the organization. You may find a few mini-missions as you listen intently and hear what your teams have to share. But the conversation doesn't stop there. You, the leader, are responsible for helping your people reach their personal visions. You can do it by asking what they need from you to be their absolute best. They may not have the answers right away, but be sure to follow up.

To ensure that a vision catches on, a little accountability goes a long way. Ask your teams how they would like you to hold them accountable to their personal visions. If you have a teacher who wants to start a new science club by the following semester and have a roster of at least fifteen students, be the leader who paves the way for guideposts, check-ins, and celebrations of progress.

Once the vision has been created, you could have the teacher prominently display the club's vision on a bulletin board with visuals. Encourage teachers to set their own "mini-visions" aligned with the bigger goal. Hold regular meetings with clear agendas focused on progress and challenges. Implement self-assessment questionnaires for teachers to track progress and identify roadblocks. Encourage peer-to-peer check-ins for mutual support. Celebrate milestones along the way with announcements, photos, or small rewards.

Use online tools to track tasks, deadlines, and responsibilities collaboratively. Conduct an annual student survey to gauge the students' experience and how well the club aligns with the vision. Encourage open communication for feedback from both students and teachers.

Remember, it's about progress, not perfection. Focus on constructive feedback, recognize individual efforts, and adapt the accountability measures as needed. This collaborative approach, paired with practical tools, will ensure the science club vision becomes a reality that benefits everyone involved. When people know their role and their contributions to a larger vision, they establish a more meaningful purpose at work, and they feel their leader genuinely cares about them, engagement soars.

Distinguishing a Mission From a Vision

If the vision focuses on tomorrow and what the organization wants to become, then the mission focuses on today and what the organization does to achieve it. Both the vision and the mission are vital to achieving success. The leader must turn the vision into a set of focused outcomes and develop time-based goals, structure, and an action plan. This is the mission.

When we're thinking of missions, we're thinking of all the approaches needed to accomplish a task. Anything you're asking someone to do can be clarified as a mission. Anything you're trying to accomplish could be classified as a mission. Anytime you're taking action steps toward teaching, learning, or safety, those steps themselves could be considered missions. In fact, the mission is often made up of mini-missions that support the vision.

The philosopher Lucius Annaeus Seneca is often credited with saying, "If a man knows not which port he sails, no wind is favorable." If you don't have a common, agreed-on destination, you are going to yield unfocused results. The common understanding of the destination allows everyone to align their improvement efforts. Time is the only cost in deciding where you want to go. Missions give strong motivations and provide us with a clear picture of what we value. Missions are the winds to our harbor vision.

Clarifying the Mission

Once the leader has established a vision, it is time for the team to clarify the mission and subsequent mini-missions. With each mission, big or small, the leader must ask, "What needs to be done? Why does this need to be done? Who is responsible? When will this take place? When will we know that we have accomplished the mission? How is our progress being measured?" The leader is creating the framework to ensure the desired impact of the mission is accomplished.

The mission can be anything from developing a school tardy policy to developing safety protocols to developing quality staff meetings. Think about it: If the school's vision is to be an excellent organization that ensures quality learning, how does the tardy policy align with that vision? A comprehensive tardy policy maximizes instruction time, minimizes distraction, and allows staff to effectively utilize their time to contribute to the vision. Even the smallest mini-missions matter. Mini-missions inspire people to adopt positive behaviors and achieve a greater vision.

Mini-missions are smaller steps within the larger mission that help you achieve your ultimate vision. You can think of them like stepping stones across a river: each stone gets you closer to the other side, but you still need to take them one by one. The following is a breakdown of milestones, subgoals, initiatives, action steps, and key results and samples of each. These samples relate to a vision of "students become confident and critical readers" and a mission to "develop strong reading comprehension skills."

- **Milestones:** Milestones are specific, measurable achievements that mark progress toward your larger mission.
    - Students can summarize the main idea of a text.
    - Students can identify key details and supporting evidence.
    - Students can make inferences and draw conclusions.
    - Students can analyze different perspectives and interpretations.
- **Subgoals:** Subgoals are smaller, more manageable versions of your overall mission. They break down the larger objective into more focused and achievable tasks.
    - Improve decoding and fluency skills.
    - Expand vocabulary knowledge.
    - Develop background knowledge on various topics.

- Foster critical-thinking and questioning skills.
- **Initiatives:** Initiatives are specific projects or actions taken to achieve a subgoal. They put your plan into motion and involve concrete steps.
  - Implement daily reading practice with diverse texts.
  - Conduct vocabulary exercises using games and puzzles.
  - Organize collaborative projects exploring different cultures and viewpoints.
  - Hold discussions and debates on thought-provoking topics.
- **Action steps:** Action steps are the smallest, most specific tasks that make up an initiative. They are the individual to-dos on your list.
  - Read aloud to students, modeling intonation and expression.
  - Guide students in identifying unfamiliar words and using context clues.
  - Have students create graphic organizers to map out story elements.
  - Encourage annotations and questioning while reading.
- **Key results:** Key results are specific, measurable outcomes that define success for each mini-mission. They help you track progress and ensure you're on the right path.
  - Students score above proficiency on standardized reading tests.
  - Students participate actively in class discussions and debates.
  - Students demonstrate independent reading habits and choose challenging texts.

With mini-missions, the important thing is to have a clear understanding of the steps you need to take and how they contribute to your overall mission and vision. Just like effective leadership starts with understanding and empowering people, achieving a vision relies on breaking it down into clear, actionable steps. Think of these mini-missions as stepping stones guided by your vision and fueled by the talents and contributions of your team. From ensuring clarity to establishing a mission, it all comes back to the people. Effective leaders must lean into their people's experiences. Everyone has something to offer. It is up to you, the leader, to help them see that too. Sometimes, helping people see their potential starts by acknowledging their potential. When we give people a vision, provide them space to develop the missions, and ensure clarity along the way, people see what can be accomplished and know where they are going. Because of this, they will be able to provide ideas and talents to help the organization get there.

Fostering Buy-In

To unlock unlimited potential for the mission (or missions), you will need collective buy-in, defined as individuals' acceptance of and willingness to actively support and participate in something. In their book *Buy-In*, Harvard Business School professor John P. Kotter and physicist Lorne A. Whitehead (2010) state that the process we use to secure buy-in is inherently flawed. We rarely approach it as buy-in at all.

In fact, we typically approach a new idea with a sell-in mentality. First, we "sell" the idea or opportunity to ourselves. Then, we ponder the ways people will resist the idea and develop airtight defenses to debunk their concerns.

Effective leaders need others to be open to their influence. When people feel sold to, they will resist new ideas. Simply put, people will not support what they do not understand. There are a few things we can do to garner buy-in when it comes to the mission.

- **Engaging in transparent and honest dialogue:** In his book *Good to Great*, Jim Collins (2001) says, "It is impossible to make good decisions without infusing the entire process with an honest confrontation of the brutal facts" (p. 88). By going beyond the data and the reasons and tapping into others' emotions, effective leaders can make great strides toward a transparent and honest dialogue. Use vivid and compelling examples to illustrate your point. Talk to your people about what can happen if you do or do not employ specific ideas. Take note of the visionary leaders you know and love. Did they speak from the heart? Did they paint an accurate picture of what was to come? Both transparency and honesty can go a long way toward garnering buy-in from your teams.
- **Chunking:** The introduction to any type of change initiative can seem overwhelming at first. After all, many people are resistant to change. To reduce the effect on your team of being overwhelmed,

you can break down your change initiatives into distinct phases and steps. Be sure to include interim goals to keep you on track. That simplicity makes the impossible very possible. As the saying goes, "How do you eat an elephant? One bite at a time."

- **Simply listening:** For you to ensure clarity, you will want to make sure you are an effective listener as well. Truly listening to others is a way to build relationships. By listening, you can also identify if your team is resistant to change.

  Rick Maurer's (2002) book *Why Don't You Want What I Want?* classifies resistance to change into three broad categories: (1) I don't get it, (2) I don't like it, and (3) I don't like you. The first category invites you to ensure understanding, whereas the second two categories are emotional reactions to the change or the messenger of change, which make listening so important. The more you know, the better you can take steps to listen fully and help your teammates discover the root of their change resistance.

- **Obtaining feedback and input:** By and large, one of the biggest challenges is when administration drives change using the top-down approach, meaning all new ideas, missions, and opportunities come from above and trickle down the "pyramid" of the leadership hierarchy. That practice is a death sentence to your organization. Research has identified common problems in top-down team structures, such as limited participation, influence from inappropriate sources, and a lack of constructive conflict (Stangel, 2016). When decisions are imposed from the top without meaningful input from those lower down the hierarchy, it can stifle creativity and innovation. While top-down management offers clear direction and efficient decision making, it can be perceived as authoritarian (Touro University Worldwide, 2015). This highlights the importance of fostering an environment where all team members feel empowered to contribute their ideas and engage in constructive dialogue, rather than solely relying on directives from above.

  The top-down approach says that whoever is at the top knows all. That isn't leadership. You have to get feedback to understand your team's dynamics, and you must obtain input on how to collectively fulfill each mini-mission to make the vision come to life. Research suggests that asking for advice doesn't just help you gain new insights; it can also make you appear more competent to others (Brooks, Gino, & Schweitzer, 2015). This is because seeking advice demonstrates a willingness to learn and grow, a quality often associated with high performers. So, don't hesitate to ask—it's a win-win situation!

- **Communicating progress:** If you fail to communicate progress, enthusiasm will wane and buy-in will dissipate. If you listen, share, communicate, make goals, obtain input, and adjust, but you fail to provide communication on progress, you will lose credibility, transparency, and collaborative investment. People feel like they are part of the solution when you keep updating them on the progress you are making together. So, we listen. We share the vision. We communicate the missions born out of the vision. We make the goals. We put in the processes and changes needed to meet those goals. We take all those actions. But if for some reason we fail to provide communication on the progress, it will all fall apart. You must either set benchmarks for your goals or mark quarterly times to report back and host a conversation about the status of the organization's goals. Transparency is essential.

Prioritizing Consistency

Achieving clarity, understanding the nuances between vision and mission, and garnering buy-in are crucial leadership skills and can transform a school culture. These are all huge endeavors. But as they take time and dedication, it becomes increasingly clear that achieving success rarely involves grand leaps or overnight transformations. Here's where the powerful sentiment of "doing little things consistently over time" comes into play.

Educational leaders often face the pressure to produce immediate, dazzling results. This can lead to snap decisions fueled by the need for instant answers. That is why the leadership cycle serves as a powerful reminder that true impact lies in the consistent cultivation of small positive actions. Each decision, each interaction, and each commitment to clarity and vision becomes a seed shaping the destiny of your organization.

If a teacher one day decides to engage with students using unconventional tools like Tinkertoys, rap music, or maybe even food, the intended results will most likely not appear on the first day. Colleagues may question those methods. Students will hopefully be delighted by the change but may be confused at first. It will take days, maybe even weeks before the intended results arise. Studies in cognitive and educational psychology have demonstrated that spacing out repeated encounters with the material over time produces superior long-term learning (Kang, 2016). Three months down the line, the students are grasping concepts they struggled with before the different learning tools were introduced. That teacher found a way to ensure learning, and the method aligned beautifully with the school's vision.

The effect is so important I'll say it once more: We don't get results from the big action we take in one day. We get results when we get the little things right the vast majority of the time, each and every day. Author Scott Ginsberg (2012) stated, "Consistency is far better than rare moments of greatness." Consistency, or the lack thereof, can be the defining factor between failure and success. Without consistent effort, few people become experts. Without diligent practice, ballplayers do not improve. Without daily practice, musicians do not become virtuosos. Without consistent steps in the right direction that align with the mission and vision, educational leaders impede transformation.

What happens when we're inconsistent? Fear and mistrust are born. Those two powerful factors can dilute the impact of the vision. You, the leader, must maintain a consistent approach with your team. If on Monday you reinforce that establishing a new attendance policy is the utmost priority, and then the following week, after expectations have been clarified, you allow three veteran teachers to arrive late without consequence, you've allowed cracks in your leadership foundation. Now your team doesn't know where they or the organizational priorities stand.

It does not stop there. Inconsistency kills ambition. If you, the leader, are inconsistent, then people will wait to act. They want to see what you will ask them to do first. They need to feel you out and determine which you they are dealing with on this particular day. This act of self-preservation they're using deadens empowerment and delays improvement. Instead of taking initiative, your people wait and see. Inconsistency creates a culture of reaction, and any area of inconsistency breeds opportunity for decay.

I see so many leaders who are fully aware of the importance of consistency yet continuously struggle to establish a consistent mindset for a sustained period of time. Their lack of consistency is painful for all. Consistency creates progress in every aspect of our lives, but somehow, we continue to falter.

It is nothing short of tragic that so many leaders find themselves consistent at one thing: starting something new. They can pilot a new project, spout off a new initiative, and get people excited about a new development. Then, these leaders stop before getting any results. Call it *shiny object syndrome*, or just a penchant for starting new things, because starting and changing are "what leaders do."

The problem here is that such leaders are all too focused on the outcome rather than the process—they see that final result, and that is all that matters. Once the process is underway, it may take too much time, or the leader may get sidetracked due to the overwhelming nature of multiple initiatives. Sometimes, a new, brilliant idea comes along, and progress stops. The leader encourages everyone to recalculate and begin at square one. Just like that, consistency is gone.

That is not to say the outcome is unimportant. Nevertheless, if we become fixated on the outcome, it will work against us, no matter how compelling. Why? Because any outcome compelling enough to excite, motivate, and inspire is probably one that won't be achieved without hard work and sacrifice over a long period of time.

Without certain processes and systems in place to help us, most of us aren't able to maintain the effort needed to accomplish worthwhile outcomes. If we want to achieve our desired outcomes, we must build consistency into our plan, which is where the leadership cycle is so important. Do we follow through with the leadership cycle? Or are we inconsistent because of time, urgency, or any number of the things that may distract us? If we follow through, then we can ensure consistency and buy-in over time. We can put it into a simple equation:

Vision + Strategic Planning + Consistent Right Actions = Success

Remember, leaders, the seeds you sow today shape the destiny of your organization. While making quick decisions to immediately change things grabs attention, it's the consistent cultivation of small positive actions that fuels true impact. Every decision, each interaction, and every commitment to clarity and vision becomes a building block, a testament to your dedication. Don't be seduced by shiny object syndrome—resist the urge to abandon ship before reaping the rewards of consistency.

Key Points

This chapter unlocked the secrets of mission clarity for leaders. It defined clarity, stressed the importance of a shared direction, and emphasized the leader's crucial role in aligning everyone with the mission's goals.

Understanding the importance of crafting a compelling vision and differentiating it from the mission is vital to success. Mutual understanding and team buy-in are key. Effective communication and a collaborative environment ensure everyone grasps their roles, their responsibilities, and the commitment needed to achieve organizational goals. Guiding questions and consistency empower leaders to sustain the vision and drive momentum toward desired outcomes.

With a clear mission understood and embraced, it's time to move from understanding to action. The next chapter dives into the essential tools and frameworks leaders need to translate vision into concrete plans and make effective decisions to move toward success.

As you leave this chapter, remember the following.

- The first step in the leadership cycle for educational leaders is to ensure clarity of the mission and vision.
- The burden of clarity always rests on the communicator, so refrain from using ambiguous words with multiple meanings.
- A great way to ensure clarity in a conversation is to ask your listener, "Would you mind sharing with me what you're taking away from our conversation?"
- The leader establishes the vision because they have a passion and motivation for the future.
- Missions are established collaboratively as long as they align with the vision.
- Buy-in can be achieved by engaging in an honest and transparent dialogue, breaking down large goals into smaller actionable steps, listening to others, obtaining and processing feedback, and communicating progress often and consistently.
- Consistency will make or break your ability to transform and cultivate change in your organization, and it starts with the leader.

Reflective Activity: Determining Mission Clarity

List a few priority missions. For each one, identify its level of clarity based on the following key (levels 1–5), list supporting evidence that proves your ranking, and identify action steps to help you ensure a higher level of clarity.

1. **Very poor:** The mission is poorly defined, it lacks clear goals and objectives, and there is no check for understanding.
2. **Poor:** The mission has some clarity, but goals and objectives are not fully defined or communicated effectively. There are few to no checks for understanding.
3. **Average:** The mission has a basic level of clarity, with goals and objectives outlined, but there is room for improvement in communication. Checking for understanding is surface level.
4. **Good:** The mission is well-defined, with clear goals and objectives and a communication plan in place. Checking for understanding is evident with the majority of individuals.
5. **Excellent:** The mission is exceptionally clear, with all stakeholders having a strong understanding of the goals, objectives, and expectations. There is evidence of understanding among all stakeholders involved.

Mission	Level of Clarity	Supporting Evidence	Action Steps to Ensure Clarity

Reflective Activity: Consistent Impact

Before diving into the following reflective questions, consider dedicating a notebook specifically to your leadership improvement journey. This dedicated space will help you track progress, revisit insights, and cultivate a consistent habit of self-reflection. Now, let's embark on this activity by exploring the areas where you shine consistently, the impact those areas have on others, and places where inconsistencies might be hindering your leadership potential. Remember, identifying challenges and barriers is the first step toward overcoming them and achieving a lasting impact. So, let's begin!

- What are three areas in which you are consistent?

- What impact is your consistency having on others?

- What are three areas in which you are inconsistent?

- What challenges or barriers are impeding your ability to be consistent?

- What is one action step you can take today to minimize or eliminate a barrier to your consistency?

Six Steps to a Strong School Culture © 2024 Samuel Nix • SolutionTree.com
Visit **go.SolutionTree.com/leadership** to download this free reproducible.

STEP 2: PLAN STRATEGICALLY AND MAKE DECISIONS

6

Working on the right thing is probably more important than working hard.

—Caterina Fake

LET'S DIVE into the second step of the leadership cycle: ensuring strategic planning and decision making. This step is crucial, yet often overlooked or misunderstood. However, as we dissect its components, you'll come to realize how even the most intricate strategic plans are built on simple foundational elements. In fact, your personal definition of strategic planning will likely transform by the end of this chapter.

Research suggests that strategic planning plays a pivotal role in organizational performance, in both the private and public sectors, across various international settings (George, Walker, & Monster, 2019). It's not merely about having a plan; it's about engaging in an informed process. This involves analyzing both internal and external environments, defining clear strategies and goals based on this analysis, and meticulously considering different courses of action before making final decisions.

Despite its significance, strategic planning is often neglected. It's not something that is commonly taught in schools, which begs the question, How can we expect our educators to incorporate it into their professional lives? As leaders, we are responsible for not only understanding strategic planning but also teaching and exemplifying it.

The beauty of strategic planning lies in its accessibility. It doesn't require additional financial resources; rather, it demands a shift in thinking and processing. Just as a pilot can enhance safety by engaging in the aeronautical decision-making thought process, organizations can mitigate risks and enhance performance by embracing strategic planning.

Of course, many companies fail to take strategic planning seriously. A 2005 report from *Harvard Business Review* (Kaplan & Norton, 2005) found that 85 percent of executive leadership teams spend less than one hour per month discussing strategy, and that 50 percent spend no time at all discussing it! The same report also revealed that, on average, 95 percent of an organization's employees do not understand said organization's strategy.

This chapter aims to give you the tools to break out of those statistics and establish a culture of strategizing and planning at your institution. In this chapter, you will learn how to plan strategically and make decisions by working around time and change, harnessing the elements that leaders can control, understanding emotional intelligence, and ensuring leaders know the foundation of effective planning.

Working Around Time and Change

Before we dive into strategic planning, consider this question: What are two things that are completely out of our control? You may be able to curate an expansive list, but the two elements we are looking for in this case are *time* and *change*. Time and change are going to happen whether we want them to or not. Both are inevitable constructs of life that are inherently neutral. They are neither constructive nor destructive. They can be optimized, or they can victimize. But any perception or notion of control over time and change is simply an illusion.

Successful leaders are defined by the way they manage time and change. After all, we become what we are as a result of how we use time and how we manage the change in our lives. In chapter 3 (page 37), we discussed fixed mindset and growth mindset. Anyone with a fixed mindset is going to use time and change as excuses to play the victim ("I don't have enough time," or "My circumstances changed and threw me off course, so I could not plan effectively"). Although these reasons may be valid, they are also fixed statements. The growth-minded leader is optimistic about finding opportunities to maximize the use of time and change. The challenges that time and change present will excite the leader with a growth mindset.

There is a statement attributed to author Stephen Keague (2012): "Proper planning and preparation prevents poor performance." Proper planning in this context will rely on the extent to which the planning includes internal and external analyses and the formulation of goals, strategies, and plans. If we take that saying and apply it to our educational systems, we can tackle multiple types of poor performance.

Proper planning and preparation prevents poor student performance, poor teacher performance, and poor institutional performance throughout a district or region, but many leaders take action without proper planning. Effective leaders plan ahead for lasting success because if you do not have a plan, you do not have a focus.

As a leader, you must navigate time and change effectively. Equipping yourself with the right tools empowers you to thrive in dynamic environments. Time-tracking apps or logs provide you with self-awareness, revealing areas to improve and enabling effective task prioritization. Calendar tools help you master your minutes by blocking time for specific tasks, scheduling meetings efficiently, and minimizing wasted time. Prioritization frameworks become your allies, helping you focus on the most critical activities with maximum impact. Finally, mastering time delegation frees up your time for strategic work. By assigning tasks to the right team members, you empower them and unlock your full leadership potential.

Determining What Can Be Controlled

After determining that 80 percent of the land in Italy was owned by 20 percent of the population, the civil engineer, philosopher, and sociologist Vilfredo Federico Damaso Pareto coined the terms *vital few* and *trivial many*. Their meaning is important to what is now known as the *80/20 rule*, which Pareto is credited with developing (Dunford, Su, & Tamang, 2014; New World Encyclopedia, n.d.); that is, 80 percent of results come from 20 percent of actions. Pareto's universal truth regarding the imbalance of inputs and outputs became immensely popular and was used in time management, leadership development, and self-help books about healthy habits across the board.

Consider these general examples of the 80/20 rule: if 80 percent of consequences occur from 20 percent of actions, then, in generalized terms, 80 percent of crimes are committed by 20 percent of the population; 80 percent of pollution comes from 20 percent of factories; and 80 percent of a company's sales are generated by 20 percent of a company's customers.

Effective leaders face a paradox in their use of time. It always feels like they do not have enough time to plan in a thorough, strategic, and collaborative way when faced with distractions and a lack of focus. Yet, they are expected to plan strategically as a core function of their job.

To leverage the 80/20 rule, leaders need to spend more time planning on the front end, using that time to get their job done right in the first place, which will supercharge productivity. When planning as well as strategically planning, leaders need to remember that in every mission (and mini-mission), there is a goal.

The first step is to identify specifically what you are trying to accomplish and what the impact will be. For you to be strategic, you have to think through the obstacles and anticipate them. You have to identify the knowledge, skills, and information you need to be successful. Then, once you've established these elements, you must identify the people whose help, support, and collaboration you will need. That's a lot of preparation, and yet, there is more.

Once you have established what you want and what the goal is, you now have to determine all the steps needed to reach that goal. Every single step. Successful leaders plan each day, week, month, and sometimes year in advance. Such leaders are not reactive. Investing the majority of your focus and time in your planning will make executing more effective.

There is a saying I have heard that goes, "If you don't have time to do it right the first time, when will you have time to do it over?" Think about that statement for a moment. Effective leaders make time to get it right. They think through every element possible. They take the time on the front end so that they don't have to make time on the back end.

Effective leaders must take the time to be strategic. You have to look around corners and proactively anticipate what obstacles could be lurking at every turn. If you apply the 80/20 rule to your daily work, you will spend much less time having to rework your plan, review your plan, revamp your plan, rewind your plan, recover from mistakes made during inadequate planning, and more. Effective leaders minimize risk. They also minimize waste.

In the next section, let's explore the definition of strategic planning.

Redefining Strategic Planning

In education, the term *strategic planning* connotes an outcome, but it is so far from that result in reality. Strategic planning is a process through and through.

When leaders define *strategy*, most will say that a strategy is a plan. But it's not just any plan. It is vital we understand the difference for ourselves. Too many leaders are comfortable with their strategy. If you become comfortable with your strategy, there is a good chance that it isn't a good one. Effective leaders understand that a good strategy will stretch their comfort zones.

Planning and other activities will always dominate strategy unless you make a conscious effort to prevent that. *Strategic planning* is a blueprint for the work you will do to achieve your goal. *Strategic thinking* is the process that you use to get there—the practice of orienting decisions with the end goal in mind. Strategic thinking is the input to strategic planning. In short, it is foresight. Strategic thinkers resist the urge to let one decision dictate future decisions. Effective leaders accept that good strategy is not the product of hours of researching, modeling, and developing the perfect conclusion. Instead, good strategy is achieved by simple and quite rough-and-ready processes of thinking about what it will take to achieve what you want. At the end of the day, strategic planning takes a lot of courage and determination, but leaders who use strategic thinking and planning will drive proactive change.

Key elements of strategic planning that have proven effective include analyzing the organization's core principles (mandate, mission, and values), dissecting its internal and external environments, pinpointing critical issues based on these analyses, and formulating robust strategies, goals, and actionable plans to address them (George et al., 2019). Outlined in more specific terms, it looks like the following.

1. **Defining your vision:** Paint a clear picture of your desired future state, outlining what success looks like for your organization.

2. **Crafting your values:** Establish the core principles that guide your decisions and shape your organization's culture.

3. **Determining desired outcomes:** Set specific, measurable, attainable, results-oriented, and time-bound (SMART) goals that represent what you want to achieve (Conzemius & O'Neill, 2014).

4. **Declaring explicit accountability:** Assign clear ownership of and responsibility for achieving each goal, ensuring everyone knows their role.

5. **Establishing leading key performance indicators:** Identify and track key performance indicators that directly reflect progress toward your vision and goals, providing data-driven insights for decision making.

Planning Strategically Using the Seven Principles

Now that you've grasped the basic elements of strategic planning, here is a helpful summary of best practices to consider when planning strategically. These seven principles should be top of mind as you ensure that the missions of your organization come to fruition.

1. **Avoid planning for the sake of planning:** Some leaders and organizations engage in planning just to say they have planned. Look at any job description of an educational leader, and you will find a section on "engaging and developing strategic plans"—but that's not what they're really doing.

   When you plan for the sake of planning, you're going to get out of it exactly what you put into it. If you've been enlightened by anything in this chapter, may it be that if you are going to take the time to do something, take the time to do it right. Conducting countless meetings and workshops for brainstorming without setting concrete goals or action steps leads to spinning wheels rather than progress. Planning sessions should spark action, not just generate further planning needs.

   There is a lot of preparation and development that must occur before a strategic plan is signed, sealed, and delivered. Effective leaders make strategic trade-offs and focus resources where they have the most impact. Put all your effort into the front end so you can see back-end results. Creating plans that please everyone instead of prioritizing key objectives dilutes the effectiveness of strategic planning efforts. Instead, prioritize key objectives and focus on actions that will have the greatest influence. Strategic plans are powerful guides that can pave the road for lasting, positive change.

2. **Plan for impact:** Anytime a leader is planning, they should always be focused on impact. Their vision must inspire the planning teams

to pay attention to changes in the culture and climate. Everyone involved needs to pay attention to the adaptive and technical aspects of the planning process. What can be solved by an expert? What requires relationship building and trust? Leaders must set meaningful priorities to pursue results. Plan to have an impact, not just to check a box.

3. **Invite the right team:** Effective leaders get the right people involved. Those charged with executing the plan should be involved at the onset. You don't want to do things to people. You want to do things with people. As a leader, you must champion those involved in planning to keep everyone on track. The right team is filled with the right motivation and desire to get things done to benefit the greater good.

4. **Monitor consistently:** Effective leaders monitor consistently. Most plans that schools develop are talked about and then forgotten. They lie collecting dust in a file folder or a binder, or perhaps never make the transition from the digital word processor to physical paper. To be effective, plans must be used and reviewed continually. People change, circumstances change, and priorities may even change. How can a strategic plan developed at the beginning of the school year address the issues that arise during the second half of the school year? (Granted, if the leaders anticipated potential roadblocks, those issues may indeed be in the plan.) The strategic plan should be seen as a living, breathing document that can change when needed. The plan must also live in the minds, hearts, and beliefs of those in charge of executing that plan. For that outcome to happen, the plan should be top of mind.

5. **Keep plans flexible:** Along with consistent monitoring, there should be a generous allowance of flexibility. Although the strategic nature of the plan is to look around corners and identify potential challenges, plans have to be nimble and adaptive to all the nuances and changes that come with working with and leading people. Effective leaders understand that. Those aspects are part of the strategic nature of plans, as most strategic plans must be malleable in order to make long-lasting change.

6. **Establish a culture of accountability:** Effective leaders must establish a culture of accountability and follow through with it. They must be resolute once a plan is developed and resources are deployed for the delivery of strategy. If and when the strategy is unsuccessfully delivered or the results do not come to fruition, effective leaders reflect on their part in ensuring clarity, support, and resources and take the necessary steps to hold people accountable. The culture of accountability is achieved by ensuring clarity of the mission, continual monitoring of the plan, and a focus on impacts.

7. **Focus:** Effective leaders avoid a lack of focus. As I said before, when leaders do not have a road map or they let distractions affect their ability to plan strategically, there will be cracks in the foundation of that strategic plan. Effective leaders avoid wasting resources and time. They spend much time on the front end preserving the stewardship of resources so they do not waste their own time or the organization's resources. Effective leaders understand that strategically developed plans must be focused and include a manageable number of goals, objectives, and initiatives. Although the planning is strategic in nature, fewer tactics in focus are better than numerous and nebulous ones.

Making Decisions Effectively

Strategy is implemented through decision. Effective leaders are decisive, and they establish clear decision-making frameworks to help them navigate difficult choices. They anticipate and manage uncertainty. In order to anticipate problems and challenges, effective leaders engage in brainstorming on their own and collectively. This brainstorming allows leaders to identify prospective conditions or events that could negatively affect the mission.

Effective decision makers understand that they are not trying to be prophetic but are working to anticipate potential obstacles and manage them. You're not going to get it all right or accurate all the time, but you will train yourself and your staff to think through potential obstacles—imagining what could happen, exploring a range of possibilities. Then, when the possibilities become reality, you and your team are prepared for the best and worst scenarios.

Identify and prepare for potential obstacles that could impact your strategy or project. Use the worksheet in figure 6.1 (page 111) as a starting point, and build

Activity	Individual	Collective
Questions to consider	• What internal weaknesses could hinder progress? • What external threats could arise? • What unexpected events could occur? • What are potential roadblocks to success?	• What concerns do others have? • What unique perspectives can others offer? • What creative solutions can we brainstorm together?
Techniques to use	Freewriting, mind mapping, worst-case scenario planning	Brainwriting, role playing, group discussion
Identified potential obstacles		

FIGURE 6.1: Individual and collective decision making.

*Visit **go.SolutionTree.com/leadership** for a free reproducible version of this figure.*

on it as you gain experience. Fill out each section for your specific situation. Adapt the methods and prompts to best fit your needs.

The second mark of effective decision makers is their ability to decipher when to rely on evidence and when to trust intuition. Most leaders believe their intelligence will always help them make the best decisions. In reality, they rely on their intelligence as a crutch when intuition is equally important in decision-making progress.

The reason intuition is so important is that it is developed over a period of time. It is largely shaped by past experiences, past knowledge, professional encounters, and more. Of course, leaders should not rely solely on intuition. One extreme or another is never ideal. They should call on a delicate balance between intelligence and intuition. Effective leaders make systemic decisions based on a combination of intuition and knowledge supported by data.

A practical example of when a campus principal might rely on intuition is during a crisis situation that requires immediate action. Let's say there's a sudden security threat on campus, such as a potential intruder. In such a scenario, the principal may not have time to gather extensive data or consult with others before making a decision. Instead, they may need to rely on their intuition, honed over years of experience dealing with various situations, to quickly assess the threat and determine the best course of action to ensure the safety of students and staff.

In this situation, the principal's intuition, shaped by past experiences and professional encounters, can guide them in making swift and effective decisions under pressure. While they may not have all the relevant data at hand, their intuition can help them draw on their knowledge of the campus layout, understanding of potential risks, and past experiences with emergency protocols to take decisive action.

Of course, it's essential for the principal to balance their intuition with any available information and to follow up with a thorough review of the incident afterward. This allows them to learn from the experience and refine their intuition for future crisis situations.

In short, evidence-based experiences guide intuition, and effective leaders rely on a combination of resources for strategic decision making.

Incorporating Emotional Intelligence

Effective leaders ensure that they can balance emotion and reason to make decisions that will benefit their organization, which is where emotional intelligence comes into play. Emotional intelligence, and an understanding of its connection to dimensions of personality, provides an additional tool for leaders to become more effective and successful (Cavaness, Picchioni, & Fleshman, 2020).

Emotional intelligence (*EQ*) is the ability to understand your emotions as well as those of others. It is one of the most important qualities of an effective leader. A central theme in the book *Leadership: The Power of Emotional Intelligence* by Daniel Goleman (2011) is awareness of a leader's degree of emotional intelligence and its direct relation to effectively motivating others, getting them to commit, and getting them in the best zone. It is worthwhile for anyone desiring to lead others, or simply to become an effective team member, to study emotional intelligence and acquire higher EQ skills. This will yield rewards in professional success and personal satisfaction (Cavaness et al., 2020).

Effective leaders bring out the best of the people they work with. Emotions are contagious (Goleman, 2011). Naturally, a leader's emotions are contagious, so being a leader who is calm in a storm is vital. A leader's mood will resonate with others and can set the tone of the entire organization.

Leaders have to make a lot of crucial decisions. They could be related to budget or personnel. They could be about classroom policies or incredibly high-stakes things that could make or break the organization. When schools rely on their leaders to make swift, tough, influential, wide-ranging decisions, that pressure can evoke emotions of frustration, fear, anxiety, self-doubt, and even anger. If a leader is engaged in planning for their educational institution and is in a heightened state of emotion, what kind of impact will that state of mind have on the people working within the organization?

Leaders do not have to be emotionless robots. I'm not suggesting they hide their feelings away. To deny an emotion is like cleaning up a room full of dirty clothes by hiding the clothes under the bed, in the closet, or under the rug. Sure, the room appears clean, but eventually, you will still have to deal with the mess you hid away. It is OK to experience emotions in the decision-making process, but effective leaders ensure that those emotions do not guide their decisions. If a leader makes an emotional decision or fails to rely on their own emotional intelligence before making a big decision, the driving emotions behind that decision will emanate throughout the organization.

Emotional intelligence consists of self-awareness, self-management, social awareness, and relationship management, which are Goleman's four quadrants of EQ. These four skills are essential for understanding the balance between emotions and decision making (and the role emotions do play). The individual skills that comprise emotional intelligence, according to Goleman (2011), can be described as follows.

1. **Self-awareness:** This is the foundation of all aspects of emotional intelligence. It means you can recognize your own strengths, emotions, values, weaknesses, and drivers. It is the ability to understand your own impact on others. Effective leaders recognize their emotions and understand how to separate emotional drivers from the decision-making process by identifying the root of the emotion and casting it aside so it does not cloud their judgment. Let's say a leader gets in a fight with their spouse in the morning before work. As the leader drives to their workplace, they get stuck in traffic, making them rush to prepare for an early morning meeting. Before the leader sits down to start the meeting, their morning has been full of emotions and even distractions. During the meeting, someone could say something that triggers an emotional response, reminding the leader of the fight with their spouse. Yet, keen self-awareness is the superpower that helps the leader calmly facilitate the meeting and be fully present.

2. **Self-management:** This ability to control or redirect your disruptive emotions and adapt to changing circumstances in an optimistic way keeps your team moving in a positive direction. Perhaps someone in this meeting says, "You seem as if you're rushed," to the leader. Rather than take offense, or jump into a defensive mode, the leader can take a deep breath and respond accordingly to the observation. "I appreciate your consideration. My commute took a little extra time from my preparation this morning, but I am glad to be here and am fully prepared to begin our meeting." That redirection aids the leader in managing their emotions, yet also drives the meeting in an optimistic direction.

3. **Social awareness:** This ability allows you to put yourself in someone else's shoes and understand how they feel and react in certain situations. If a teacher is having a rough week or a student is really struggling with emotional management, social awareness gives the leader the lens to see from the teacher's or student's point of view and make decisions accordingly.

4. **Relationship management:** This is vital for leaders, as is relationship awareness. Awareness of your own distractions will help you foster meaningful relationships with your teachers and colleagues. To build trust, leaders must always manage relationships in order to forge new relationships and strengthen existing ones. Effective leaders do both by being genuine, decisive, transparent, and knowledgeable.

The mastery of emotional intelligence is like a magnet, inviting others to trust the leader.

Addressing the Roots and Fruits of the Decision-Making Process

So often in leadership, we are conditioned to address the fruit. What is fruit in a school system? A student misbehaves—that is fruit. A teacher appears dysfunctional—that is fruit. An administrator is always turning in reports late—that is fruit. Each circumstance has a root cause.

At a particular middle school where I worked, discipline left much to be desired. When assistant principals would walk into their offices, they would be greeted by a line of students waiting to be addressed for disciplinary issues. The issues could be classroom misbehavior, fighting, dress code violation—you name it. The moment the assistant principals cleared the line of students, a new slew of misbehaving students would come down the hall to their offices. It was a never-ending cycle.

Because of that issue, the assistant principals were unable to get into the classrooms, attend meetings, monitor the hallways, or do a range of responsibilities. They were always tied up addressing the line of misbehaviors. The teachers would get frustrated with the students and send them to the assistant principals for discipline. The assistant principals would dole out disciplinary actions and send the students on their way (be it to in-school suspension, out-of-school suspension, or another disciplinary measure).

The constant revolving door–like process did not contribute to a productive or enjoyable environment. The teachers didn't appreciate having to stop their curricular activities to address the misbehaviors. The assistant principals felt ineffective because they couldn't attend to their other duties, which quite possibly could have prevented some of the misbehaviors from occurring. Most of all, the students were not happy. They didn't feel as if they belonged. They didn't feel successful. They didn't feel motivated. There was a lot of leaf picking and fruit picking of the tree at this school. With every pick, something grew back. Progress went backward. Something had to be done.

The principal made the controversial decision to spend the majority of his time, energy, and effort working to identify and address the root issues causing the majority of the fruit problems. The administration engaged in strategically planning how they would identify the 20 percent of the teachers experiencing—and in some cases, causing—80 percent of the issues. They worked collectively on an aligned approach to provide targeted support, training, development, and progress monitoring to ensure improvement. That approach meant that there would be short-term, temporary sacrifices in order to focus on long-term, sustainable results. Students sent for discipline would have to be sent back to class. Attempts to reduce recidivism with discipline weren't even working, so this shouldn't be much of a sacrifice. Yes, it would upset some teachers; however, the administrators would help them understand and manage such changes for the greater good.

If the administration could get into the classrooms more frequently and identify the challenges before they escalated, they could work with the teachers to develop strategies to get the students feeling motivated, engaged, valued, and desirous to be successful. What else happens when administrators spend more time in classrooms, hallways, and cafeterias, meeting with and talking with students and teachers?

The presence of the administrators is a proactive deterrent to off-task behavior for both teachers and students. The administrators' visibility, participation, and collaborative efforts would have a positive impact on the middle school's culture and climate. The administrators could gain a more in-depth understanding of exact issues and build stronger connections to support improvement.

Their attention identified the root.

What was the root? Students were misbehaving and requiring discipline because they were not engaged with the learning. Bored students wanted attention. They were seeking connection and felt that acting out was a way to achieve it. When students are not engaged and do not understand the lesson at hand, they have no relationship with the teacher and no connection to the learning environment.

Based on this discovery, the assistant principals worked with teachers on the technical aspects of engagement and alignment as well as the adaptive aspects to motivate, engage, and empower both the teachers and the learners. Those teachers needed the resources to determine how to handle behavioral situations before they occurred instead of dealing with the issues after the disruption. Even technical actions such as greeting each student at the door and checking in on their mood had a huge impact at the root level, minimizing the fruit. And by supporting improvement in just one teacher who had a direct correlation to student achievement, spending 20 percent of time working on the root solved 80 percent of the issues. The root was there all along. It just needed to be uncovered.

Imagine a school where students consistently perform poorly on standardized tests. The administrators, teachers, and parents may focus on implementing short-term solutions such as extra tutoring sessions or test-taking strategy workshops to improve scores (addressing the fruit of poor performance). However, if they were to delve deeper and identify the root causes of the poor performance, they might discover issues such as inadequate resources, ineffective teaching methods, or lack of student engagement.

To address these root causes, administrators could allocate resources to provide additional training for teachers on innovative teaching methods, invest in updated educational materials, or implement programs to enhance student motivation and engagement. By targeting these underlying issues, the school can create a more conducive learning environment where students are better equipped to succeed academically, leading to improvements in test scores and overall academic achievement.

If leaders start to embrace a mindset of identifying the root cause of an issue, instead of picking at the problem, there will be more sustainability in the results and achievements. Understanding root causes is believed to help everyone decide future action (Gnepp, Klayman, Williamson, & Barlas, 2020).

Strategic planning falls under the umbrella of how we approach issues and problems as well as the thinking that takes. In the long term, we develop teachers who have the skills, mindset, resources, tools, and perspective that drastically minimize fruit-bearing activities.

A widely popular method of root cause identification and analysis is known as the *five whys*. It's a structured method for mapping out all the potential culprits behind an issue, ensuring you tackle the real problem (roots), not just its symptoms (fruits). Think of it as a detective's blueprint, revealing the hidden connections and underlying issues that fuel recurring challenges.

But what about when you don't have all the answers? To create a comprehensive map of possibilities, even with limited information, start with a binary issue. Ask the initial *why* and frame it as a choice: either this, or not that. Then, delve deeper from the chosen path, exploring its implications and potential branches. See the example in figure 6.2 for an illustration of the breakdown.

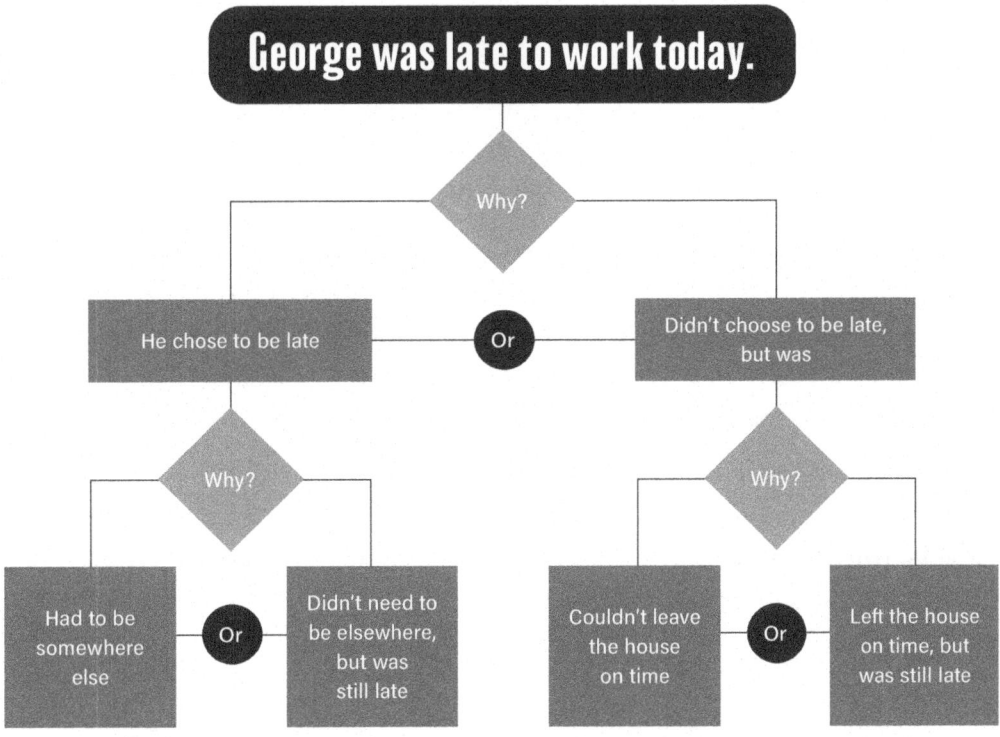

FIGURE 6.2: "George was late to work today" possibility map.

But where do you start? It's simple, really. Channel your inner five-year-old and unleash the power of why. Ask why five times, digging deeper with each answer until you reach the core, the root cause. This five whys approach is just one way to get your root cause map rolling.

But what good is a map without a plan? Once you've identified the root cause, it's time to take action. Use your newfound knowledge to develop solutions that address the core issue and will prevent it from resurfacing. Root cause analysis isn't just about solving problems; it's about developing a structured problem-solving mindset, a valuable skill applicable in any situation. Let's take a look at the following example:

> *George (also Daddy) was late to work.*
>
> *Why?*
>
> *Because he didn't leave the house on time.*
>
> *Why?*
>
> *Because he couldn't find his shoes.*
>
> *Why?*
>
> *Because they were not in the usual place.*
>
> *Why?*
>
> *Because his four-year-old son hid them under the bed.*
>
> *Why?*
>
> *Because his son thought it would be funny and could reach them.*
>
> *Solution: George should keep his work clothes and essentials out of his son's reach!*

When incorporating the five whys method, remember that you may not always get to exactly five whys. Don't force it—focus on uncovering verifiable problems within your control, even if it takes fewer or more than five questions. Stop when you hit the root cause you can address. Figure 6.3 (page 119) is an example of how to use root cause analysis to map out why current results are below par.

After mapping your information, strategically prioritize your findings by allocating one hundred points across potential root causes based on their likelihood of being true and accurate. This weighted voting system helps you visualize which causes are most deserving of investigation.

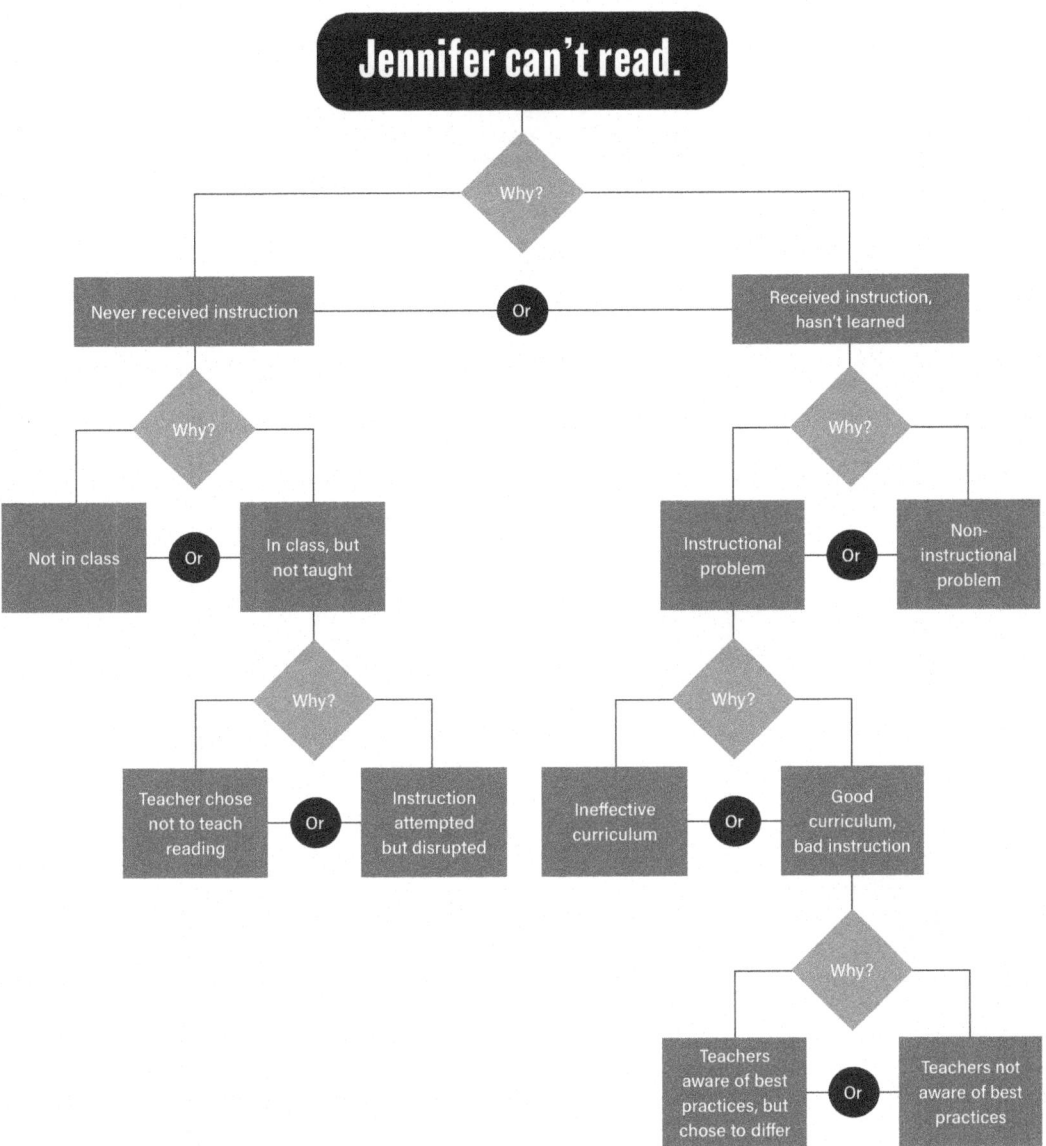

FIGURE 6.3: "Jennifer can't read" possibility map.

Next, list your root causes in descending order of their weight. This clarifies the focus. Now, create a plan to disprove each possible cause, starting with the most likely. By systematically testing each weighted cause, you'll not only pinpoint the true culprit more efficiently, but also uncover potential solutions to move forward. See figure 6.4 (page 120) for a sample.

Allocate 100 points across the potential root causes based on their likelihood of being accurate.

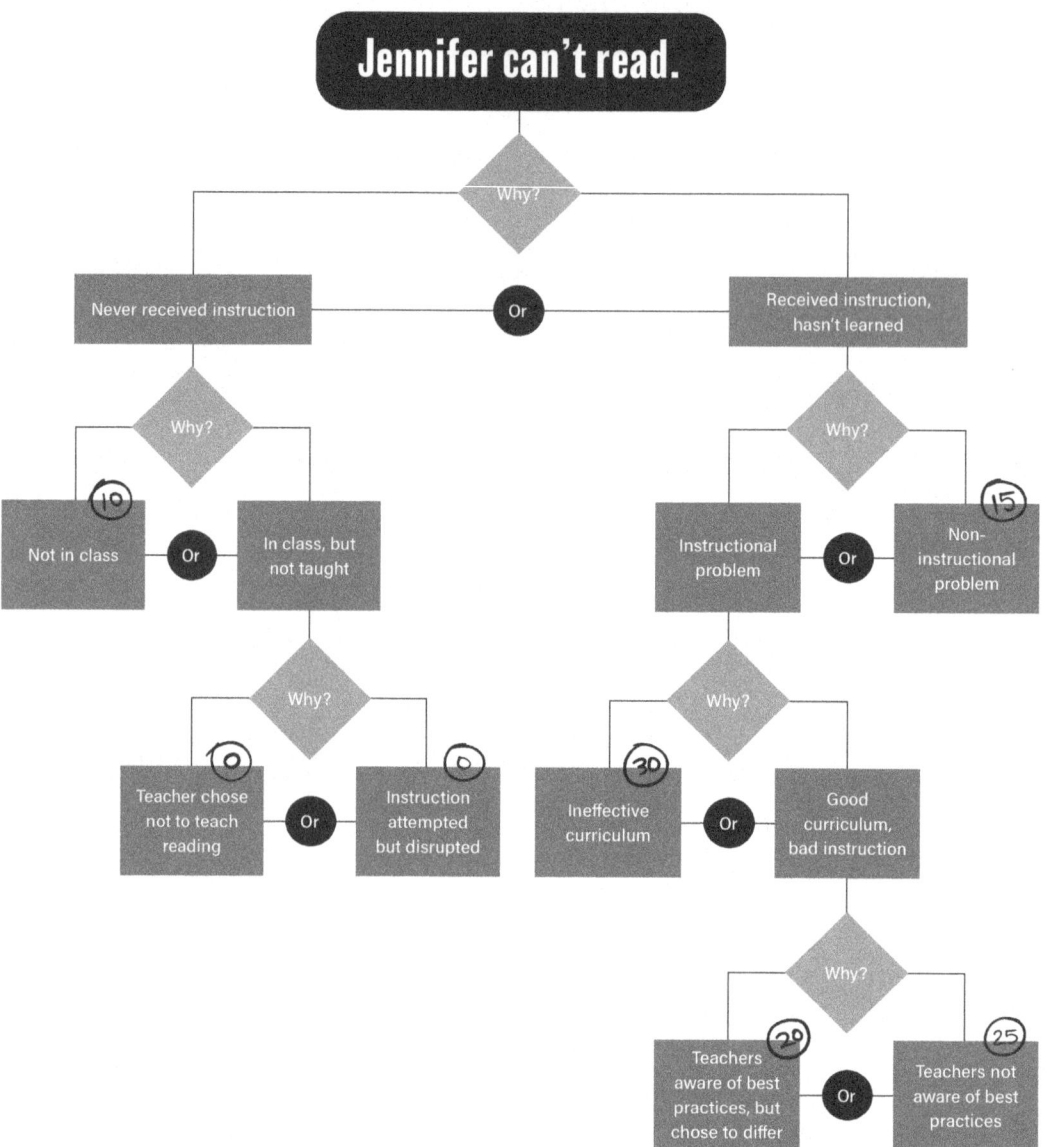

FIGURE 6.4: Point allocation for a possibility map.

Define your problem statement; then consider the bigger picture. How widespread is the issue? For instance, our example problem is Jennifer's inability to read. Now, consider the broader scope. Are many other students struggling? In our example, only 45 percent of students are reading proficiently, but nearby districts boast rates of 65–75 percent. This context helps paint a clearer picture.

Next, ask yourself, "Is this an isolated case or a recurring pattern?" If it's a pattern, determine the time frame. Maybe our district has consistently scored below 45 percent on fourth-grade reading tests for the past decade. Understanding the context, whether it's widespread or isolated, recent or ongoing, will guide prioritization and action steps.

Using Root Cause Analysis

Reflect on a current issue you are experiencing, its likely root cause, and possible solutions using the template in figure 6.5. Analyze the problem by filling out the next levels of the root cause map (as sampled in the figure). Strive to get to root causes that are verifiable.

Example Problem

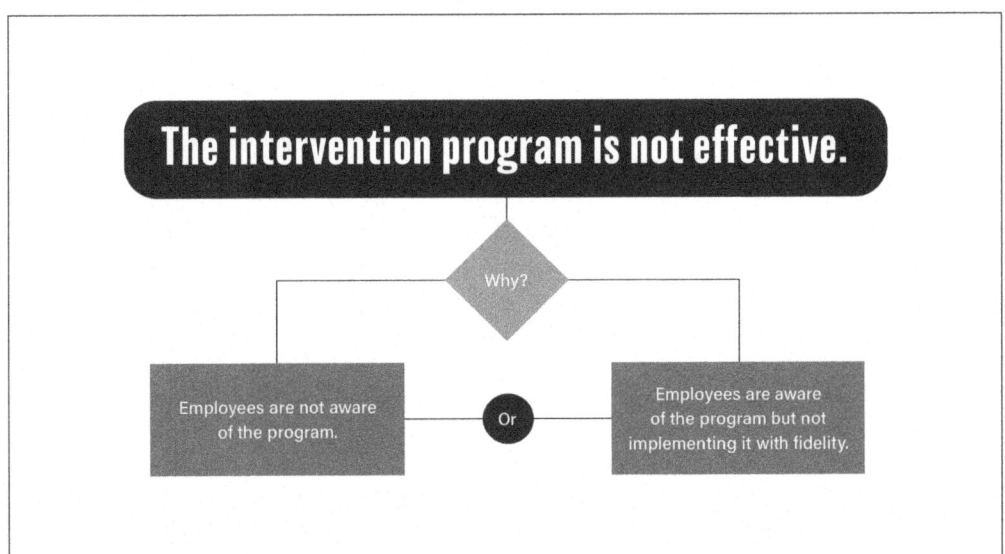

Map the Problem

1. Define the problem.
2. Break the problem into its component parts.
3. Assign points to prioritize which components to solve first.

Investigate and Verify

1. Take action steps.
2. Analyze.
3. Synthesize and communicate.
4. Solve.

FIGURE 6.5: Root cause analysis. continued →

Issue	
Description	**Impact on Student Learning**
Lack of instructional alignment to the standards	Students are not learning to the level of the standards.

Likely Root Cause		
Description	**Adaptive Challenges**	**Technical Challenges**
Teachers have not received sufficient training or professional development on how to effectively implement the standards in their classrooms.	Teachers may need to shift their mindset and instructional practices to align with the standards, which can require changes in attitudes, beliefs, and behaviors. This may involve moving away from traditional teaching methods and embracing more student-centered, inquiry-based approaches.	Teachers have diverse needs and levels of expertise, so providing differentiated support to meet these needs can be challenging. Tailoring professional development opportunities to address specific skill gaps or instructional priorities requires careful planning and resource allocation. Teachers may struggle to find time for professional development amid their busy schedules, and schools or districts may face resource constraints in providing ongoing support.

Possible Solutions
Provide ongoing support rather than one-off sessions, allowing teachers to gradually implement new strategies and receive feedback.
Incorporate research-based instructional practices and examples of successful implementation to inspire and guide teachers.
Provide opportunities for reflection and dialogue to address teachers' attitudes, beliefs, and concerns about adopting new instructional practices.
Empower teachers to take on leadership roles and share their expertise with colleagues.

Description	Risks	Measures of Success
Transition to ongoing support by establishing a PLC for collaboration and feedback. Explore coaching or mentoring programs to connect teachers with experienced educators for personalized guidance. Establish a way for teachers to share reflections to refine their practices and foster continuous improvement in teaching effectiveness.	Potential risk of overwhelming teachers with added responsibilities and expectations Challenge in maintaining a consistent quality of support across various initiatives Resistance from entrenched organizational cultures or individuals Resource constraints or logistic hurdles impeding implementation	Measure the frequency and duration of support sessions provided to teachers. Monitor the implementation progress over time, tracking the adoption of new strategies. Evaluate lesson plans and teaching materials to ensure they align with research-based instructional practices. Monitor student performance and engagement to assess the impact of the implemented strategies.

*Visit **go.SolutionTree.com/leadership** for a free reproducible version of this figure.*

Key Points

This chapter highlighted the crucial roles strategic planning and effective decision making play for any leader. While time and change are constant, how we manage them defines our impact. The 80/20 rule, where 80 percent of results come from 20 percent of actions, emphasizes the need for prioritization and resource efficiency.

Strategic planning starts with setting clear goals, engaging the right team, consistently monitoring, and adapting to changing circumstances. Effective decision making goes further, anticipating challenges and leveraging emotional intelligence to motivate and lead others. Addressing root causes, not just symptoms, leads to sustainable solutions and lasting improvement.

By implementing these principles, leaders can navigate complexities, drive proactive change, and foster a culture of accountability, innovation, and success. But this journey doesn't end there. As we move to chapter 7, we'll explore how effective leaders truly thrive: by empowering themselves and others.

Empowerment fosters a culture of motivation and engagement. Team members become active contributors to sustainable solutions and long-term improvement. Strategic planning and decision making remain crucial, requiring leaders to prioritize, assemble the right team, and adapt. However, it's through empowerment that this framework comes alive, generating ownership, innovation, and lasting success.

As you leave this chapter, remember the following.

- Two things that are out of everyone's control are time and change.
- The 80/20 rule states that 20 percent of actions yield 80 percent of consequences. You can manage your time by adopting the 80/20 rule in your daily life to supercharge your productivity.
- Strategy is implemented through decision.
- Effective leaders have focus and do not let distractions or emotions affect decision-making processes.
- Effective leaders anticipate roadblocks and check around corners when planning strategically.
- Emotional intelligence (EQ) is the ability to understand your emotions as well as those of others. It is one of the most important qualities of an effective leader.
- When you are addressing any issue, any problem, or any emotion, it is paramount to determine the root cause. If you tackle the fruit of the issue, it will always grow back. You must address the roots for change to last.

Reflective Activity: Planning Time

Before delving into this activity's thought-provoking questions, take a moment to acknowledge your current relationship with planning. Are you feeling stretched thin, reacting to demands instead of proactively shaping your future? Consider this a chance to reclaim control and unlock your potential through effective planning. Remember, there's no one-size-fits-all answer, so approach these questions with an open mind and a readiness to tailor your schedule for maximum impact. Let's dive in and design a planning approach that empowers you!

Consider the following questions as you reflect on your own planning time.

- What percentage of your time is currently devoted to planning?

- What are three influential adjustments you can make to your weekly schedule in order to increase the time you invest in strategic planning?

Reflective Activity: Strategic Planning

When it comes to ensuring a quality strategic planning process, asking reflective questions is key. Consider the following questions as you reflect on your own strategic planning.

- What two or three specific objectives are you planning to accomplish?

- What impact will your objectives have on student learning?

- How will you measure success with each objective?

- Who owns each objective? Who will lead the efforts to ensure results?

- How will you know you have the right people involved in the process?

STEP 3: EMPOWER YOURSELF AND OTHERS

If your dream only includes you, it's too small.

—Ava DuVernay

DURING THE 2016 Summer Olympics, the star-studded U.S. team consisting of Tianna Bartoletta, Allyson Felix, English Gardner, and Tori Bowie prepared to compete in the 4 × 100 meters relay (Mather, 2016). All eyes were on them as they hoped to defend the United States' gold title from the 2012 Olympic Games.

In the qualifier heat, these four women were prepared to earn their spot in the championship relay. Bartoletta, Felix, Gardner, and Bowie had trained hard for that moment. They had eaten to fuel their bodies and made countless sacrifices to compete on the world's biggest athletic stage. Each competitor had put in thousands of hours of training individually and as a team. There was a lot of pressure and a lot of expectation on the defending champions' shoulders.

At the sound of the gun, Bartoletta shot off the block to get a strong lead for her team. Felix held her arm behind her back, eager to receive the baton from Bartoletta. If you watch a relay race closely, you will see that the runners rarely look at their teammate delivering the baton. Instead, their eyes are forward, and they trust their teammate to get the baton in their hand.

After a clean handoff, Felix took off. She made her way around the track and approached Gardner, who, like Felix before her, awaited the baton. But something wasn't right. A runner from the Brazilian team bumped Felix's arm, and she dropped the baton onto the track. It was a relay athlete's worst nightmare come true.

However, the U.S. team would learn the importance of empowerment that day. As you'll see, they returned from the brink and won.

Leadership is like a relay race, where the baton is a baton of empowerment. You see, it is one thing to develop a plan strategically, but it is an entirely different thing to empower others to follow through with the plan. The latter is why the next step in the leadership cycle is empowering yourself and others. It only makes sense to empower people after a plan has been decided, and feedback can only be fair and effective after your people are empowered.

What do I mean by *empower*? For our purposes, to empower is to encourage and stimulate an individual to think, behave, and make decisions toward the mission. Empowerment is permission to take a proactive approach to learning and experiencing what is currently affecting, or will eventually affect, yourself and others.

By now, you've ensured clarity of the vision and mission. You're well versed in planning strategically. Instead of having employees ask for permission or wait for direction, you, as an effective leader, will empower them to become more responsible and accountable as a result of self-direction. Empowered people add value to the mission. They can change the culture and climate of an organization from one of reactivity to one of proactivity. Empowered people do not wait for change to affect them. They initiate change to influence results.

Two Focus Areas of Empowerment

Effective leaders must focus primarily on two different perspectives of empowerment. These are (1) self-empowerment and (2) empowerment of others.

Sounds easy, but what does it really mean? A leader's job is to take the necessary steps to gain the proper insight, understanding and knowledge required for them to empower others. You can't teach what you don't know—and you can't provide an experience for others if you have not experienced it yourself.

Self-Empowerment

Self-empowerment, in the context of the leadership cycle, is the process of gaining that insight and understanding to empower others. It is possible to inform and plan at a surface level of understanding and to not be empowering. The goal of empowering yourself is to maximize your potential and everyone else's.

Effective principals build up their teachers, provide those teachers with the resources for them to learn from, help teachers realize their leadership potential, and then trust those very same teachers to do their work. As a leader, if you attempt to solve everyone's problems, you will eventually burn out. You will create an atmosphere of dependence on your availability and reliance on your knowledge. If everything revolves around your decision making, you could be missing out on the creativity, experiences, and collective wisdom of great contributors. But if you can establish a culture of proactive consumers of information, the momentum you will build and the time you will save will be instrumental in achieving a greater level of success in a timelier manner.

Empowerment in leadership is like a relay race—not a sprint. Leadership is about not just how fast you run your leg, but how effectively you pass the baton to the next runner so they can run their leg of the race. You do not win a relay on your own. The whole team wins, and the key to the win is successfully passing the baton in the exchange, or empowerment, zone.

Effective leaders model a mindset of continuous improvement. They are constantly leading the learning. Self-empowered leaders are never satisfied with surface-level knowledge. These leaders constantly analyze their strengths and weaknesses, and they foster a continuous hunger for learning and growth.

Here is an example to illustrate self-empowerment. Let's say there is a room full of principals. They are hearing for the first time from their district leadership that the state will unveil a new teacher evaluation system for the upcoming year. The way the teacher evaluations have been done for years will be optimized and will change. In fact, to prepare for the change, the state has rolled out trainings on the new system along with evaluation templates for principals to get familiar with.

The principals are halfway through the current school year. They know the current system backward and forward. In fact, they could evaluate teachers in their sleep! Why bother taking time out of their busy days to poke around the new system? They can learn it when it is time to use it.

That approach is a complete and utter lack of self-empowerment. When the new system replaces the old, these principals will become victims of change. If they're focused on the old way and not learning the new way, they will become frustrated and look for excuses as to why they are failing at implementing the new system in a way that yields the desired results.

Instead, self-empowered principals find small chunks of time to get to know the new system. They take the time to strategically review the old evaluation and compare it to the new one, observing similarities and differences, and begin to think through potential obstacles and challenges with implementation as well as to formulate ideas and plans to overcome those. If they wait for someone to direct and guide them, their responses will be purely reactive when the time to change comes.

Self-empowered leaders are proactive. They take advantage of everything available to them so that when the change comes, they've practiced and prepared for that very moment. And remember, leaders are models in the organization, so if they are not engaging in self-empowerment, they are also creating a culture of the following.

- "I'll know it once I'm informed."
- "I'll do it once I'm directed."
- "I'll understand it once I'm taught."
- "I'll pay attention once it becomes important."

That mindset is dangerous because a reactive approach breeds an attitude of dependence. When you depend on others to show you the way, you put accountability on everything and everyone but yourself. That is how rumors start. That is how frustrations are born. That is what encourages a fixed mindset. Reactive people gather together and complain, "This school doesn't care about teachers," or "This school doesn't invest in students," or any other statements that blame the organization at large. Reactive people are often bred in a culture of dependence, and a culture of dependence stems from a lack of empowerment. To empower yourself means you are a proactive consumer of information, not a reactive recipient.

When leaders engage in self-empowerment, they demonstrate the priority of a growth mindset by leading the learning. Their modeling is a powerful way to ensure that a growth mindset permeates throughout an organization. Effective leaders establish credibility by learning and engaging in the discussion of a deeper level of understanding and by building trust.

I'll say it again: leadership is a team sport, and there is no weakness in demonstrating a growth mindset. Leaders' participation will foster trust throughout the organization. Finally, when a leader engages in self-empowerment, they minimize the chance of being victimized by someone else's timeline. When you know what is coming, you can prepare for it.

Leaders are always learners. They're always learning about what they are accountable and responsible for.

Empowerment of Others

When we start talking about empowering others, oftentimes many people think to empower is to inform. Information is a part of empowerment, but it is not the only part. Empowerment extends far beyond information.

To empower is to provide information and experience. People can have information, but the experience is what fosters beliefs. Beliefs shape actions, whereas actions produce results. You can't read a dissertation and say, "Oh, I'm empowered." A leader can't hand teachers a binder and say, "You'll be empowered after reading this." They will be informed, not empowered. Effective leaders have to think about how to provide experiences to engage with the information. Information and experience are what foster empowerment.

We learn by experience. Imagine if I tried to teach you how to tie a bowline knot by reading the instructions aloud to you. Would you be able to translate that information and tie the knot? Maybe. However, if you and I practiced tying the knot together, and I walked you through each step after demonstrating the knot, would you pick up the practice faster? Yes, because I provided you with an experience to use the information I wanted to relay. Providing information is helpful and will inform, but providing an experience based on that information is more helpful and will transform. Moreover, people feel empowered when they have what they need to solve their own problems, which simultaneously frees up time for leaders to address bigger, more macro-level issues.

Need proof? An employee job satisfaction and engagement study conducted by the Society for Human Resource Management (2016) found that "70 percent of employees [rank] being empowered to take action . . . as an important element of their engagement." When people have the knowledge to do their jobs, they feel good. Add on authorization to do their jobs along with resources, and they feel even better. So, how do effective leaders empower others?

- **Effective leaders empower others by delegating:** Such leaders appropriately share organizational authority. Now, *share* doesn't mean the leader dumps busywork onto subordinates or gives away tasks they do not enjoy doing. That's not empowerment. When the leader delegates tasks of importance, though, others feel empowered. They feel the leader trusts them.

  In turn, the leader provides opportunities for innovation, creativity, and increased morale. Everyone has a stake in the mission, and delegation solidifies that sentiment. It is also important to note that we cannot confuse empowerment with abandonment. When I say "empower people," it doesn't mean provide them with information and experiences and then leave. Information and experience are not replacements for the leader. They are supplements. Empowerment is collaborative in nature, with the leader leading the learning effort and delegating appropriately.

- **Effective leaders empower others by educating them:** The growth and development of people is a vital priority in effective leadership. Part of that comes through educating. Effective leaders are also effective teachers. They don't just give information—they ensure clarity and give experiences and opportunities to engage in that information.

- **Effective leaders empower others by encouraging them:** Courage is a special type of power. It is a mental strength to face fear and step outside the box. Many effective leaders are masters in the art of inspiration. They have the right words to lift someone up when they have fallen. They have the right lesson to share when someone has failed. Those talents can be life changing and empowering. But they must be genuine and personal. Personal encouragement is far more influential than a generalized complimentary statement. Leaders who engage in active listening are better positioned to tailor encouragement to individual needs and aspirations. This builds trust, personalizes support, and empowers individuals to overcome challenges and achieve their goals. Ultimately, it fuels growth through genuine and meaningful encouragement.

- **Effective leaders empower others by providing experiences that allow others to engage in the knowledge:** How often do we see teachers hired as assistant principals and immediately realize they might not have been as prepared as even they originally thought? They look great on paper and passed all their certifications, but when they get into that role, all that theory, all that information now has to be put into practice.

Look at medical students; they start as interns and slowly gain more responsibility as their knowledge and experience accumulate. However, educational leaders do not often receive this type of experiential training. If a teacher turned assistant principal hasn't experienced being cursed out by a parent with a line of students waiting out their door as the phone rings and email notifications ding like there is a fire, then have they really been empowered by their background?

The same can be said for principals. Many are former assistant principals. Now they're each the head of their school and in charge of the school's budget. Sure, they may have seen the budget, but did they have opportunities to practice allocating funds, identifying academic priorities for financial alignment, dealing with district pressures, and getting stakeholders on the same page? Those examples show why it is so important for leaders to empower others and offer experiences in addition to the knowledge. Knowledge is necessary, but experience practicing and using that knowledge is required to be empowered and successful.

Impact Without Imposition

Some leaders will try to impose their wills and beliefs onto the people they lead. That is not empowerment. Effective leaders understand that empowerment is not about imposition, but about influence. In order to understand the importance of having an impact without imposition, though, we must first understand the dynamics of influence on empowerment.

Effective leaders recognize that influence, not forceful mandates, unlocks true potential. This translates to inspiring and guiding, rather than dictating and demanding. Impact is about results, but the *how* matters deeply. How a leader builds trust, fosters collaboration, and empowers individuals shapes the outcome's sustainability, cultural impact, and long-term success. Ultimately, their goal is to cultivate an environment where people feel valued, empowered, and intrinsically motivated to achieve shared goals, not coerced into compliance.

The beliefs of an effective leader come out in their principles and behavior. They lead in learning, go the extra mile, practice consistency, and believe in the best of other people. When working with others, effective leaders provide opportunities and experiences to move people toward what is best for the organization. Sometimes, that momentum means leading people out of their comfort zones. Improvement isn't always comfortable. To motivate and inspire others to move into a realm of discomfort, effective leaders require influence. Influence is more important than power.

Power demands, but influence suggests. Power is forced, but influence is voluntary. Power is a one-way dialogue, but influence creates conversation. Power leads to an increasingly disengaged organization, but influence boosts employee retention, engagement, and morale. The following are examples of good influencing behaviors.

- **Focus on collaboration and shared goals:** This involves working together to understand others' perspectives and seeking solutions that benefit everyone. It prioritizes consensus and avoids manipulation of others.
- **Emphasize persuasion and reason:** Present clear arguments, evidence, and data to support your position. Encourage open dialogue and address concerns respectfully.
- **Empower others and build trust:** Delegate tasks, share information, and provide opportunities for others to contribute. This fosters a sense of ownership and engagement.
- **Respect diverse perspectives and feedback:** Value different viewpoints and actively listen to understand them. Be open to adjusting your ideas based on valid feedback.
- **Promote transparency and ethical practices:** Share information openly and honestly, avoiding deception or manipulative tactics.
- **Focus on long-term benefits and sustainability:** Consider the consequences of your actions on individuals, the organization, and society as a whole.

The following are examples of bad power-seeking behaviors.

- **Use intimidation, coercion, or threats:** This creates a climate of fear and discourages open communication.
- **Manipulate information or withhold key details:** This undermines trust and prevents informed decision making.
- **Discredit or dismiss opposing viewpoints:** This creates an environment of silence and discourages collaboration.
- **Focus on personal gain or advancement over the common good:** This leads to unfairness and resentment within the organization.
- **Make promises or commitments you cannot keep:** This erodes trust and damages credibility.
- **Take credit for others' work and achievements:** This demotivates and disengages team members.

Leadership and Emotional Security

Why would a leader refrain from, or actively work against, empowering others? Isn't the whole goal of leadership to empower, inspire, and mold future leaders to continue an evolution of transformation? There are many reasons. The first is the obvious scapegoat: a lack of time. Leaders are pulled in many different directions and can easily become victims of their time. Giving someone something to read is so much easier than providing an experience for empowerment. The latter is much more effective, but the first one checks the box.

The second reason is even more complex and often stems from a deeper issue: insecurity. Unfortunately, some leaders are hesitant to empower because they are driven by exploitative leadership tendencies, as outlined in research by Hongda Liu, Jiejun Geng, and Pinbo Yao (2021). These leaders prioritize their own self-interest above all else, reflected in behaviors like being genuinely egotistical, taking credit, exerting pressure, undermining development, and manipulating. This exploitative leadership style not only harms the individuals involved but also has detrimental effects on the organization (Schmid, Verdorfer, & Peus, 2019). These leaders fail to produce leaders and they make sure there are no empowered leaders around them. They fear competition and challenge, and therefore create an environment devoid of diverse perspectives and innovative thinking. This ultimately hinders the organization's ability to adapt, evolve, and thrive.

Effective leaders, in contrast, understand the power of empowerment. They see it as an investment in the future, not a threat. They welcome diverse perspectives and encourage healthy discourse, recognizing that challenges can lead to growth. They understand that true leadership is not about clinging to power but about creating a legacy of empowered individuals who can carry the torch forward.

Effective leaders understand that nonconformists will question the system because the established system isn't working anymore. Effective leaders understand that they have blind spots, and it is often the nonconformist who will have the gall to help the leader identify where those blind spots are. Nonconformists provide new ideas that break up old traditions. Ineffective leaders feel secure in old traditions, since those traditions protect their positions.

Be careful to understand that empowerment is not the same as entitlement—which is the greatest weakness in leadership. People who are entitled think that benefits, privileges, and results should come automatically. Leaders who are entitled feel that everything is everyone else's fault. Leaders who are empowered, on the other hand, are humble. They make sure they do not let down the people who gave them power. Ineffective leaders put paperwork before "people work."

Yet, the goal of leadership is to help others discover their potential. Effective leaders pass the baton in such a way that they and others collectively and collaboratively run the race together. Effective leaders are not afraid of empowering others, including nonconformists, because they understand the dynamics of the race. They are focused on both the short- and long-term success of the individuals and the organization. They realize they could be here today and gone tomorrow. They do not want the people or the organization to suffer in their absence. Remember Martin Luther King Jr., who had a dream but said he may not be around to see it. That's the mindset of effective leaders. They have a vision, and even if they're not around to see it come to fruition, they have empowered others to step up and be leaders and carriers of the vision.

Effective educational leaders know that their role is not about them. Everything they do is for the students, the teachers, the organization, and the community. Effective leaders don't want an organization with a leader. They want an organization full of leaders.

The Relay Race

It's important to say this again: leadership is a relay race of empowerment. When you observe a relay race team, you see each person has their individual training that they do on their own. Maybe it involves sprinting, or practicing push off the blocks, or timing strides and turnover rates. The individual athlete watches what they eat and drink and is cognizant of their individual actions because they know those things can affect the team. Once the individual training and preparation is complete, the racers come together as a team. They display team preparation, team commitment, team practice, unity, and a clear and unified mission.

When asked what is the most important part of a relay race, many people say it is the running. After all, they think, the fastest team wins. Running fast is important, but it is not the most important part.

The most important part of a relay race is the passing of the baton in a small area called the *exchange zone*. It won't matter if an individual runner is the fastest in a leg if they miscalculate the handoff or violate that exchange zone. All the training, commitment, and hours of preparation will feel as if they were for nothing.

That is exactly how the U.S. women's 4 × 100 meters relay team felt on that fateful day in Rio. English Gardner picked up the baton and ran it to the next point. Despite disqualification, the women finished their race. They appealed their disqualification, citing interference from the competing team. After a review, the women won their appeal and were given a special heat to qualify for the championship relay. They would run on an empty track. There would be no excuses for a failed baton pass or error. Fortunately, they ran the fastest qualifying time without incident and were off to the finals. But the challenges didn't end there. Right before the momentous championship meet, Gardner realized she did not have both her cleats. Allyson Felix gave her a backup pair, despite the size being off. The team could have viewed the situation as another setback and gone in with a disempowered attitude. Instead, the teammates empowered each other. They had come this far and faced some pretty bizarre adversity. The U.S. team went on to win back-to-back gold medals in the 4 × 100 meters relay, successfully defending their title.

In the context of leadership and empowerment, every mission is a relay race. The most important part is not how fast the leader runs, but how well they hand off the baton and what happens next. In fact, a good team has "spares"—substitutes who are trained to step in at any point for their particular role in the race.

After the handing of the baton, the runner doesn't simply turn their back on their teammate and walk away. Instead, they observe, focus, and encourage their teammate to run fast and exchange smoothly. During a relay race, it is amazing to see how much trust the runners have in each other. The only way the team can win is if everyone empowers one another.

Imagine you have a runner who says, "I'm faster than all of you. I can do this all myself." Sure, they may be fast, but there is nothing like having another runner with a fresh set of legs and lungs ready to sprint after a handoff. The egotistical solo runner will grow tired and weary; they can't outpace the collective ideas, efficacy, and brainchild of multiple leaders.

You want those fresh legs and lungs on your team. A lot of leaders disqualify themselves because they think they are in a solo race. They may not like or trust the team they have, but when they and their teammates empower one another, the end result will be a better likelihood of success.

Key Points

This chapter emphasized the crucial role of empowerment in effective leadership. Both self-empowerment and empowerment of others are essential. To empower yourself, be a proactive learner, embrace change, and model a growth mindset. To empower others, delegate thoughtfully, be an effective educator, and offer personalized encouragement. Remember, leadership is about influence, not force. Insecure leaders might resist empowerment, but truly effective leaders see it as an investment in building a legacy of empowered individuals who can thrive together. Embrace continuous learning, collaboration, and the power of empowerment to achieve lasting success.

Having established the importance of empowerment in fostering a thriving team, the next chapter naturally delves into the art of measurement and feedback. By effectively measuring progress and providing constructive feedback, we can empower individuals and teams to continuously learn, adapt, and achieve their full potential. This focus on data-driven insights and growth builds on the foundation of trust and ownership established through empowerment, enabling individuals to take ownership of their performance and trajectory.

As you leave this chapter, remember the following.

- To empower is to encourage and stimulate an individual to think, behave, and make decisions toward the mission.

- Empowerment is taking a proactive approach to learning and experiencing what is currently affecting, or will eventually affect, yourself and others.
- There are two types of empowerment: (1) self-empowerment (the process of gaining insight and understanding to empower others) and (2) empowerment of others (the process of providing information and experiences to enhance, engage, educate, and inspire others to take action).
- Some leaders fail to empower others because they are insecure, they tie their position to their self-worth, or they fear competition.
- Empowerment is not the same as entitlement.
- Leadership is like a relay race, and the most important part is the handoff.

Reflective Activity: Empowerment

When it comes to ensuring the empowerment of others, consider these questions.

Information

- In what ways are you preparing yourself beyond surface-level knowledge of the information?

- In what ways is information being shared with others? Are those ways conducive to how people best absorb information?

Experiences

- What practical experiences are being provided for people to engage with the information in a meaningful way?

- What potential for failure is being provided?

- What lessons are being learned through failure?

- How are you working with others?

Feedback

- How regularly are you providing quality feedback?

- How are you measuring the quality of your feedback?

- What systems have been established for you to obtain transparent, honest, timely, and meaningful feedback?

- How are you responding to, acting on, and communicating adjustments or improvements based on received feedback?

STEP 4: MEASURE AND GATHER FEEDBACK

If you want people to be flexible, adaptable, and open to feedback, so must you.

—George Raveling

IN 2010 a good friend of mine had an idea that we should rent motorcycles and take a road trip from Dallas, Texas, to New York City. It would be a ten-day round trip, and everything we needed to survive would have to fit on the bikes.

I was teaching eighth-grade U.S. history at the time and thought I could use the road trip experience to highlight what students were learning about the thirteen colonies. I planned on collecting memorabilia on the trip and sharing it with my students when I returned. So my friend and I packed ten days' worth of clothes and resources and hopped onto our 2007 Harley-Davidson Road Kings full of vigor, optimism, and a bit of naivety.

Now, weeks prior to the trip, we strategically planned our route and even mapped out contingency routes in case of unforeseen hazardous road conditions. Our goal was to avoid major highways as much as possible to witness the serene beauty of each county and town that the states had to offer. Seeing as how the 2007 Road Kings did not come equipped with technology such as GPS and navigational resources found on modern bikes, we had to rely on the accuracy of a good old-fashioned sixteen- by twelve-inch Road Atlas map. My friend had an innate sense of direction that eludes me to this day. Therefore, his responsibility was handling our daily briefings regarding the route and weather. My responsibilities were handling the bike maintenance and identifying the safest places for us to rest.

There is something to be said for the thrill, excitement, and adrenaline that come with being on the open road. On the second day of our trip to New York, I felt inspired. Although we had already agreed on roles and responsibilities, I wanted to handle the daily briefing that day. I woke up early, got the bikes ready, and shared the itinerary with my buddy. This time, I would take the lead and handle our stops and exits.

We rode for about nine hours. As the sun set and we rode in the darkness, things felt a bit odd. Remember, we didn't have GPS on the bikes, and our phones did not have reception at the time. So as we approached our tenth hour, I pulled us over to check the map. Well, where we were did not seem to be on the map at all. My friend trusted me. After all, my enthusiasm to take the lead for day two really won him over—that is, until his directional intuition kicked in.

"Sam, are we headed in the right direction?" he asked.

"Yeah, we are," I responded confidently.

At the next little town, he suggested we pull over and find the town on the map.

Well, it turned out we had been going in the wrong direction for over an hour. We were far from home, and limited with what we had for energy and resources. We did not have the means to be driving in the wrong direction for an entire hour. We were headed south when we needed to head north. I really messed up.

I was monitoring our movement, but I wasn't measuring it. Just because you are moving doesn't mean you're moving in the right direction. My inability to understand where we were cost us valuable time and resources. Now, we did get on the right path and eventually made it to our destination safely. I'm proud to say my friend and I have successfully navigated North America on four motorcycle road trips since then, with destinations ranging from Alaska to Nova Scotia—but the point of this story is that movement doesn't always mean progress. You need to measure your progress for movement to be productive. That's where measurement and feedback come into play.

In this chapter, we will define what it means to measure and monitor leadership initiatives for efficacy by gathering metrics, weighing factors like time and attention, and prioritizing efficient time usage.

Defining Measurement and Monitoring

This step is incredibly important, because without providing timely and concise feedback, and without establishing a system to monitor and measure that feedback, you cannot go on to the next step in the leadership cycle. It all falls apart. How can you adjust and improve if you do not know how effective your feedback is? There is no blueprint to follow. There is no baseline for growth.

How often are the terms *measurement* and *monitoring* used interchangeably? The answer is often. The fact is measurement and monitoring have very different meanings, especially for our purposes in education and leadership.

To *monitor* is to determine the status of an activity. Monitoring typically entails critically observing an activity or process. You can monitor a classroom lesson or students' progression of a classroom experiment, but monitoring in this sense may not involve specific measurements of quality or impact.

Measurement is a process used to determine value. If a leader is monitoring teaching, they're looking at the teaching. If a leader is measuring teaching, they are concerned with the value, quality, and specific evidence of learning. Measurement is a subset of monitoring and involves specific parameters.

Their difference is paramount because, in the leadership cycle, you don't monitor continuous improvement. You measure continuous improvement. You look for evidence of impact. Effective leaders understand the principle of quality versus quantity. In fact, effective leaders are nearly obsessed with this question: What is the evidence that this decision, this activity, or this system is having the intended impact? Or this question: What is the evidence that this lesson is in alignment with what students need in order to ensure learning?

Effective leaders are always on the lookout for ways to measure impact, so one of the worst mistakes a leader can make is to assume. If ineffective leaders make assumptions about team members who are new to the organization, untested, unmonitored, or even unskilled, results and impact can be stunted.

Now, you may be thinking, Well, if the ineffective leader assumes the new members of the team can't do their jobs, then morale and trust go out the window. While that's true, we're not necessarily talking about negative assumptions. We're talking about ineffective leaders' assumption that because a new addition has great character, a strong intellect, and a passion for their profession, they can be handed a map and sent on their way. Sure, the new person looks great on paper, but having great attributes doesn't mean the leader can forgo measurement of impact and feedback. Unless the leader checks in regularly to ensure the person is clear about the mission, is on track, and has the resources and support they need, and the leader provides quality feedback, there are likely to be unexpected and often disappointing results.

So, leaders cannot assume everyone knows what they are doing and they are striving for excellence. Leaders must monitor and determine evidence of such, in addition to providing quality feedback for improvement. If you are the recipient of quality feedback, it means you are valued. Effective leaders do not assume. Instead, they develop systems to ensure the measurement of quality. They use those systems to glean knowledge so that they themselves, and others, can make wise choices.

Effective leaders do not want to waste their finite resources of time, energy, and effort. Therefore, these leaders accomplish goals and get missions completed through and by people. They inspect what they expect. To do this, the leaders design positive measurement processes that thoughtfully and strategically assess the fulfillment of key expectations, ensure continued alignment, provide needed support, reinforce progress, and promote learning. One such effective measurement process is effective feedback.

Understanding Feedback

To really understand it, we need to explore feedback as it behaves in the real world. Here is a little story.

Nicole manages a coffee shop in Seattle. As she cleans off the counter, her eyes land on a customer finishing his coffee. He reaches into his pocket, takes out his cell phone, and begins to make a call. The coffee shop is unusually quiet today, so Nicole can't help but overhear the customer's conversation.

"Hi. I'm calling about the regional manager position you posted online a few months ago," the customer says. Intrigued, Nicole stops wiping the counter.

"Oh, I see. The position has been filled. Are you satisfied with the new manager? You are? That's great. Thank you." The customer hangs up the phone and carefully places it back into his pocket. He stands up, gathers his things, and approaches the counter to leave a tip in the jar for the quality service he has received.

"I couldn't help but overhear," Nicole says. "I'm sorry the job wasn't available."

The customer looks confused for a moment, and then he laughs. "What? Oh, that!" he says in a voice different from the one he used on his call. "That's my job, actually. I was calling to see how I have been doing."

Effective leaders actively seek feedback because they understand it's the only way to course-correct and improve performance. Feedback is a response to a person's activity with the purpose of helping them adjust to become more effective. Feedback comes in various forms, including evaluative (how you did and where you are), appreciative (how you are valued and recognized), and coaching (how you can improve; Hardavella, Aamli-Gaagnat, Saad, Rousalova, & Sreter, 2017). No leader is perfect, and there is always room for improvement and elevation. Quality feedback establishes a point-in-time "here" and suggestions to get to "there."

Perhaps there is no better analogy for the importance of feedback and follow-through than that of sports. Coaches are notorious for providing feedback to the best of the best. Players welcome that feedback because they understand and value improvement. Baseball pitchers need the proper follow-through to manipulate the ball appropriately. Golfers need the proper follow-through to perfect their drives and putts. Basketball players must have the correct positioning and footing on their free throws in order to increase their percentage and optimize their form. Tennis players are constantly told by their coaches to follow through on their swings to achieve maximum accuracy and power. Follow-through is essential for leaders too. For leaders, it is about the consistency of following up with others, and themselves, during and after the completion of a task. Giving and receiving feedback effectively is as important for leaders as follow-through is for athletes. Without it, leaders alienate their people and leave loose threads hanging.

Team members often will assume they are doing the right thing only to produce lackluster results. Or team members will do the right thing but be unsure of its impact due to a lack of feedback. It works both ways.

Regular delivery and reception of feedback, especially when it's objective and focused on improvement, fuels an environment of engagement and increased productivity. This ultimately leads to an organization that's more aligned with its vision. Studies even suggest that offering objective feedback can lead to measurable performance improvements (Warrilow, 2017).

Effective leaders understand the importance of continual communication. It means establishing a culture where giving and receiving feedback is a regular occurrence. Gone are the days when teacher evaluations were the only times teachers received feedback. Leaders who rely only on teacher evaluations as the vehicle for feedback delivery face several potential issues. First, teachers may dread evaluation day because it feels like they themselves are being graded. Second, teachers may produce results leading up to the evaluation but then resume their old way of doing things afterward. Third, teachers may feel evaluations are unimportant if there is a lack of follow-through and if the evaluation has no impact correlated with it. Therefore, feedback should be honest, timely, and continual.

Receiving Feedback

You can spot an ineffective leader a mile away when they take feedback personally and see continual communication as a threat. It is the effective leader who responds to feedback by saying, "Thank you," and not attempting to explain or defend themselves. Effective leaders are aware that listening is a tool for clarity and understanding, but that it doesn't equal agreement. If the feedback requires a response, effective leaders may say, "Thank you. I will take time to process that feedback and would like to continue this conversation at another time."

To truly benefit from feedback, embracing a learner-centered approach is key. This means actively listening with an open mind, reflecting on the input, and demonstrating a genuine desire for improvement. Ideally, feedback should be delivered directly and promptly. By viewing feedback as an opportunity to identify strengths and weaknesses and build on existing skills, you pave the way for increased confidence, greater independence, and stronger connections with others. Remember, the effectiveness of feedback hinges on its reception. How you interpret and respond plays a crucial role in shaping the teacher-learner dynamic and unlocking future learning possibilities (Hardavella et al., 2017).

Unfortunately, quality feedback is often lacking in organizations because people get so caught up in doing work that they don't take time to evaluate the work that they do. Also, sometimes egos are fragile, so honest feedback is not given. In addition, feedback can be lacking if an organization as a whole has a fixed mindset and thus tends to be too comfortable with where it is. If feedback is provided, it is often ambiguous and lacks timeliness.

When employees feel empowered to speak up, their sense of belonging, trust, and impact grows. It fosters a culture where challenging the status quo isn't just accepted, it's encouraged, leading to better ideas and outcomes. Here are seven suggestions for how to introduce a culture of feedback in your organization and how to get engagement from your team members.

1. **Make it easy to give feedback:** A common problem people face when trying to give feedback is that there's not always an obvious

way to do it. Give people plenty of easy ways to share their thoughts, and you'll find that people are more inclined to share their thoughts.

Host question-and-answer sessions, share engagement surveys, and get into the habit of asking for feedback during one-on-one sessions.

2. **Allow for ways to give anonymous feedback:** Positive feedback is easy to come by, but honest, actionable criticism can be harder to find. Anonymous feedback channels create a safe space for team members to share their true thoughts, helping you gain a clearer picture of what's working and what needs improvement.

3. **Help your teams build a habit around feedback:** When something becomes a habit, people are more likely to do it. So, it's important to find ways to help your team build a habit of regularly giving and receiving feedback.

    Make every meeting a springboard for dialogue. In one-on-ones, actively seek feedback, and offer a dedicated space for your team to do the same. Carve out "questions and ideas" on stand-up agendas to spark discussions. Regular "ask me anything" sessions with leaders and team-specific feedback forums create safe spaces for sharing thoughts and concerns. Don't let the conversation stop there! After check-in meetings, send out a quick survey or feedback request to gauge experiences and gather suggestions. By consistently showing you value team members' input, you'll build a habit of open communication, leading to a more engaged, empowered, and communicative team. Remember, lead by example, ensure psychological safety, listen actively, and celebrate feedback.

4. **Introduce feedback training:** Sometimes, people hold back on giving feedback because they're not sure how to do it. This is especially relevant in cases where they want to raise negative feedback or concerns. Help your team members find the best way to navigate this with feedback training.

    Bring in a professional trainer to teach everyone how to give effective feedback. Empower your people with training on how to give positive feedback, how to give constructive feedback, and how to handle feedback that may not be favorable. Incorporate this practice as part of the onboarding process, and host refresher sessions for existing employees.

5. **Adopt a culture of feedback from the top:** For your feedback culture to succeed, it needs to be championed from the top. Engage your leadership team and let them lead a healthy feedback culture by showing everyone else how it works.

    Create opportunities for everyone to see critical feedback in action. Let your team members see healthy feedback play out in front of them so they feel reassured on how to handle it and know they can freely share their own thoughts and concerns.

6. **Have a process for managing feedback:** Encouraging people to share their concerns is only half the battle. To build trust and address their feedback, implement a solid feedback process. This empowers you to manage concerns transparently and fairly and ensure each issue receives a proper response.

    Work with your senior leadership team to come up with a process that effectively deals with both positive and negative feedback. Set timetables, identify priority concerns and who is responsible for addressing them, and determine how you'll share feedback updates with all employees. Share this policy or workflow with everyone so there's transparency around what should happen.

7. **Show that you'll act on feedback:** A major barrier to having people give their honest opinion is that they feel it won't get acted on. Break down that barrier by actively demonstrating transparency and commitment to feedback. Follow up with team members and contributors who have brought up ideas or issues. Share updates on initiatives sparked by their specific input, showcasing progress in a public channel. This reinforces the message that their feedback is valued and acted on. It is best to ensure people give feedback in a timely manner—that is, as soon after the event as possible (Hardavella et al., 2017).

Imagine a game of cornhole where your target is hidden by a dense fog. Everyone is playing the game, tossing the beanbags to the hole. Now, what if you are given just three bags each day to throw to the best of your ability, and the results of your daily tosses are consolidated and given to you at the end of the month?

Depending on the results, you're either rewarded or punished for the accuracy of your aim, with the usual encouragement to improve. And yet, you can't see where your beanbags are landing. You have no idea how to adjust your technique to be more successful each day because you are not getting feedback until the end of the month. That's what receiving feedback too late is like—the total sum of your cornhole tosses, no matter the environmental factors at play. Put quite simply, delaying feedback impacts learning (Freedberg, Schacherer, & Hazeltine, 2016).

Giving Effective Feedback

Feedback is essential to learning. Feedback needs to be timely, direct, and specific and have parameters built around it to measure success and effectiveness in the future. The lack of quality feedback is a large contributor to organizational, team, and personal paralysis. Consider the following four key components, or pillars, of effective feedback.

Goal Referenced

Both goal-setting theory and ample evidence support the idea that people need feedback comparing progress to goals in order to adjust their efforts and strategies to reach those goals or standards (Gnepp et al., 2020).

Effective feedback requires that a person has a goal, then takes action to achieve the goal, and then receives goal-related information about their actions. We've already established that the major goal in an educational institution is to ensure student learning. If you lack clarity on the goal, or if you fail to pay attention to the goal as the ultimate priority, then feedback you give can easily focus on actions that are unlikely to culminate in the achievement of the goal.

Information becomes feedback when a person is trying to achieve something and the information tells them whether they are on track or they need to change course.

Actionable

The second pillar of effective feedback is that the feedback is tangible, specific, and useful. That description sounds like a bunch of mini-pillars, but ultimately, the feedback provides actionable information. Thus, giving a C+, for example, or saying, "Good job!" or "You did not do that right," is not feedback at all. Learners may ask themselves, "What specifically should I change next time, based on the information?" They do not know what was "good" or "wrong" about what they did.

Actionable feedback must be provided in such a way that it is received as helpful. Many so-called feedback situations lead to frustrations because the givers are insufficiently descriptive. They jump to an inference from data instead of simply presenting the data. For example, a supervisor may make the unfortunate but common mistake of stating that "many students were bored in class." That remark is a judgment, not an observation. It would be far more useful, and perhaps even less debatable, if the supervisor said something along the lines of, "I counted ongoing inattentive behaviors in ten of the twenty-four students once the lecture was underway. The behaviors included texting under desks, sleeping on desks, and talking with other students about off-topic subjects. However, after the small-group exercise began, I saw this behavior in only two students." Such care in offering neutral, goal-related facts lies at the heart of great feedback. Supervisors and coaches diligently observe and comment based on predefined goals, leading to clear understanding of both areas needing improvement and metrics for success.

Effective leaders know that in complex performance situations, actionable feedback about what went right is just as important as feedback about what didn't work (Freedberg, Glass, Filoteo, Hazeltine, & Maddox, 2017).

Contrary to intuition, studies suggest people actually crave constructive feedback more than praise. A *Harvard Business Review* study found that 57 percent of people prefer it over compliments or recognition (Zenger & Folkman, 2014). Why? Because we inherently recognize its value for learning and growth.

However, positive feedback remains crucial. Positive feedback has been found not only to enhance performance but also to be an efficient intervention to manipulate perceived self-efficacy (Peifer, Schönfeld, Wolters, Aust, & Margraf, 2020). It boosts confidence, leading to better performance. It fosters appreciation, fueling motivation and engagement. It communicates support, strengthens relationships, and reduces turnover. Most importantly, positive reinforcement makes accepting occasional criticism easier, creating a balanced feedback loop.

Timely

A major problem in education is untimely feedback. Vital feedback on key performances often comes days, weeks, or even months after the work has been completed. Effective leaders work to ensure that students get timely feedback and opportunities to use it while the attempts and effects are still fresh in their minds.

Few things are worse than receiving feedback for an issue that occurred months ago. When effective leaders deliver timely feedback, it tells the recipient, "I value you and your contributions to this organization; therefore, I want to address this with you right away." When feedback is put on a to-do list or seems retroactive, the recipient doesn't feel as valued.

Ongoing

The final pillar of effective feedback is that feedback is a continual dialogue. Adjusting performance depends on not only receiving feedback but also having opportunities to use it. The more feedback a person can receive in real time, the better their ultimate performance will be.

Highly successful video games work that way. If you play goal-based computer or phone games, you know that the key to substantial improvement is that the feedback is both timely and ongoing. When you fail, you can immediately start over—sometimes even right where you left off—to get another opportunity to receive and learn from feedback.

You will be hard-pressed to find a good reason to avoid creating a culture of communication and feedback within any organization. Feedback is a monumental tool that provides real results and creates a strong and productive organizational culture. It costs you and your organization nothing at all. While overhauling policies and making sweeping changes may seem tempting, consider this: effective feedback hinges on conversation, not mass action. Let's explore some different feedback models for incorporating genuine dialogue into your daily interactions. Not all these models are applicable in every daily case of providing feedback.

THE FEEDBACK SANDWICH

Instead of layering praise with criticism, the feedback sandwich approach starts and ends with positive feedback, sandwiching the constructive criticism in between. While this can be useful in everyday interactions, overusing this approach can dull its effectiveness. The recipient might anticipate the *but* and tune out the positive aspects. To combat this, offer genuine praise independently whenever possible. Daily recognition fosters a more receptive environment for all types of feedback. Here are two examples of the feedback sandwich in action:

> "I really enjoyed observing your math lesson on fractions today. It was clear you put a lot of thought and effort into creating an engaging and interactive learning experience for your students. I noticed a few students seemed to struggle with the concept of equivalent fractions. Perhaps incorporating some more visual aids or manipulatives could help solidify their understanding. Overall, I was very

impressed with your lesson. Your students were actively participating and seemed to be having fun while learning. Keep up the great work!"

"Your use of differentiation strategies during the lesson was impressive. By providing varied activities and resources, you effectively met the diverse needs of your students and fostered a supportive learning environment. However, I noticed that the pacing of the lesson seemed a bit rushed toward the end. Perhaps allocating more time for certain concepts or activities could ensure that all students have ample opportunity to grasp the material. Nevertheless, your ability to adapt and tailor your instruction to the needs of your students is commendable. Your dedication to their academic growth is evident, and I have no doubt that with minor adjustments, this lesson will continue to thrive."

CHRONOLOGICAL FASHION FEEDBACK

In chronological feedback, observations are relayed in order, reminding the learner of the session step by step. It's like the observer is walking through the learning experience again, sharing insights along the way. This is helpful for short feedback sessions but can bog you down in detail during long sessions. Here is an example of chronological fashion feedback:

"The first thing you did really well when you entered the room was to garner the attention of the students and direct them to the warm-up. Then, you proceeded with taking roll and monitoring student progress on the warm-up activity. You identified four students who were struggling to master the concept and created a small group with those individuals. It was after that when you engaged the entire class in a demonstration of learning."

Pendleton Model Feedback

In 1984, the Pendleton model emerged as a learner-centered alternative to traditional feedback methods. This conversation-based approach prioritizes joint action planning, known as *reflection for action*. Before diving in, the facilitator ensures the learner is receptive to feedback. Then, the learner sets the stage by sharing context and self-identified strengths, fostering a safe environment through positive reinforcement. Building on this foundation, the facilitator prompts the learner to suggest areas for improvement. This shift in focus, from dissecting weaknesses to prompting self-reflection, unlocks opportunities for growth. The facilitator then offers suggestions and collaboratively constructs an action plan with the learner.

Open-ended questions, such as the following, are key throughout the process; they empower the learner to think critically and reflect deeply on their own learning journey. In this way, the Pendleton model empowers learners to take ownership of their development, fostering a more engaged and effective learning experience (Hardavella et al., 2017).

- "What do you think went well?"
- "What do you think could be done differently?"
- "What could be further improved?"
- "How can this be achieved?"

Feedback reinforces individual accountability. An organization—whether large or small, corporate or not-for-profit, complex or traditionally structured—cannot function to its fullest if individuals do not take accountability for their projects, tasks, and behaviors. Feedback is crucial when reinforcing an individual's accountability to their commitment. Feedback provides support, guidance, and direction in a way that builds confidence.

Praise

Be mindful of the use of praise as a go-to feedback tool. Praise is a useful tool, but it doesn't directly map performance the way feedback does. Praise can even be counterproductive. If you're accidentally giving praise when you think you're giving positive feedback, you won't see the results you expect.

What do praise and positive feedback sound like? Here are seven examples of both praise and positive feedback. See if you can pick out which are which.

1. "Congratulations on such a great lesson."
2. "You properly planned how to check for student understanding, which translated perfectly during class when students demonstrated confusion. Great job!"
3. "Thanks for jumping in to help cover classes this morning."
4. "I saw that you submitted your information on time. Great job!"
5. "I saw that you led by example and submitted your information on time while also reminding your department of the deadline. Leading by example and setting your team up for success help build capacity moving forward. Please keep it up."
6. "I see that you have been coaching Bobby on alignment during PLCs, and today, all three components of his lesson (cognition,

context, and content) were aligned. Thank you for your impact on student learning."

7. "Nice job. How you are moving those data in the right direction is impressive."

The answers: 1, 3, 4, and 7 are praise; 2, 5, and 6 are positive feedback.

We often use the terms *praise* and *positive feedback* interchangeably, but there are a few key differences.

- Praise is a simple but powerful tool. A quick "good job" or "thanks" acknowledges someone's effort and accomplishment; it's a thank-you for a job well done. It looks back on their past actions and usually is steeped in feelings and opinions.
- Positive feedback goes a step further. It highlights specific behaviors and their impact, fostering development. Think of it as saying, "Keep doing that!" or "More like this, please!" It points toward future improvement and growth.

While praise can be offered publicly or privately, feedback usually thrives in private conversations. However, this rule can bend at times. Publicly sharing positive feedback can be impactful, but tread carefully. Ensure the recipient will appreciate it in that setting.

Effective feedback is what follow-through looks like in the world of leadership. So, if you're looking for methods to improve your leadership, you should focus on the way you give and receive feedback. Measure your progress—don't just monitor it—so you avoid wasting precious time and resources.

Skipping the Step

Those were a lot of benchmarks for a positive and effective measurement process. Even the most seasoned strategic thinkers and planners may feel overwhelmed by that list. Indeed, out of all the steps in the leadership cycle, assessing progress is the most neglected. There are a number of reasons for this, which are detailed as follows.

A Lack of Time and Attention

"I just don't have the time to give everyone feedback."

"I don't have time to follow through on the feedback I give."

"I provided feedback, and I hope everyone takes it to heart."

Effective leaders understand that whatever you allow, you cannot complain about. That's why developing those systems that measure what is critical to the organization is so important to effective leaders. Measurement and feedback are not "check the box" actions. They are vital tools that can transform an educational institution once everyone is on the same page and working toward a common mission.

Schools dream of a positive learning environment where student discipline isn't a concern. But achieving that dream takes action. Effective leaders understand this and dedicate time and attention to establishing clear end goals for behavior. This seemingly simple act is immensely influential, as illustrated by the following example.

Let's say that discipline is a challenge for a school. An effective leader reviews trend data for the past three to five years on teachers, grade levels, cohorts, times of day when disciplinary issues most frequently occur, and more. That effort is where knowledge gathering comes into play. The leader doesn't assume they know why discipline is an issue (even though they may have some intuitive ideas). Instead, they review the data for trends. But they don't stop there. They take the data and ensure everyone in the organization is aware of the key findings. The effective leader engages in dialogue about the impact that the data have on student and staff morale. They investigate the data for impacts on teacher workload, administration workload, and ultimately student achievement.

As a team, everyone establishes one goal to determine where discipline markers should be each month, each semester, and at the end of the year. The right people are engaged in the strategic planning and decision-making process to determine the method of "root" intervention. That's right—there will be no fruit picking in this scenario. Campus leaders are empowered to engage in the development and support of the root intervention process.

Each month, the campus leaders report back to our effective leader on the impact their support is having on student discipline. Together, they review the data and highlight what is working, what needs to be improved, and what needs to be adjusted. They discuss their measurement and obtain feedback from everyone.

Together, everyone established a system where they could have a comprehensive understanding of exactly what is happening in the school related to discipline within the scope of a few meetings and some research. No decisions were made unilaterally. No assumptions were made. The root interventions made discipline much less of a challenge for the school and enriched the student experience. What if we took the same system and process and applied them to everything else that needs to be measured in the educational realm? Some examples would be classroom observations, the quality of PLCs, and reduction of student tardiness with evidence of impact, to name a few.

Monitoring, Measurement, and Micromanagement

The second reason that leaders may skip the step of measuring progress in the leadership cycle is that they do not want to give others the impression they are micromanaging them. Checking in and providing feedback can often be misconstrued as helicopter leadership (like helicopter parenting).

But effective leaders nip that preconceived notion in the bud straightaway. The difference between micromanaging and measuring success is the perception of intent. If people see a leader checking in with a genuine attitude, a genuine interest in the work being done, and a supportive instead of critical demeanor, they will see that monitoring as a measurement of success.

On the other hand, if people see a leader coming in to criticize, demand, direct, berate, and hold accountable, they will perceive it as micromanaging. There is no trust, no belief, and no empowerment.

A Lack of Metrics to Track Improvement

Metrics are like gauges on a dashboard, providing insight into areas that require improvement and highlighting those that are performing well. When leaders do not establish clear metrics, or clear benchmarks to track improvement, then ensuring measurement and feedback is an easy step to skip (but detrimental to the success of your organization). Leaders must set clearly defined metrics that can be discovered through data research and thoughtful discussions. Leaders can't measure progress if they don't have a benchmark for determining where they started and where they need to be. The following are some examples of metrics you can reasonably use to track improvement.

- **Metric:** Graduation rate for students with individualized education plans (IEPs)
    - *Benchmark*—Increase the graduation rate for students with IEPs by 5 percent within two years.

- *Data source*—School records, state (or provincial) testing data
- *Action*—Implement targeted interventions, provide additional support to IEP students, and monitor progress regularly.

- **Metric:** Average student growth on standardized mathematics assessments
  - *Benchmark*—Increase average mathematics scores by ten points within one year.
  - *Data source*—Standardized test scores, classroom assessments, student feedback
  - *Action*—Implement differentiated instruction, provide professional development for teachers, and analyze data to identify areas of weakness.

- **Metric:** Proficiency levels of English learners (ELs) in English and native language reading skills
  - *Benchmark*—Increase proficiency levels by one level for 70 percent of EL students within one year.
  - *Data source*—Language assessments, student portfolios, teacher observations
  - *Action*—Offer targeted language support, use culturally relevant teaching methods, and track individual student progress.

Taking the time to diligently track these metrics will provide insight into opportunities to improve. At the core of feedback are the raw data of metrics.

Wasted Time

The fourth and final reason why some leaders skip this step in the leadership cycle is that they see it as a waste of time. Steve Jobs is widely attributed with the assertion, "It doesn't make sense to hire smart people and tell them what to do; we hire smart people so they can tell us what to do" (Schwantes, 2017). His statement is absolutely true. However, just because people are smart and driven, it doesn't mean that they can navigate through all the technical and adaptive nuances of dealing with people and their beliefs and actions.

The right measurement establishes vital feedback loops that provide information on whether the chosen approaches are moving an organization toward its goals.

Accurate measurement helps separate the useful work from the useless work, saving everyone time in the process. Effective measures are tools that reveal whether all the training, activities, actions, planning, processes, and professional development sessions are producing results. Those tools help leaders see through the dust storms produced by so many particles of enthusiastic busywork, which can create the illusion of progress.

Remember, just because you're moving forward, it doesn't always mean you're progressing. My friend and I found that out the hard way when we went an hour off our course to New York. If the biggest argument for not providing measurements and feedback is time, isn't it ironic that this step in the leadership cycle saves time in the long run?

Key Points

Effective leadership hinges on measuring impact and cultivating a culture of feedback. This chapter highlighted the difference between monitoring, which simply observes activities, and measurement, which assesses their value and impact. Leaders should focus on the latter, seeking out evidence of continuous improvement. Additionally, embracing feedback is crucial. Receiving it with an open mind and utilizing it for growth fosters stronger connections, confidence, and independence. Building a culture of feedback requires making feedback easy to give and receive, encouraging anonymity for honest criticism, and actively demonstrating feedback's value by acting on it. Finally, remember the four pillars of effective feedback: it should be (1) goal oriented, (2) actionable, (3) timely, and (4) ongoing. By mastering these principles, you can unlock the immense power of feedback and drive positive change within your organization.

While understanding the impact of our actions and embracing feedback are critical steps, true leadership and transformation lies in taking action based on these insights. In the next chapter, we'll dive into the art of adjusting and improving, transforming observations and feedback into steps that propel your team and organization toward excellence.

As you leave this chapter, remember the following.

- To monitor is to determine the status of an activity. Monitoring typically entails critically observing an activity or process.
- Measurement is a process used to determine value.

- Effective leaders are always looking for ways to measure impact and actively seek feedback. Ensuring measurement and feedback is the step most often skipped in the leadership cycle.
- For leaders, follow-through is about the consistency of following up with others, and themselves, during and after the completion of a task.
- Effective leaders establish a culture of continual communication and feedback to meet organizational goals.

Reflective Activity: Determining Measurement Challenges

Identify challenges that may impede your ability to effectively measure for improvement. Then, brainstorm possible solutions that will help you overcome those challenges.

Challenge	Possible Solution

Six Steps to a Strong School Culture © 2024 Samuel Nix • SolutionTree.com
Visit **go.SolutionTree.com/leadership** to download this free reproducible.

Reflective Activity: Measuring the Quality and Frequency of Feedback

When answering the following reflective questions in your reflective journal, consider providing detailed insights into your feedback process. Use the provided checkboxes to indicate the frequency of feedback provision, and utilize the template chart to outline your next steps for enhancing feedback quality and frequency.

- How do you provide feedback?

- In what ways are you measuring the quality of your feedback? What evidence supports the level of quality identified?

- How frequently are you providing quality feedback to your staff?
    - ☐ Weekly
    - ☐ Monthly
    - ☐ Yearly

- Which of the four pillars of effective feedback would most enhance the quality of your organization?

- What are your next steps for improving the quality and frequency of your feedback? Use the following chart as a template for your work.

Action	Timeline for Improvement

STEP 5: ADJUST AND IMPROVE

9

The things we fear most in organizations—fluctuations, disturbances, imbalances—are the primary source of creativity.

—Margaret J. Wheatley

IN THE previous chapter, I shared my story of my friend's and my first-ever motorcycle road trip across the United States and my failure to measure our progress. For a good while, as I naively navigated us farther south, I was trusting the process. We were moving forward, in what I thought was the direction we needed to go. But, as we now know, it was not. Once we determined we were an hour out of our way, it was time to adjust our course to improve our progress toward our mission.

Leaders are always going to be faced with two options after ensuring measurement and feedback. The first option is to trust the process, rely on intuition, and see if the kinks smooth out over time. The second option is to make adjustments. Either decision will have an impact on the mission. It is important to note that adjustment does not always equal improvement. However, improvement does require the right adjustments. Being able to identify when to trust the process and when to make adjustments is vital to a leader's success. That is why ensuring adjustment and improvement is the penultimate step in the leadership cycle. But first, let's distinguish between the two. In this chapter, you will learn about the crucial difference between adjustment and improvement within the context of your mission. Also, this chapter equips you with the knowledge and tools to discern when each is necessary and guides you through the decision-making process.

The Difference Between Adjustment and Improvement

There is a vast difference between improvement and adjustment. When something is improved, it is made better, as evidenced by increased value or productivity. Improvement provides a tangible benefit, usually a saving of time, money, space, effort, and other resources. Defining adjustment is slightly more complex. Adjustment is the practical, physical, and behavioral modification required to accept and implement new practices or ideas.

Adjustment may not lead to a tangible benefit. When I talk about making adjustments, I do not mean adjusting the goal or mission—I mean adjusting the execution of a plan or process to achieve the mission. Adjustment and improvement work hand in hand. Effective leaders understand the dynamic relationship between the two and ensure that people are not overwhelmed by the pressures of either. Often, leaders focus only on technical adjustments associated with measurement and feedback and neglect the adaptive adjustments that also need to be considered.

As you may recall from chapter 3 (page 37), technical challenges are easy to identify and solve with existing resources. Adaptive challenges are fluid and change with circumstances. Solutions to those types of challenges usually require people to learn new ways of doing things; change their attitudes, values, and norms; and adopt an experimental mindset. Fortunately, effective leaders have an eye for adaptive adjustments because they realize it is critical to address employees' attitudes toward change (Ahmad & Cheng, 2018).

Resistance could stem from fear, past negative experiences, or feelings of pressure due to a perceived lack of time to implement the needed changes. It could even be due to a perceived lack of support. Effective leaders take the time to identify what is impeding the change effort.

Knowing precisely when to make adjustments varies. The reality is that leaders must know their milestones in relation to their final destination, or end goal, and the timeline to get there. Effective leaders ensure alignment of activity and evidence of impact. Reviewing progress and reviewing measurement indicators should be normal parts of weekly team meetings, department meetings, and one-on-ones. The right discussions lead to the right adjustments. The right adjustments lead to the right improvements.

Some organizations, notably low-performing ones, are characterized by a remarkable inability to sense that they have problems. In such organizations, people spend much of their time fighting organizational boundaries and broken processes. They often are not clear on the mission, so they don't even know if they are moving in the right direction. They fail to detect misalignment even when presented with feedback and measurement indicators. Thus, they have little ability to anticipate and adapt to changes when it becomes necessary. That effect is commonly observed when technological changes shift rapidly.

When dealing with levels of engagement for influencing improvement with a person or situation, follow this good rule of thumb: If the needed adjustment or improvement affects a single person, then engage at a single-person level. However, if the adjustment or improvement affects a large group or organization, then engage at the organizational level. In other words, address the action at the level of impact—small impact, small involvement; large impact, large involvement.

So, let us say that, based on quality and timely feedback, you are seeing that improvement is needed and will require some change at the organizational level. You need to be able to ease the change and allow the adoption of technical and adaptive transformation for a positive outcome. When you are dealing with improvement, it is always best to introduce the improvement in chunks when possible. You shouldn't expect total transformation in a single stroke. Again, the saying goes, "How do you eat an elephant? One bite at a time."

An example of a metaphorical elephant could be something as simple as a districtwide form going from physical (hard copy) to electronic. Let's say that by a certain date, everyone in the district will be expected to fill out and submit a form electronically; paper copies will not be accepted. That requirement sounds simple, but when you have had hundreds of people filling out the same paper form for the same situation for years, switching to the new method will be perceived as a huge change.

The elephant can be introduced in two chunks. The first step is to roll out the form in printed form. Everyone can get familiar with how it looks. If anyone has questions about the hard copy, they can get those questions addressed. The second step is to complete the form electronically. As you can see, one small change at a time, to sort out the issues, listen to the feedback, acknowledge the challenges, and lead people through the change before introducing the greater change, provides people the time to adapt.

Once the process is in place, it is important that leaders do not make assumptions. Measurement and feedback must be a continual process. Once adjustments are made, leaders then go back, continue to monitor, measure, and provide feedback to and receive feedback from anyone impacted by the change. After taking those steps, effective leaders continue to monitor and continue to receive and provide more feedback.

However you choose to measure, the most important thing is that you do it. Don't let measurement fall by the wayside. If it fails to be a priority, you may neglect it. Understanding how close you are to where you need to be can, unfortunately, take a backseat due to busyness. But how else can you tell if something is truly an improvement or just another misaligned adjustment? How else will you know if you're going to reach your destination? If my friend had not stopped to ensure we properly measured our progress on our trip, we would have driven all the way to the southern border of the United States when we needed to head north. His feedback and my willingness to adjust got us where we needed to be.

When to Make Adjustments

Data based on measurement—or information based on feedback—indicating the need to adjust or improve are critical. However, clarity about the alignment of measurement and feedback to the goal is just as critical. Effective leaders understand that some feedback is not in alignment with the mission. An example of this would be feedback in the form of criticism or praise. Criticism often relies on subjective opinions and feelings, lacking specific examples or constructive feedback. It can be couched in phrases like, "I'm just being honest," but masked honesty can come across as rude and unhelpful. Imagine someone saying, "No one likes you, just being honest," or "This report is terrible, just being honest." These statements offer no room for improvement and leave the recipient feeling attacked.

Now, both unhelpful criticism and excessive praise can be detrimental. While praise doesn't directly harm, it lacks the specificity needed for growth. People need to understand why they're being praised to truly learn and improve. Telling them, "Good job," without explaining what specifically made their work good provides little value.

Although paying too much attention to the wrong type of information can derail or prolong the process of improvement, information gleaned from such measurement or feedback shouldn't necessarily be dismissed. In fact, it could be useful for reflection.

Effective leaders are always reflecting on how they can improve. But it is important for you to remember that misaligned measurement or feedback may not necessarily justify the need for adjustment or improvement. The reason for that is because measurement or feedback is useful when it aids you in accomplishing the mission. Some feedback is without value because it is based on bias, prejudice, guesswork, hearsay, and sometimes ignorance. Also, measurement indicators that focus on things that will not get you to the goal are superfluous. A leader must be clear about where they are going and what they are trying to accomplish.

By this point in the leadership cycle, clarity has been ensured, strategic planning and decision making are evident, the leader and involved personnel have been empowered, and quality feedback has been provided based on the right measures. Although transformation and improvement is a process that can come with doubt, challenges, and even resistance, trusting the process is important. But even those who tend to trust the process have an identified line of demarcation—a point when they confront the brutal fact that they need to make adjustments or initiate improvement. It's important to remember that "the process" itself is not inherently harmful; however, blindly adhering to it without critical evaluation or adaptation can lead to negative outcomes. The key takeaway is to understand the limitations of any process and have the flexibility to adjust when necessary.

I have asked multiple leaders this question: "Which of the following mistakes have you most frequently made—the mistake of waiting too long to make the necessary adjustments for improvement, or the mistake of acting too quickly instead of being patient?" In response to this question, most leaders indicate that they have made the mistake of waiting too long before taking decisive action.

The fact is that every leader struggles with the tension of knowing when and how to make the proper adjustments for improvement. No leader gets it right every single time. There is no algorithm to memorize, no road map to follow, no secret hack to crack that says when to stop trusting the process and make adjustments.

Effective leaders care about their people and honor the process of change, but they never lose sight of the mission. With time, effective leaders improve their decision-making process for judging when and how to help people adjust and improve based on the right measurement and quality feedback.

Six Questions for Adjustment Reflection

How do you know when you have crossed the line of demarcation? When is the right time to make the shift from trusting the process to adjusting or improving? While there is no secret formula to determine when to adjust and when to trust the process, effective leaders have several questions they can reflect on to guide their decision making. Ask the following six questions (in no particular order) to stimulate your thinking when you face the decision to continue trusting the process or to make adjustments.

1. **Is the decision to continue doing things the same way having a negative impact on the mission?** It is one thing not to be making the progress you want to make; it is quite another thing to experience challenges that are damaging to the mission. If what we're doing is having a negative impact on the mission, that's a good indicator it is time to make the necessary adjustments for improvement.

2. **Does the challenge with progress have to do with the will or the skill of the people executing the mission?** When we talk about will or skill, it is critical to define both. Skill is something you can teach, provide an experience for, and empower people with. It is a technical thing. Will is an adaptive approach. It is the willingness to want to execute the mission. One challenge of progress is to ask yourself, "Am I dealing with a technical situation or an adaptive situation?"

3. **What uncontrollable factors are at play that could cause temporary or permanent challenges to the mission?** We can only control what we can control. As in most organizations, uncontrollable factors arise in schools, and we have to take them into consideration. Sometimes, uncontrollable factors prohibit accomplishment of the mission; the mission is not the problem. If that is the case, then helping others focus on controllable factors in the uncontrollable situation can minimize frustrations and maximize productivity.

4. **What is the timeline for progress?** If you have six weeks to get something done, you cannot wait five weeks to see if it's effective. Or if it is not effective, you cannot wait five weeks to make the adjustment. You need to be cognizant of the timeline and the

progress to meet the goal. At the bare minimum, a measure of alignment toward the mission should occur at the halfway point in the process. A healthy formula to consider is based on a three-measure approach. The first measure is to ensure clarity. The second measure is to ensure effective implementation based on clarity. The third measure is to ensure impact and alignment based on implementation.

5. **Are our measurement indicators the right indicators that will ensure the success of the mission? What are we measuring?** In education, the most important factor to ensure quality learning is quality teaching. A universal example of that concept in education is when educational leaders focus on the number of classroom observations that have been conducted over a period of time. Touting the number of classroom visits is not an effective indicator to measure impact toward improving teaching and ensuring learning. Sure, measuring the time that educational leaders spend monitoring classroom instruction is key to development and improvement, but effective leaders want to measure administrators' impact being in those classrooms.

   Instead of just measuring the number of classroom walkthrough observations, effective leaders measure the alignment of the lesson objective to evidence of student learning. They measure the quality of feedback provided to the teacher to determine whether growth and improvement are occurring. They measure the right indicators in order to ensure the success of the mission. When effective leaders want to support quality teaching, they engage in coaching conversations. They also reflect with the teacher and develop a coaching cycle. Putting those tactics into practice is a better method of measurement.

6. **Is the provided feedback for change of good quality and based on factual evidence that will help achieve the mission?** Remember, feedback can be steeped in several things that are unproductive (bias, prejudice, or fear). When looking at a mission, really examine the feedback for change to determine whether there is factual evidence or empirical measures that will help people reach the goal.

Thinking through these six questions is a good, but not surefire, way for leaders to understand whether to continue trusting the process, work out the kinks because a plan is in place, or adjust and improve. Reflection and adjustment an evolving process that takes time, effort, and practice to master. But if you've followed every step in the leadership cycle, you are already on your way to making exceptional progress.

Key Points

This chapter has been your guide to navigating the delicate dance between trusting the process and making necessary adjustments. Remember, adjustments are about adapting existing practices, while improvements enhance them with tangible benefits. To make informed decisions, seek data-driven feedback and avoid subjective opinions. When faced with a crossroads, ask yourself six key questions: (1) Is the current approach hindering the mission? (2) Are challenges related to skill or motivation? (3) What uncontrollable factors are at play? (4) Does the timeline necessitate adjustments? (5) Are measurements aligned with success? and (6) Is feedback based on factual evidence? Remember, sustained successful leadership is an evolving process that requires continuous effort and practice. But by applying these insights, you can confidently navigate the path to exceptional progress.

Now that you have the tools to navigate the process of adjustments and improvements, it's time to ensure they stick. Chapter 10 delves into the crucial strategies for embedding lasting change within your organization.

As you leave this chapter, remember the following.

- Leaders are always going to be faced with two options after ensuring measurement and feedback. The first option is to trust the process; the second option is to make adjustments.
- When something is improved, it is made better, as evidenced by increased value or productivity. Improvement provides a tangible benefit, usually a saving of time, money, space, effort, and other resources.
- Adjustment is the practical, physical, and behavioral modification required to accept and implement new practices or ideas.
- Change is often met with resistance. Effective leaders take the time to identify what is impeding the change effort.
- Measurement and feedback have to be a continual process.

- Misaligned measurement or feedback may not necessarily justify the need for adjustment or improvement.
- Engaging with reflective questions may help you determine whether to adjust or to trust the process.

Reflective Activity: Perspective for Adjustment

Select a mission and use it to complete the following chart.

Mission	Reflective Question	Your Perspective	Your Action Steps
	Is the decision to continue doing things the same way having a negative impact on the mission?		
	Does the challenge with progress have to do with the will or the skill of the people executing the mission?		
	What uncontrollable factors are at play that could cause temporary or permanent challenges to the mission?		

Mission	Reflective Question	Your Perspective	Your Action Steps
	What is the timeline for progress?		
	Are our measurement indicators the right indicators that will ensure the success of the mission? What are we measuring?		
	Is the provided feedback for change of good quality and based on factual evidence that will help achieve the mission?		

STEP 6: BE ACCOUNTABLE AND GIVE REWARDS

Leaders inspire accountability through their ability to accept responsibility before they place blame.

—Courtney Lynch

THE FIRST day of school has a ritual, a tradition of sorts, that the teacher and the students in every single classroom carry out. On that very first day, students learn what is expected of them while they are learning in the classroom. The teacher discusses the classroom rules and regulations. The teacher explains what additional supplies the students need to be productive. The teacher outlines the curriculum or, at the very least, the consequences of not turning assignments in on time. The teacher defines success and failure. Students learn what happens if they misbehave, if they're late, if they don't do their homework, if they cheat, if they get into a fight with their peers, if they're sent to the office, if their name is written on the board, if they receive three strikes, and the list continues. This process is called *clarifying the consequence of decisions*.

By ensuring the expectations and consequences on that first day, teachers set the stage for a culture of accountability. Some teachers have students sign pledges acknowledging they are aware of the expectations set before them. Teachers will even go as far as to send a memo home for the parents to sign, acknowledging their receipt and understanding of the student expectations.

Just like the first day of school sets the stage for student success, establishing clear expectations and consequences creates a culture of accountability in our organization. By involving everyone in defining desired outcomes and potential roadblocks, we create a shared road map for achieving our goals. Just like students are more likely to succeed when they understand the rules, our team members thrive when they know what's expected and how their actions impact collective success. This means open communication, support, and celebration of individual and team achievements rather than punishment.

This chapter challenges negative perceptions of accountability and guides leaders to build a positive culture around it. It explores how ineffective leaders contribute to the accountability problem and equips you with essential questions to assess your own practices. You'll learn about the three major roadblocks to accountability and how to overcome them. The chapter then dives into fostering a culture of ownership and action, emphasizing the leader's role in creating a safe and supportive environment. Finally, it highlights the power of recognition and its impact on employee morale and performance. By the end, you'll gain valuable insights and tools to transform accountability from a burden to a driving force for success in your organization.

Accountability as a Positive Thing

Ensuring a culture of accountability and reward is the final step in the leadership cycle. Too often, people associate accountability with reprimand and negativity. Being held accountable, by nature, can get a bad rap, especially in a world with ineffective leaders. Ineffective leaders are those who assume that professionalism equals automatic clarity of expectations. This "you know what's expected of you because you're a working professional" attitude can undermine an organization, because the moment someone doesn't know what is expected of them and they are held accountable to any degree, they feel targeted and unfairly reprimanded. *Accountability* is defined as a complex, three-dimensional concept: (1) the individual takes responsibility for their actions (responsibility); (2) the individual agrees that their decisions or actions will be assessed by a meaningful audience (transparency); and (3) the individual acknowledges that rewards or sanctions will be imposed in accordance with this assessment (answerability; Drach-Zahavy, Leonenko, & Srulovici, 2018; Srulovici & Drach-Zahavy, 2017).

The lack of a culture of consistent, clear communication frustrates so many schools and organizations. In these organizations, there is a vivid disconnect among the mission, the vision, the lived values, and the consistency of accountability. Some people are held accountable; others are not. Perceived favoritism ensues as trust and respect are damaged. The employees held accountable take little to no ownership of their actions, instead opting to pull the victim card and blame anything and anyone else.

Individuals high in victim sensitivity harbor a constant fear of exploitation. They become hypervigilant to any hint of untrustworthiness, interpreting even neutral cues as potential threats. This heightened sensitivity can lead to seemingly antisocial and egotistical behavior, which can be understood as a defense mechanism. By acting uncooperatively first, victim-sensitive individuals attempt to preemptively protect themselves from being taken advantage of (Gollwitzer et al., 2015).

The second they are held accountable for their actions, these people automatically assume termination is on the table. They mistrust their leader because now they fear the leader is "out to get them." Those feelings and perceptions can drive an employee to contact their local union representative, vent their feelings of unfair treatment to their colleagues, and rally to find supporters who sympathize with their plight. But that reaction can be avoided or at least minimized. Accountability is not a negative thing, nor does it ever have to be met with fear, anxiety, and mistrust.

Here are three very important questions about accountability for every leader.

1. Do your employees know the measures being used to hold them accountable?
2. Are your employees clear about the impact of accountability on them personally and professionally?
3. Do your employees understand what accountability looks like, sounds like, and even feels like?

Somewhere along the way, consequences came to be viewed as unfavorable. The truth is that consequences can be either positive or negative. The origins of the word *consequence* come from two Latin words: (1) *con*, meaning "together," and (2) *sequi*, meaning "to follow" (Consequence, n.d.a). Combined, they make a neutral word meaning "something that logically or naturally follows from an action or condition" (Consequence, n.d.b).

Often, the discomfort of consequence is rooted in the misbelief that the hidden agenda of *consequence* means "punishment." However, the word can also mean "reward." In my experience, the people who don't like consequences are those who consistently underperform in their jobs. High performers, on the other hand, love consequences. To them, the word is synonymous with recognition and reward.

Individual accountability is the cornerstone of a thriving organization. When it's absent, employee morale declines, productivity dips, and performance suffers. This, in turn, fuels turnover, especially among top performers who crave a culture of ownership and responsibility (Trivedi, 2013). Organizations that fail to cultivate personal accountability create confusion and frustration for their high achievers. These individuals, often the backbone of their company's success, find themselves seeking opportunities elsewhere, where accountability is valued and rewarded. The link between individual accountability and organizational performance is undeniable. Studies consistently show that employees who take ownership of their work outperform those who don't (Trivedi, 2013). By fostering a culture of accountability, organizations unlock their full potential and gain a competitive edge.

Imagine what would happen if a principal took the same approach with their staff as teachers take with their students at the beginning of the school year. Everyone gathers together as the principal communicates, not simply to be heard but to be understood. The school's expectations for teachers are clearly written and articulated in the meeting. Teachers are informed about the consequences of their own actions in a comprehensive and supportive manner.

Principals may go as far as to discuss what actions warrant each consequence. For example, the principal may create a hypothetical scenario to articulate what decisions may warrant a memorandum of concern, a written reprimand, peer coaching, and even termination from employment. Then, take it a step further and explain the impact each corrective or coaching action will have on an individual's career, personnel file, evaluation, or contract. The purpose of this is not to instill fear within the teachers, but rather to lay out the expectations in a clear and concise manner so that teachers can perform their duties with knowledge and within a culture of accountability.

Imagine a principal who engages in discussion, answers questions, and listens to concerns. The principal establishes transparent practices in alignment with the mission, vision, and values of the campus. The principal takes the time to get feedback from staff about ways to improve the process and incorporates input that is reasonable and feasible and adds value to the process. The approach will not stop employees from violating rules and expectations, but it does eliminate the anxiety, fear, and uncertainty that often come with accountability.

Clarity improves a team's ability to execute plans. It enhances a team's ability to confidently change directions and elevates a sense of ownership. When clarity is abundant in terms of consequence, the feeling of being targeted or singled out is drastically minimized. When clarity of expectations is delivered in a supportive and caring manner, individuals realize that a culture of accountability is a positive force for the individual, the students, and the organization at large.

A Culture of Accountability

Establishing a culture of accountability is paramount for the success of the organization, and encompasses the students, teachers, faculty, staff, and administration. I often ask educational leaders two questions. The first is, "What is your definition of accountability?" I follow this question with, "How do you establish a culture of accountability?"

Here's what I've learned. Some leaders say something along the lines of, "Holding someone accountable means following up with them, discussing the situation at hand, or reminding them of the expectation." Other leaders are dogmatic in their approach and think accountability means beating people over the head with memoranda of concern and threatening corrective action based on every mistake. Neither of those approaches will be successful in transforming an organization from a mindset of apathy and lack of ownership to one of passion and buy-in.

The first answer sounds good. It is a common definition of accountability. It might actually be where accountability got such a bad rap. But "reminding them of the expectation" and "following up with them" are passive approaches. Sure, the leader is active in the delivery of communication, but the recipients, those who failed to meet expectations, are passive. They are reminded. They are asked to listen. Where is the action in that approach? Where is the transfer of ownership from the leader to the colleague?

In a nutshell, accountability is giving an account of one's conduct and reporting on one's progress. It is also admitting motives and reasons for taking certain actions. When building a culture of accountability, effective leaders understand their role in the process. They understand most people have been trained not to solve problems, but rather to bring problems to a person higher up in the organization to solve. That mindset is a challenge. It takes time for leaders to establish a culture where problems are reasonably and effectively solved at the lowest level. However, while understanding the definition of accountability is crucial, the key lies in moving beyond passive approaches and fostering a culture of active ownership. This is where the specific questions effective leaders ask come into play, shifting the focus from merely following up to empowering problem solving and collaboration.

Two Questions That Impact the Accountability Process

There are two questions effective leaders can ask that have a powerful impact on the accountability process. When dutifully presented with a problem, effective leaders can ask, "How are you planning to overcome this challenge?" That question may take employees aback, for they are used to presenting problems to their leaders and walking away from them. Therefore, the second question is equally important: "What support is needed to assist you?" Accountability doesn't mean the leader shoulders the weight of every single problem in the organization. It also doesn't mean the employees must navigate problems and issues alone, without counsel.

By asking those questions time and again, effective leaders create the understanding that they are not there to solve every problem, but they can provide the resources, support, coaching, and training to help others be successful. Conversely, ineffective leaders cannot fight off the urge to solve other people's problems, which is what limits their ability to be highly successful. Each time someone goes to an ineffective leader with a problem and the leader solves it, a loop of dependence is strengthened. That act in turn develops a culture of reliance instead of a culture of ownership. It fosters a mindset of compliance instead of comprehension. Additionally, it perpetuates a reactive disposition instead of a proactive belief system.

The culture of dependence is rarely built from an egotistical place. In most cases, the ineffective leader is not intentionally forcing their employees to depend on them. The pattern comes from a willingness to be there for everyone and create positive progress. However, solving everyone's problems will not encourage accountability.

Three Major Accountability Inhibitors

There are three major inhibitors to accountability.

1. **Planning in place of action:** In education, we are so good at planning. We have lesson plans, classroom management plans, five-year plans, districtwide plans, statewide plans—the list goes on. We can plan our hearts out. But when action does not take place in the midst of all our planning, it is impossible to establish a culture of accountability. Effective leaders ensure the elimination of the gap between planning and action.

2. **Excuses instead of execution:** There will always be barriers to knock down when executing plans in any system. However, developing excuses that barriers are "impenetrable" will quickly destroy any semblance of a culture of accountability. Remember, accountability isn't about excuses. It's about empowerment, ownership, and action. An established culture of excuses will lead to inconsistency in accountability. Effective leaders are skilled at redirecting any attempt to justify or provide excuses as well as at leading people through the thinking process to take ownership of their situation. Such leaders focus their time, energy, effort, resources, and dialogue on impacting what they can control.

3. **Focus on busyness rather than on impact:** "I'm so busy." "I'm so overwhelmed." "I don't have time for anything else." If you hear those phrases often, you know you have a culture where busyness is shown as a badge of honor. But busyness is not that. Busyness is an excuse for not achieving results. Busy is hurried. Busy is overwhelmed. Busy is fast and careless. Busyness is sprinting around the track, ignoring exchange zones, and gripping that baton with the selfish ambition of finishing the team race all by yourself. Certainly, there are moments when life gets busy. We all know that. But when being busy extends to being exhausted without evidence of impact, it is not productive. We never want to look back at life and say, "Wow, I was really good at being busy."

   When you hear language such as, "What is my impact?" and "What evidence do I have that I am being effective and efficient?" you know you have a culture where results are far more important than any level of activity.

The Seeds of a Culture of Accountability

The beauty of accountability is that the leader only needs to start the ball rolling. The effective leader plants seeds of accountability, steps back, and watches the team water those seeds. Once accountability takes hold in the organization, more and more people will come to your aid. Teams hold one another accountable, even in the leader's absence. It all starts with creating a psychologically safe environment where people challenge one another in a supportive manner and look into collaborating for success. Is accountability working that way in your school? Why or why not?

Conventional wisdom holds that lack of accountability is a worker problem. Ineffective leaders lament that declining work ethic and rampant apathy within an organization are due to the job. A lack of loyalty is a "worker issue"; employees rent their jobs instead of owning them. That way of thinking encourages the ineffective leader to blame employees, make accountability personal, and default to punitive consequences.

An Accountable Leader's Mindset

What if conventional wisdom is wrong? What if lack of accountability is purely a leadership problem? It all adds up. The difference between inspiring ownership and having employees who trade time for money has less to do with strategies and techniques and everything to do with the leaders' mindset.

The best leaders are guided by the following three beliefs.

1. **Employees want to do a good job and succeed:** Yes, it is a job, but most people are driven by personal success and grow from witnessing their impact in their organization.

2. **Consequences should be taught and sustained rather than used to mandate compliance:** Consequences used to mandate compliance can feel demotivating. That methodology generates a huge feeling of mistrust throughout the organization, as well as a culture of fear.

3. **Relationships, not positions, are the ultimate tool for influencing the performance of others:** The difference between mandated compliance and volunteered commitment can be traced to the relationship between the leader and the follower. People will do what they are told to do because it is their job. They will run through walls to succeed for a leader they trust and admire. Employees show up on their first day at work wanting to take ownership and succeed. Somewhere along the way, some will decide to do as little as possible. How many employees take that path may very well depend on you.

Leaders who get accountability right know that most people want to do great work. These leaders view their job as creating an environment where commitment and self-discipline are volunteered.

An Accountable Leader's Actions

Effective leaders are clear about what they expect from themselves, their organization, and those who work for them. They walk the walk. They communicate those expectations. Remember, people can't hear what you think. You really don't want to make people guess what you want them to do. Unspoken expectations lead to resentment. Here are three things you can do right now to build a culture of volunteered accountability.

1. **Adjust your mindset:** There may be a few people on your team who do not want to do a good job, but that number is small—probably 2–5 percent. Stop thinking of the other 95–98 percent as part of the problem.

2. **Make sure you are doing your part:** Be honest with yourself on areas where you are not fulfilling your responsibility, and make a plan to improve. Solicit feedback if you're unsure of blind spots. Determine in which areas you are lacking processes and systems to ensure impact.

3. **Focus relentlessly on relationships:** People will always be your greatest asset. Your ability to connect with, inspire, and motivate them matters. The organizational structure is rooted in relationships, not titles. When employees feel psychologically safe and valued and they understand their impact, relationships are strong throughout the organization. Accountability is not a thing to be feared, but rather a culture to be embraced.

In his book, *Good Authority*, leadership trainer Jonathan Raymond (2016) says, "The right question isn't, 'How do I get my people to engage?' The right question is, 'How do I engage better with my people?'" (p. 1). Raymond suggests that true engagement comes from empowering individuals to take responsibility. By actively engaging with people, leaders can create a culture where accountability is shared, ownership is encouraged, and the blame game is replaced by collaborative problem solving. The idea that leaders should focus on "engaging better" with their people instead of waiting on their people to initiate the change is an excellent example of ownership and accountability.

When Ownership Is Dormant

Nothing is as destructive as irresponsibility, which I define as not being answerable to authority. It means lacking a sense of accountability. It also means being fickle, careless, thoughtless, undependable, and unstable. To be irresponsible is to transfer blame for your behavior to someone else.

Ineffective leaders allow people not to take responsibility for their actions, decisions, situations, or circumstances. People with a propensity to disavow ownership are experts at blaming the past for their future. A by-product of their attitude is a culture of irresponsibility where everyone engages in the blame game. The principal blames the teachers for test scores. The teachers blame administration for student behavior. The administration blames the teachers for student behavior. The upper-grade teachers blame the lower-grade teachers for unprepared students with learning deficiencies. The parents blame the teachers for their children's not passing a test, or even the entire grade. The teachers blame the parents for their children's not engaging in classroom activities and their own education. The principal blames the central office for the campus situation. In turn, the central office blames the campus for their situation.

The blame goes back and forth, around and around, and improvement doesn't happen, trust breaks down, and no one wins. If you notice a lack of ownership in your organization, consider the following action steps.

1. **Model accountability:** Leaders must set the tone by demonstrating personal accountability for their actions, their decisions, and their team's performance. This includes owning mistakes, taking responsibility for outcomes, and consistently delivering on commitments.

2. **Shift the blame game:** Leaders should actively challenge the blame game narrative. Encourage open communication and focus on solutions instead of assigning blame. Facilitate discussions that identify root causes and work toward improvements.

3. **Empower and delegate:** Granting employees ownership and responsibility for their tasks fosters a sense of accountability. Provide clear expectations, resources, and support while allowing space for autonomy and decision making.

4. **Recognize and reward responsible behavior:** Celebrate individuals and teams who demonstrate accountability, ownership, and initiative. Public recognition reinforces these positive behaviors and motivates others to follow suit.

5. **Hold people accountable:** When individuals fail to meet expectations or they demonstrate irresponsible behavior, address it constructively and consistently. Provide clear feedback, offer coaching and support, and implement consequences when necessary.

The Differences Between a Culture of Accountability and a Culture of Nonaccountability

To ensure clarity, let's explore a culture of accountability and a culture of non-accountability in a simple chart. See table 10.1 (page 186) for lists of beliefs, foci, and results that characterize accountability and nonaccountability.

Imagine two organizations. In Organization A, mistakes are met with hushed whispers and pointed fingers. Challenges are seen as dividers, pitting colleagues against each other. This is a culture of nonaccountability, a breeding ground for stagnation, low morale, and high turnover.

Across town, Organization B hums with a different energy. Mistakes are openly discussed and seen as opportunities for growth. Challenges are tackled collaboratively, uniting team members toward a common goal. This is a culture of accountability, where ownership and learning reign supreme, leading to constant progress, high engagement, and a thriving team spirit.

The information you hold is the map to navigate from Organization A to Organization B. It reveals the stark contrast between two belief systems and their resulting behaviors and consequences. Understanding this dynamic empowers you, as a leader, to cultivate the latter belief system within your organization. Here's how you can use this information.

- **Recognize that beliefs drive actions:** Foster a growth mindset where challenges are seen as opportunities to learn and improve. Encourage ownership, not blame. Remember, people are the solution, not the problem.
- **Shift the focus from finding faults to finding solutions:** Encourage fact finding and open discussions about issues, not individual punishments for past mistakes. Help your team focus on the future and on learning and doing the job better.
- **Move from assuming and informing to ensuring and empowering:** Equip your team with the information and resources they need to succeed. Foster a culture of open communication and feedback, where everyone feels heard and valued.

Table 10.1: Culture of Accountability Versus Nonaccountability

	Culture of Nonaccountability	Culture of Accountability
Belief	"People are the problem."	"People are the solution."
	"Challenges divide."	"Challenges unite."
	Fixed mindset	Growth mindset
	Blame	Ownership
Focus	The person	The issue
	The past	The future
	Punishment and embarrassment	Correction and restoration
	Fault finding	Fact finding
	Compliance to do the job	Learning to do the job better
Result	Assuming	Ensuring
	Informing	Empowering
	Lower levels of trust	Higher levels of trust
	Reactive behavior	Proactive behavior
	Confusion	Clarity
	Status quo	Risk taking
	Unclear priorities	Clear priorities
	Stagnation or regression	Constant growth
	Lower levels of team morale	Higher levels of team morale
	Higher rates of turnover	Lower rates of turnover
	Less employee engagement	More employee engagement

The consequences of both cultures are clear. In a culture of accountability, you'll see increased trust, proactive behavior, clarity, risk taking, and ultimately, growth. By using this information as a guide and leading by example, you can usher your organization into an era of accountability where everyone thrives.

Reward and Recognition

Reward and recognition are so powerful that these two elements can renew employees' sense of loyalty, ownership of the mission, and pride. Recognition connects employees to the organization, elevates performance, and increases retention. Reward lets employees know that you value their efforts and want to make them feel that way with a meaningful gesture that benefits them.

From an early age, we crave recognition from our parents, our teachers, and our friends. That craving never truly goes away. The desire for recognition—that is to say, the desire to have the approval, esteem, consideration, or respect of those around us, whether as individuals or as members of social groups—has, in fact, been described as a vital human need (Gomes, 2017).

Acknowledging your employees can be a powerful tool for improving their mood and productivity (Amer & Obradovic, 2022). Research has shown that effective recognition occurs in organizations that have a strong, supportive culture; understand the psychology of praising employees for their good work; and apply the principles of employee recognition (Amer & Obradovic, 2022).

Affirmation during development builds trust in received feedback. It is a strong motivational tool that enriches employees' energies toward the accomplishment of organizational goals and objectives (Imran, Ahmad, Nisar, & Ahmad, 2014). Employee recognition helps retain top talent, increase employee engagement, and encourage high performance (Rahim & Daud, 2013).

Punke (2013) emphasizes the importance of incorporating three distinct methods of recognition: (1) formal (structured programs), (2) informal (peer-to-peer or manager-driven recognition), and (3) day-to-day (spontaneous appreciation).

Formal recognition involves structured programs with clearly defined objectives, processes, and criteria. These programs reward and recognize individuals, teams, or departments across the organization for achieving specific goals, exemplifying core values, or going above and beyond expectations. As Punke (2013) highlights, this organized approach celebrates employees for their contributions, including long-standing service.

Informal recognition celebrates individual and team achievements, focusing on milestones reached monthly or quarterly. This can take the form of low-cost awards, refreshments, point-value incentives, gift cards, or certificates. The key benefit of informal programs lies in their immediacy, acknowledging employee contributions at the right moment within a dynamic work environment, ultimately reinforcing their value (Amoatemaa & Kyeremeh, 2016).

Day-to-day recognition is a powerful tool that involves acknowledging employee contributions frequently (daily or weekly). Unlike traditional rewards, it typically has no cost and relies on interpersonal skills for positive feedback that can be shared widely across the organization. This approach offers immediate reinforcement of desired behavior and sets a clear example for others. Importantly, it empowers individuals and teams at all levels to recognize each other's good work, fostering a culture of appreciation and personal accountability (Amoatemaa & Kyeremeh, 2016).

Effective recognition in the workplace fosters a positive work environment and motivates employees to become committed and excel in their roles. This high level of motivation translates into a competitive advantage for the organization, as the employees' performance drives achievement of goals, strategic objectives, and ultimately, growth and high levels of achievement (Imran et al., 2014).

My challenge to leaders is this: Channel that first-day-of-school excitement with your staff. Pair it with a transparent conversation about expectations, what-if scenarios, and the personal, professional, and organizational impact that specific choices and behaviors will have on the mission as a whole. When everyone knows what is expected and is given the tools, resources, and support to course-correct when necessary, a culture of accountability will continue to grow. A culture of accountability will be welcomed.

Key Points

This chapter emphasized the importance of fostering a culture of accountability and reward. It clarified that accountability is not about punishment, but rather about responsibility for and ownership of actions. Leaders play a crucial role in establishing this culture by setting clear expectations, empowering others, and building trust. The chapter highlighted three major inhibitors to accountability and suggested ways to overcome them. It also emphasized the power of rewards and recognition, stressing the importance of positive, frequent, and personalized approaches. Ultimately, the chapter encouraged leaders to build a culture where accountability and reward work hand in hand to drive employee engagement, ownership, and organizational success.

As you leave this chapter, remember the following.

- Ensuring a culture of accountability and reward is the final step in the leadership cycle.

- In an organization where the culture of accountability is muddy, employees held accountable take little to no ownership of their actions, instead opting to pull the victim card and blame anything and anyone else.
- When clarity is delivered in a supportive and caring manner, individuals realize that a culture of accountability is a positive force for the individual, the students, and the organization at large.
- Nothing is as destructive as irresponsibility.
- People with a propensity to not take ownership are experts at blaming the past for their future.
- When building a culture of accountability, effective leaders understand that most people have not been trained to solve problems; rather, they have been trained to bring problems to a person higher up in the organization to solve.
- There are three major inhibitors to accountability: (1) planning in place of acting, (2) offering excuses in place of executing, and (3) focusing on being busy rather than on having an impact.
- Reward and recognition are so powerful that these two elements can renew employees' sense of loyalty, ownership of the mission, and pride. Recognition connects employees to the organization, elevates performance, and increases retention.

Reflective Activity: Culture of Accountability

Read each of the following questions, and select the number that best correlates with your current organizational culture of accountability.

- To what degree do people at all levels take ownership of solving problems with a focus on continuous improvement, instead of playing the victim and blaming others?

Low									High
1	2	3	4	5	6	7	8	9	10

- To what degree is the culture directly linked to student achievement and measured?

Low									High
1	2	3	4	5	6	7	8	9	10

- To what degree are people regularly recognized for their value and contributions, as opposed to only acknowledged with formal, structured recognitions or awards?

Low									High
1	2	3	4	5	6	7	8	9	10

- To what degree is busyness valued compared with productivity and impact?

Low									High
1	2	3	4	5	6	7	8	9	10

- To what degree are poor performers addressed, coached, supported, or removed instead of ignored, transferred, or promoted?

Low									High
1	2	3	4	5	6	7	8	9	10

- To what degree do people openly surface and effectively resolve problems and conflicts rather than avoiding them?

Low									High
1	2	3	4	5	6	7	8	9	10

- To what degree do people at all levels have a clear sense of direction, a clear sense of purpose, and clear priorities rather than fragmented, competing, or overwhelming priorities?

Low									High
1	2	3	4	5	6	7	8	9	10

- To what degree are student outcomes, teacher team execution, and campus outcomes tracked and measured, instead of only generic metrics?

Low									High
1	2	3	4	5	6	7	8	9	10

- To what degree do administrators effectively collaborate, problem-solve, and include others in the decision-making process rather than operate in isolation?

Low									High
1	2	3	4	5	6	7	8	9	10

- To what degree do people initiate and execute change rather than resisting or avoiding change?

Low									High
1	2	3	4	5	6	7	8	9	10

Score	Results
0–60	Your score indicates a critically low level of accountability. This means that your organization very likely has inefficient practices and low morale.
61–79	Your score indicates a low level of accountability. This means that your organization is experiencing breakdowns in execution that may negatively affect student achievement, compounded by wasted resources, employee frustration, and low levels of efficiency.
80–89	Your score indicates a moderate level of accountability. This means that your organization is fairly accountable. In order to be even more influential to ensure student achievement, the organization must improve its execution of good practices as well as cross-functional teamwork and engagement.
90–100	Your score indicates an excellent level of accountability. Congratulations! Your organization is a great place to work where all stakeholders are treated well, and the organization exhibits high-level execution and cross-functional teamwork.

HIRE WITH PRECISION

People are not your most important asset. The right people are.

—Jim Collins

CONGRATULATIONS! YOU have made it all the way through the leadership cycle. I hope you have gleaned important lessons and knowledge that will help you transform your educational leadership landscape. Remember, everything you need to make monumental changes is already within you. Just follow the steps of the leadership cycle and you will see results.

But before we conclude the collection of lessons, there is one more important topic I want to address. It is not a step in the leadership cycle, but is undoubtedly related to everything you are trying to achieve as a leader—especially fulfilling the mission and vision.

The two most important decisions regarding staff that a leader will make are (1) whom they hire and (2) whom they fire. If the first is not done well, the second will be done frequently. There are a plethora of hiring methods that can positively affect the likelihood of success. The following information is by no means prescriptive. However, it contains proven strategies you can deploy that align with best practices for hiring and increase the probability of success.

Effective principals hire quality teachers. They are able to use the interview process to identify characteristics of quality teachers who will positively respond to leadership. It should come as no surprise that principals directly affect their students' levels of achievement. Principals are in a unique position to use the hiring process to increase student achievement. For example, Gregory F. Branch, Eric A. Hanushek, and Steven G. Rivkin (2012) examined value-added scores and found that just one year of having a highly effective principal who hires the right teachers and provides proper support increased student achievement from the 50th percentile to more than the 54th percentile.

When you hire high-quality teachers who respond well to leadership, you are cultivating a culture of trust and accountability, which translates to an environment in which alignment with the mission is more prevalent. More than any reform strategy or campuswide policy, effective teaching that ensures learning is the best way to improve student achievement.

Conversely, hiring teachers who focus more on teaching than on student learning can lead to a lack of student achievement, and can create much more work for everyone around those teachers. Students will notice a teacher who is unwilling to respond appropriately to leadership direction or who is not intrinsically motivated to learn, grow, and develop in alignment with the mission and vision of the organization, staff members, and parents. Once that deviation occurs, the mission is in jeopardy, and the culture is compromised.

Ultimately, it is the principal's job to ensure a healthy culture and climate. Have you heard the adage attributed to management consultant Peter Drucker that says, "Culture eats strategy for breakfast"? That declaration is true regardless of the strategies employed to ensure learning. Culture sets the standard for building a high-performing environment. Forget traditional hiring methods! This chapter shows how finding the right teachers, who align with your school's values and possess emotional intelligence, can transform your climate, culture, and ultimately, student achievement. Learn how to conduct behavior-based interviews and avoid red flags to ensure you hire the perfect fit for your school community.

Hiring With Climate and Culture in Mind

We have talked about organizational culture and climate many times throughout this book. Those terms are often used interchangeably, but they are not synonymous. When we are defining *climate* in an educational setting, the term refers to the characteristics that differentiate one school from another and includes the feeling that stakeholders have when they are in the school. School climate represents the attitude of the organization.

In a healthy climate, teachers are happy. The collective mood is positive and focused on student achievement. Leaders must create conditions where positivity, proactiveness, and happiness thrive. Unfortunately, some leaders do not research the most effective strategies for creating a healthy climate, and instead rely on extrinsic rewards. An extrinsic reward is something that comes from an external source. Rewards can be financial (a bonus, an incentive, or a commission) or nonfinancial (praise, a training badge, a development opportunity, or a coveted project assignment). In contrast, an intrinsic reward is intangible; it might be the sense of satisfaction you get from mastering a new skill, successfully completing a complex project, or working on a project that has personal significance.

Bringing the teachers muffins each week may give a few teachers that needed extra boost, but the act will not affect the morale of the building. Activities designed to address low morale by creating a more positive climate need to be scrutinized using the following criteria.

- How much of an investment in time and energy is involved?
- What is the span of time it takes for the activity to have an impact?
- Will the activity impact an individual or the group?
- Is the activity focused on intrinsic or extrinsic rewards?
- How does this activity align with the culture?

Activities that go deeper include open and honest town halls with the staff, team-building activities, and brainstorming sessions where actionable items are deployed within certain time frames (and not just strategized and talked about), to name just a few examples.

Descriptions of culture go deeper than those of climate. *Culture* includes the history of the school (or any organization), such as the traditions and rituals that develop over time. Culture is developed from or composed of three levels: (1) artifacts, (2) values, and (3) basic assumptions.

Artifacts are aspects of the school that are observable. They include the physical layout of the building, the dress code, the feel of the building, and even the smell of the building. Values are the ideologies and philosophies that guide how things should be done. Last, basic assumptions are the processes and feelings that guide the behaviors and actions of individuals within the school. For example, when an individual is provided with feedback for improvement, is the prevailing assumption one of self-reflection, positive intent, and a continuous improvement mindset? Or is it one of deflection, blame, criticism, and a lack of ownership?

When we're talking about culture, we're talking about mindset, behavior, and experience. In a healthy, student-focused culture, people respond appropriately to stressful or challenging situations and keep the focus on learning instead of teaching. People create the culture's energy through their responses and their collaborative work in teams, departments, pods, and small groups. People are the life force of the organization, so it is vital that you hire contributors, not detractors.

The impact of hiring high-quality teachers spans past establishing a culture and a climate that ensure student achievement. Hiring effective educators affects the school budget. School administrators witness thousands of dollars in savings accrue when they do not have to spend scarce resources to retrain, reorient, micromanage, support, counsel, or release ineffective teachers. Every time an administrator has to replace a poor hire, it costs the organization money. The hiring process, training, onboarding, and orientation for new hires are not cheap. Beyond finances, they take up valuable time, resources, effort, energy, and focus. Based on those factors alone, it is crucial to hire the best teachers the first time around.

You would be hard-pressed to find a principal who does not admit to having made at least one hiring mistake in their career. Many try to correct those mistakes by investing a great deal of resources, time, and effort in supporting improvement and attempting to change the mindset of the bad hire. Then, there are others who default to releasing hires who do not meet expectations.

So, how can school leaders ensure they effectively identify quality teachers before they indulge in restorative practices aimed at salvaging poor hiring decisions? It all starts with the interview. Start by defining your ideal culture: What are your core beliefs, and what kind of atmosphere do you cultivate? Then, delve deep into the candidate's values, work style, and experiences in similar settings. Utilize various interview methods, like behavioral questions, group interactions, and case studies, to gain a holistic understanding. Empower your team by involving them in the process, allowing them to assess the candidate's cultural fit. Finally, onboard new hires by immersing them in your culture and making them feel welcomed and integrated. Remember, transparency is key. Be clear about expectations, challenges, and rewards, and showcase your unique and positive culture to attract top talent who will thrive within it. By prioritizing both climate and cultural fit, you'll build a team that fosters a positive and productive work environment and ultimately contributes to your organization's success.

Examining the Interview Process

Throughout the years, the hiring process in education has been criticized as both bureaucratic and ineffective. After all, if the goal of hiring the best is to ensure student achievement, why do so many students not achieve when the best have been hired? The demand for teachers remains remarkably high, so the process is often rushed and ill-advised. The hiring window is often short and sandwiched between the end of the school year and the beginning of the next one. A compressed timeline presents many challenges, but it should also inspire administrators to develop highly impactful interview processes and procedures that truly explore the talents, determination, skill set, and passion of each candidate.

Traditionally, the interview process is meant to provide insight into a candidate's future performance through questions and oral responses. Yet, researchers who have studied many facets of the interview process have seen mixed results related to the predictive validity of the employment interview (Lynn, 2008).

People tend to present their best self at the interview, and that presentation may not always correlate to day-to-day job performance. Despite that factor, a carefully designed interview process can still provide administrators a unique opportunity to determine how people accomplish results, not just what they have accomplished in the past.

Teacher or administrator selection deserves rigorous examination to ensure alignment between the candidate and the school's core values and pedagogical practices and to identify teachers and leaders with the greatest likelihood of increasing student outcomes. Educational consultant Michael Fullan (2008) argues that effective hiring consists of not just matching candidates to profiles but finding those who fit in the organizational culture. Successful candidates are more than their GPA and certifications; they are individuals who understand the nuances of relationship building, the importance of impact, and the value of a growth mindset, and yearn to add value to the environment.

All too often, I have witnessed the interview process be nothing more than a question-and-answer session in which more credence is given to how someone answers a question than to strategic aspects of the process. An example would look something like this:

Dr. Eloquent, a charismatic speaker with a seemingly endless bag of educational buzzwords and passionate anecdotes, wowed the committee during his interview for the principal position. He painted a vivid picture of innovative practices, differentiated instruction, and data-driven decision making. He spun stories of transformative student relationships and soaring test scores. His passion was palpable, and his responses aligned perfectly with the school's vision statement. He seemed like the missing piece the school desperately needed.

Unfortunately, Dr. Eloquent's interview persona translated poorly to the daily grind. His "innovative practices" turned out to be recycled slideshows and borrowed lesson plans. His "differentiated instruction" amounted to assigning different busywork to different groups. His "data-driven decisions" were based on misinterpretations of spreadsheets. Most importantly, his "transformative relationships" were one-sided pep talks devoid of genuine connection.

Dr. Eloquent's carefully crafted facade began to crumble under the pressure of actual teaching. Frustrated students, confused colleagues, and disappointing assessments exposed the stark gap between his interview performance and his actual abilities. Morale plummeted, and parents voiced concerns.

Situations like this, which occur all too often, remind us that hiring beyond the interview requires a multifaceted approach. Don't be blinded by charisma; seek genuine competence and ensure a good fit. Only then can you avoid a crash and truly ensure student success.

Applying Emotional Intelligence in the Interview Process

It is a fair assumption that the higher a person's IQ, the higher their intelligence. However, psychologists assign more factors to determine an individual's intelligence. Now, emotional intelligence (EQ), including the social, personal, and survival components of an individual, is considered equally important, particularly for work performance. In fact, the foundational competency of great performance is considered to be based on EQ.

Adele B. Lynn (2008), author of *The EQ Interview*, states that 70 percent of abilities essential for effective performance are related to emotional competencies and not to personality. How beneficial would it be for hiring managers to assess candidates' emotional intelligence as part of the interview process?

Afsaneh Ghanizadeh and Fatemeh Moafian (2010) conducted a study designed to explore how a teacher's emotional intelligence influences their pedagogical success. The result? There is a high correlation between the two. After all, teaching involves management of critical situations. It involves interpersonal relationships and the ability to motivate and inspire others. Teachers constantly have to read the room to determine the best way to ensure learning. Let's not forget the many emotional situations that occur inside and outside the classroom, with parents and students alike.

Properly assessing EQ can provide information that is critical to organizations and can greatly improve the hiring process. An effective way to accurately predict a candidate's EQ is to engage in behavior-based interviewing to identify past behaviors, activities, and results. Behavior-based interviewing allows everyone on the hiring side to assess whether candidates are reflective, they tend to act with intention, or they react to certain stressors. In addition, interviewers can assess whether the applicants take ownership of their responsibilities, they tend to blame others, or they display an offensive arrogance or defensiveness. A candidate's reflections provide a wealth of information about their personality and behaviors, which can help distinguish the benefits and risks associated with hiring them.

You may be wondering how one can determine a candidate's EQ. What questions does one ask? What scenarios can one play out? Interviewers can use behavior-based interview questions to explore whether candidates have exhibited certain job-related behaviors in previous work situations. The underlying premise of the behavioral interview is that past performance is a good predictor of future performance.

Behavioral interviews utilize questions that encourage more detailed responses from candidates than traditional interview questions, which focus more on skills and qualifications. Consider these examples.

- "Tell us about a situation in which you had to adjust to changes over which you had no control. How did you handle that?"
- "What kinds of challenges did you face on your last job? Give an example of how you handled them."
- "Developing and using a detailed procedure is often important in this job. Talk about a time when you needed to develop and use a detailed procedure to successfully complete a project."
- "How did you go about making the changes (step by step)? Answer in depth or detail." (Additional context-specific prompts include, "What were you thinking at that point?" "Tell me more about

meeting with that person," and "Lead me through your decision-making process.")

- "What is the toughest group that you have had to get cooperation from? Describe how you handled that situation. What was the outcome?"

While behavioral interview questions offer valuable insights into a candidate's past performance, they're just one piece of the puzzle. Pay close attention to the candidate's attitude and behavior throughout the interview. By observing their communication, problem-solving approach, and overall demeanor, you can uncover deeper potential and identify who truly possesses the skills and drive to excel within your team.

Shaking Up the Interview Process

In the introduction to this book (page 1), I shared my experience as a first-time principal. I didn't get everything right the first time around. I came into the role wanting to change everything and did not quite follow the leadership cycle in order. In time, I understood the impact I could make on the school. I developed ways to ensure learning and clarity in the mission.

Later in my career as a principal, my high school was recognized as one of America's Best Urban Schools by the National Center for Urban School Transformation. In the span of four years, we earned twenty-two distinctions. A single distinction is hard to come by in Texas, let alone twenty-two. We didn't close achievement gaps at a staggering rate simply based on how intelligent the teachers were, how good the faculty believed they were, or even how hard everyone worked. We accomplished amazing feats as a team due to our ability to respond appropriately to the adversities and challenges that came with ensuring teaching and learning. We were intentional about our culture, our climate, our systems, our beliefs, and whom we invited to align themselves with the work of our mission and vision. Setting clear core values upfront, empowering teams to evaluate cultural fit, and delving deep into candidates' values, work styles, and experiences through various methods like behavioral questions, group activities, and even mock lessons revealed the candidates' true potential and compatibility far beyond a résumé could.

The rationale behind this was that nothing affects learning more than the teacher you put in front of the students. As principal, I developed a team that invested a lot of time in interviewing and scrutinizing the hiring process; we made sure we developed an effective process that got us the right people in the right seats. Sometimes, that meant we were interviewing twenty to thirty people for one position. There were times, due to untimely resignations or other issues out of our control, when we had to hire the only candidates who were available. Still, we had to make quality hiring decisions based on a quality hiring process.

And if we wanted to gauge EQ proactively, we needed to find ways to have candidates demonstrate their EQ. One way we accomplished that was, prior to our interview meetings, we gave interviewees a data set with clear directives to bring the data with them to the interview. At the time of the interview, if they had not interacted with or analyzed the data, or if they didn't even remember the data, that shortfall gave us great insight into their level of preparedness, proactiveness, communication, and so on. On the other hand, some interviewees would call us before the interview to inquire about the data, looking for clarity to ensure understanding. And that was all we were looking for; the team wanted to see their mindset. Some people analyzed the data, looked things up, and took notes. We were interested not so much in the data but in how they approached the data, how they communicated when they lacked clarity, how they prioritized the provided directions, and how they took ownership of their decisions. Those behaviors told us how the candidates would approach the job at hand.

Another method we used was a lesson demonstration. We provided interviewees a lesson plan in advance and asked them to prepare a ten-minute lesson for the committee. Now, that request is not an abnormal practice. Plenty of schools have interviewees teach a lesson, some even in front of students. However, the focus here was a bit more intentional. Our hiring team purposely gave them way too much material, making it impossible to cover in the short time frame. Some interviewees did try to finish the whole lesson in the time allotted, and they did a great job trying it. Most of these interviewees never checked for clarity or understanding.

Later, during the discussion portion of the interview, we would ask each candidate the following question: "Is it more important to you that you cover all intended material on pace with the scope and sequence, or that you ensure student learning prior to moving forward with lessons?" We would then sit and listen to 99 percent of the interviewees pontificate about how they wholeheartedly believed in ensuring student learning prior to moving forward with a lesson.

I would then interject with the question, "Then why did you fly through the lesson we provided for you?" Their response would always be, "Well, I only had ten minutes and wanted to get through as much as possible." See, we were not trying to trip them up, but without that question, they would not have told us anything of value. By having a way to correlate their behavior to their response, we were able to glean much more about how they think.

On the flip side, we also saw candidates who only made it through a fraction of the lesson in the ten minutes. These interviewees would state something like, "I do not want to move forward until I'm sure you are comfortable with what we just covered." That answer was the golden ticket. It was the teaching approach we wanted to see in each and every one of our classrooms.

Those were just a couple of the interview exercises that allowed us to see how the candidates thought and processed information. Also, during my experience as a principal, I learned how to identify clear red flags in the interview process, which I would like to share with you.

Identifying Interview Red Flags

The person or group responsible for selecting the right candidate must have an interviewing radar that goes far beyond detecting basic qualities of a candidate. Signs such as nervousness, thoughtful pauses, and a slightly tense demeanor can safely be ignored during the interview process, but here are nine red flags that should never be ignored.

1. **The candidate shows up late or not at all:** There are extenuating circumstances that can be overlooked. These are situations that are beyond one's control, such as hospitalization, family emergencies, and unforeseen transportation issues. However, those instances are rare and usually warrant a courtesy call for being late. When you have a no-call and no-show, that is a clear sign of disregard and disrespect for the opportunity and the interviewer's time.

2. **The qualifications on the candidate's résumé don't match up with their responses:** When you ask about specific qualifications and the candidate has difficulty answering your questions, there is a chance they falsified stated qualifications. Needless to say, a person who falsifies their qualifications is more likely to be dishonest in their work. Trust and dependability are everything, so do not let this red flag fly.

3. **There is a disconnect between the candidate's activity and evidence of their impact:** You have a candidate who can rattle off the list of committees they have served on, the list of plans they

have developed, or the litany of professional developments they have facilitated or attended. The problem is these admissions are just "busy lists" when the candidate fails to articulate any evidence of their impact on student achievement. That red flag indicates the candidate may be more focused on activity than on results.

4. **The candidate's enthusiasm is anything but present:** There are some incredibly good reasons why someone might avoid showing enthusiasm. Perhaps they don't want to appear too eager or they have trouble regulating emotions. But, in most cases, if a candidate doesn't interact positively with a firm handshake, eye contact, and a smile, they're not truly enthused about the job. Often, a disengaged interviewee makes for a disengaged employee.

5. **The candidate is disrespectful, arrogant, or overly self-assured:** The humblebrag is difficult to master, and a candidate always walks a fine line between being confident and being arrogant. Notice how the candidate interacts with everyone in the building. If they talk down to the janitorial staff or front office, that is a red flag. If they are inconsiderate of space in the waiting room, or are busy texting instead of making a good impression, that is a red flag. In the interview, a red flag should pop up when a candidate tries to control the conversation by interrupting and consistently steering the conversation back to them.

6. **The candidate speaks badly about their previous employer:** Speaking poorly of a previous employer can imply a lack of responsibility for one's actions and the inability to deal with difficult situations. That revelation is especially concerning if the candidate plays the victim card. Additionally, a complainer can bring down the morale of an entire department, so any bad-mouthing at all is a red flag that the candidate is not worth investing in.

7. **The candidate demonstrates no evidence that they researched your organization:** A candidate who goes into an interview not knowing about the entity shows a lack of preparation as well as little genuine interest in the institution and how their prospective role would fit within the organization's goals and values. Each school is different. Each origin story and organizational makeup is different. A solid candidate will take time to explore the things that make your

school stand out from others and will ask thoughtful questions about their findings.

8. **The candidate doesn't take responsibility for failed projects, teams gone awry, or mistakes:** Another red flag shows up in a candidate who admits no responsibility for past mistakes and instead blames others, such as coworkers, bosses, a lack of resources, or a lack of skilled team members. When you ask, "Tell me of a time you faced a difficult project or challenging work situation," listen to what the candidate has to say. You can tell right away if they blame others for the challenges or if they take responsibility for their actions based on what anecdote they choose to share.

   If the candidate was released by a former employer, it's important to listen carefully to their rationale. If they indicate they consider themselves blameless and cannot admit to errors, you likely do not want to hire this individual. The right candidate will reflect on mistakes, identify possible areas of improvement, and articulate steps taken to ensure success in the future.

9. **The candidate's most recent supervisor is not listed as a reference:** Current or previous employers have the most in-depth knowledge about an interviewee's work ethic. Leaving their most recent supervisor off their reference list can give the impression of a hidden reason that the interviewee does not want their future employer to contact their past employer.

   A primary goal of the reference check is to get a third-person assessment of the candidate's achievements. A good way to do this is to ask references open-ended behavioral interview questions like those used to interview the candidate. Set a positive tone from the outset, and let the reference speak freely and without interruption. Avoid leading questions, negative language, or anything that will put the reference on the defensive. Avoid asking broad questions such as, "What can you tell me about John?" Ideally, you would refer to specifics gleaned from the candidate during the interview process. A few examples would be, "I understand John helped implement a new tracking system. Can you tell me more about his role in that?" and "I understand there was tension in the department. Can you give me an example of how John galvanized his coworkers to work as a team?"

Follow up these behavioral assessments with general questions about communication skills, management skills, organizational skills, and especially people skills. Ideally, your questions will elicit detailed, specific examples without a lot of thought on the part of the reference.

Ensuring the Right People Fill the Right Seats

While one-on-one interviews remain common, they can be susceptible to unconscious bias creeping into the decision-making process. Forming an interview team of three to five individuals offers several advantages to combat this. First, getting diverse perspectives from people of different backgrounds offers a broader and more objective assessment, reducing the chance of overlooking qualified candidates due to personal biases. Second, having multiple evaluations provides a richer picture of the candidate, minimizing the risk of focusing on a single, potentially biased perception. Beyond reducing bias, team interviews also make team members more invested in the hiring process and make them feel more responsible for the new hire's success, which leads to a warmer welcome and stronger team dynamics. Additionally, candidates get a realistic job preview by interacting with future colleagues, which fosters a better cultural fit. Finally, the collaborative process reinforces teamwork and shared responsibility, solidifying the team's identity. Remember, effective team interviews require clear structure, bias training for all participants, and diverse team composition.

Assembling the right support for your interview team goes beyond just gathering numbers. While a crowd might offer multiple perspectives, it's crucial to curate a team with the specific expertise and diversity needed to truly optimize the process.

Start by identifying team members whose skills and work experience directly align with the open role. This ensures each interviewer can assess the candidate against relevant criteria, from technical proficiency to cultural fit. Don't stop at expertise. Prioritize diversity in demographics, experiences, and perspectives. This broad range of viewpoints challenges potential biases and leads to a richer, more objective evaluation. Imagine the difference between a team that solely focuses on technical skills and one that also considers communication style and team dynamics—with the latter, a much more comprehensive picture emerges. Even the most diverse team can be susceptible to unconscious bias. Ensure all participants undergo training to recognize and mitigate these biases so that you can create a fairer and more inclusive interview process.

Throwing a group of people together isn't enough. Define clear roles and responsibilities for the different interviewers. This avoids confusion, ensures everyone contributes effectively, and keeps the discussion focused on the candidate's suitability for the role.

Remember, the key to meeting educational demand is to hire individuals who are highly qualified and good fits. High-performing institutions that use behavior-based interviewing greatly increase their probability of successfully inviting people onto the team who will add value in the intended areas. Such new team members often improve morale and student achievement. It is paramount to get hiring right the first time as much as possible. Your current students, teachers, and faculty depend on it.

Key Points

Hiring the right teachers isn't just about filling positions; it's about shaping the school's environment and ensuring student success. This chapter emphasized creating a healthy school climate focused on positivity and achievement, and a culture embedded with shared values and a growth mindset. To achieve this, the hiring process needs to check more than just résumés—it should assess candidates' EQ, cultural fit, and alignment with the school's vision. The chapter emphasized the importance of watching out for red flags like negativity, dishonesty, and blame of others. By utilizing diverse interview teams and focusing on behavior-based questions, you can identify candidates who will truly add value to your school community. Remember, this is an investment that impacts everyone, so take the time to get it right.

As you leave this chapter, remember the following.

- The two most important staff decisions that a leader will make are (1) whom they hire and (2) whom they fire. If the first is not done well, the second will be done frequently.
- When you hire high-quality teachers who respond well to leadership, you are cultivating a culture of trust and accountability.
- An effective way to accurately predict a candidate's emotional intelligence is to engage in behavior-based interviewing to identify past behaviors.
- When employees have high emotional intelligence, they can manage critical situations in both their personal and professional lives.

- One method for eliminating interviewing bias is to establish an interview team of three to five individuals with experience in the particular job.
- Climate refers to the characteristics that differentiate one school from another and includes the atmosphere stakeholders feel when they are in the school.
- Culture includes the history of the school or any organization, such as the traditions and rituals that develop over time.

EPILOGUE

THE PATH to fostering a culture of sustainable success begins with the leadership cycle. But it's not merely a framework; it's a transformative journey demanding unwavering commitment and consistent action. This journey starts with you, the leader. Embody the values you expect from your team, making your dedication tangible through your choices. Prioritize long-term solutions over quick fixes, demonstrating a commitment to building a lasting foundation.

Hundreds of testimonials attest to the transformative power of the leadership cycle. Take the case of an elementary principal in a small urban district. By embracing the cycle, she underwent a strategic shift in thought that allowed her to anticipate challenges, ensure clarity, empower others, and deliver feedback within a culture of accountability. This transformation revitalized her school. Morale soared, with teachers rarely absent and buy-in for initiatives nearly unanimous. Most impressively, student achievement skyrocketed—21 percent in mathematics and 23 percent in reading.

The principal of one of the largest high schools in North Texas, composed of almost five thousand students, discovered the leadership cycle was a game changer. He was so impressed that he trained his entire leadership team to use this approach for every project. The results were amazing! Different groups within the school that were once disconnected now worked together toward clear shared goals. Leaders, feeling confident and equipped, made smart decisions based on specific goals they wanted to achieve. They established a culture of accountability in which ownership was the expectation. This led to a wave of positive changes: fewer students missing class, more effective interventions to help students who needed them, and most importantly, more students graduating! By embracing the leadership cycle, this principal showed that it wasn't just a set of tools; it was a cultural shift that transformed his school for the better.

Becoming a better educational leader begins with the recognition that the purpose of school is not just to teach students. Rather, the purpose of school is to ensure that students are learning. That simple but, sadly, rare idea will put you miles ahead of most leaders in this space. Instead of focusing on equipping and training teachers as the end goal, such efforts should be the means by which student learning is fostered. An effective leader will drive all organizational activity toward the singular goal of ensuring that students are learning.

An easy step that you can take to become a better leader is to increase your investment in the people around you. No person is an island, and your subordinates and colleagues will appreciate your acknowledgment of their roles in the broader mission. When engaging with people, seek to understand rather than be understood. Your teachers especially will have important things to tell you, given that they are closest to the target of your entire enterprise—the students. Good leaders allow teachers to talk, but great leaders actually listen.

Once you recognize that school is about learning and that you need to invest in your people, you need to ensure that your teachers are following through with the message. An effective leader will help their teachers in developing a learning environment for the students. Follow up with your teachers and emphasize their role in fostering a culture of fun, experiential learning. You'd be surprised by the number of leaders who remain in the shadows, keeping their teachers at arm's length. Be available and be personable, and you'll be off to a great start.

You can transform yourself into a better leader by following the leadership cycle that I've detailed in these pages. Be the rare leader who respects the importance of details that many leaders would dismiss as trivial. No matter what challenges your school faces, you have the tools, the knowledge, and the ability to tackle those challenges head-on. You do not have to spend thousands of dollars on restructuring a program. You just need to tap into your most precious resource: time. Use that resource wisely, and go transform your school. Be the change, lead the change, and ensure the change! The future of student learning depends on it.

REFERENCES AND RESOURCES

Aboulsoud, S. H. (2011). Formative versus summative assessment. *Education for Health Change in Learning and Practice*, *24*(2), 651.

Acar, O. A., Tarakci, M., & van Knippenberg, D. (2019). Creativity and innovation under constraints: A cross-disciplinary integrative review. *Journal of Management*, *45*(1), 96–121. https://doi.org/10.1177/0149206318805832

Adams, R. J. (1993, February). *How expert pilots think: Cognitive processes in expert decision making*. Washington, DC: U.S. Department of Transportation. Accessed at www.tc.faa.gov/its/worldpac/techrpt/rd93-9.pdf on November 3, 2023.

Adams, R. J. (1994). How expert pilots think. *SAE Transactions*, *103*(1), 2086–2091. Accessed at www.jstor.org/stable/44615036 on November 3, 2023.

Adams, R. J., & Ericsson, K. A. (1992, June). *Introduction to cognitive processes of expert pilots*. Washington, DC: U.S. Department of Transportation. Accessed at www.tc.faa.gov/its/worldpac/techrpt/rd92-12.pdf on November 3, 2023.

ADFILMS WORLD—Commercials. (2018, October 28). *Apple Watch series 4: Better you—Adfilms, TV commercial, TV advertisements* [Video file]. Accessed at www.youtube.com/watch?v=0cBJBj_tbHM on November 3, 2023.

Ahmad, A. B., & Cheng, Z. (2018). The role of change content, context, process, and leadership in understanding employees' commitment to change: The case of public organizations in Kurdistan region of Iraq. *Public Personnel Management*, *47*(2), 195–216.

Albrecht, J. R., & Karabenick, S. A. (2018). Relevance for learning and motivation in education. *The Journal of Experimental Education*, *86*(1), 1–10. https://doi.org/10.1080/00220973.2017.1380593

Alexander, P. A. (2018). The relevance of relevance for learning and performance. *The Journal of Experimental Education*, *86*(1), 124–135. https://doi.org/10.1080/00220973.2017.1380592

Altarriba, J., & Basnight-Brown, D. (2022). The psychology of communication: The interplay between language and culture through time. *Journal of Cross-Cultural Psychology*, *53*(7–8), 860–874. https://doi.org/10.1177/00220221221114046

Amer, A., & Obradovic, S. (2022). Recognising recognition: Self-other dynamics in everyday encounters and experiences. *Journal for the Theory of Social Behaviour*, *52*(4), 550–562. https://doi.org/10.1111/jtsb.12356

American Federation of State, County and Municipal Employees. (n.d.). *"I've Been to the Mountaintop" by Dr. Martin Luther King, Jr.* Accessed at www.afscme.org/about/history/mlk/mountaintop on November 3, 2023.

Amoatemaa, A. S., & Kyeremeh, D. D. (2016). Making employee recognition a tool for achieving improved performance: Implication for Ghanaian universities. *Journal of Education and Practice*, *7*(34), 46–52. Accessed at https://files.eric.ed.gov/fulltext/EJ1126683.pdf on March 4, 2024.

Ayivor, I. (2014). *Daily drive 365: Daily thoughts for positive living!* CreateSpace Independent Publishing Platform.

Blackwell, S. E. (2019). Mental imagery: From basic research to clinical practice. *Journal of Psychotherapy Integration*, *29*(3), 235.

Blanchard, K., & Kearin, T. (2014). *Fit at last: Look and feel better once and for all.* San Francisco: Berrett-Koehler.

Bond-Barnard, T. J., Fletcher, L., & Steyn, H. (2018). Linking trust and collaboration in project teams to project management success. *International Journal of Managing Projects in Business*, *11*(2), 432–457. https://doi.org/10.1108/IJMPB-06-2017-0068

Boser, U., & McDaniels, A. (2018, June). *Addressing the gap between education research and practice: The need for state education capacity centers.* Washington, DC: Center for American Progress. Accessed at www.americanprogress.org/article/addressing-gap-education-research-practice on November 3, 2023.

Branch, G. F., Hanushek, E. A., & Rivkin, S. G. (2012, February). *Estimating the effect of leaders on public sector productivity: The case of school principals* (Working Paper No. 17803). Cambridge, MA: National Bureau of Economic Research. Accessed at www.nber.org/papers/w17803 on November 3, 2023.

Brooks, A. W., Gino, F., & Schweitzer, M. E. (2015). Smart people ask for (my) advice: Seeking advice boosts perceptions of competence. *Management Science, 61*(6), 1421–1435. https://doi.org/10.1287/mnsc.2014.2054

Brown, G. (2020, April 21). *Difference between teaching and learning.* Accessed at www.differencebetween.net/language/words-language/difference-between-teaching-and-learning on November 3, 2023.

Bryk, A. S., Gomez, L. M., Grunow, A., & LeMahieu, P. G. (2015). *Learning to improve: How America's schools can get better at getting better.* Cambridge, MA: Harvard Education Press.

Cakir, S. G. (2015). The effects of teacher immediacy and student burnout on empowerment and resistance among Turkish pre-service teachers. *Learning and Individual Differences, 40,* 170–175. https://doi.org/10.1016/j.lindif.2015.05.002

Carson, C., Armstrong, T., Carson, S., Clay, A., & Taylor, K. (Eds.). (2005). *The papers of Martin Luther King, Jr., volume V: Threshold of a new decade.* Berkeley, CA: University of California Press.

Carter, D. (2022). *School improvement plan: Updating curriculum, technology and classrooms for education 4.0* [Capstone project, Northwestern College]. NWCommons. https://nwcommons.nwciowa.edu/education_masters/456

Cavaness, K., Picchioni, A., & Fleshman, J. W. (2020). Linking emotional intelligence to successful health care leadership: The big five model of personality. *Clinics in Colon and Rectal Surgery, 33*(4), 195–203. https://doi.org/10.1055/s-0040-1709435

Collins, J. (2001). *Good to great: Why some companies make the leap—and others don't.* New York: Harper Business.

Coloroso, B. (2002). *Kids are worth it! Giving your child the gift of inner discipline.* New York: Quill.

Connors, C. B. (2021). Summative and formative assessments: An educational polarity. *Kappa Delta Pi Record, 57*(2), 70–74.

Consecutive. (n.d.). In *Merriam-Webster's online dictionary.* Accessed at www.merriam-webster.com/dictionary/consecutive on February 16, 2024.

Consequence. (n.d.a). In *Online Etymology Dictionary.* Accessed at www.etymonline.com/word/consequence on November 3, 2023.

Consequence. (n.d.b). In *YourDictionary.* Accessed at www.yourdictionary.com/consequence on November 3, 2023.

Conzemius, A. E., & O'Neill, J. (2014). *The handbook for SMART school teams: Revitalizing best practices for collaboration* (2nd ed.). Bloomington, IN: Solution Tree Press.

Covey, S. R. (2004). *The 7 habits of highly effective people: Powerful lessons in personal change*. New York: Simon & Schuster.

Dlamini, N., Mazenda, A., Masiya, T., & Nhede, N. T. (2020). Challenges to strategic planning in public institutions: A study of the Department of Telecommunications and Postal Services, South Africa. *International Journal of Public Leadership, 16*(1), 109–124.

Dolin, J., Black, P., Harlen, W., & Tiberghien, A. (2017). Exploring relations between formative and summative assessment. In J. Dolin & R. Evans (Eds.), *Transforming assessment: Through an interplay between practice, research and policy* (pp. 53–80). Cham, Switzerland: Springer.

Drach-Zahavy, A., Leonenko, M., & Srulovici, E. (2018). Towards a measure of accountability in nursing: A three-stage validation study. *Journal of Advanced Nursing, 74*(10), 2450–2464. https://doi.org/10.1111/jan.13735

Dunford, R., Su, Q., & Tamang, E. (2014). The Pareto principle. *The Plymouth Student Scientist, 7*(1), 140–148.

Dweck, C. S. (2006). *Mindset: The new psychology of success*. New York: Random House.

Dweck, C. S. (2016). *Mindset: The new psychology of success* (Updated ed.). New York: Random House.

Fischhoff, B., Crowell, N. A., & Kipke, M. (Eds.). (1999). *Adolescent decision making: Implications for prevention programs—Summary of a workshop*. Washington, DC: National Academies Press.

Freedberg, M., Glass, B., Filoteo, J. V., Hazeltine, E., & Maddox, W. T. (2017). Comparing the effects of positive and negative feedback in information-integration category learning. *Memory and Cognition, 45*(1), 12–25. https://doi.org/10.3758/s13421-016-0638-3

Freedberg, M., Schacherer, J., & Hazeltine, E. (2016). Incidental learning of rewarded associations bolsters learning on an associative task. *Journal of Experimental Psychology: Learning, Memory, and Cognition, 42*(5), 786–803.

Fullan, M. (2008). *The six secrets of change: What the best leaders do to help their organizations survive and thrive*. San Francisco: Jossey-Bass.

Gabriel, A. S., Cheshin, A., Moran, C. M., & van Kleef, G. A. (2016). Enhancing emotional performance and customer service through human resources practices: A systems perspective. *Human Resource Management Review, 26*(1), 14–24. https://doi.org/10.1016/j.hrmr.2015.09.003

George, B., Walker, R. M., & Monster, J. (2019). Does strategic planning improve organizational performance? A meta-analysis. *Public Administration Review, 79*(6), 810–819. https://doi.org/10.1111/puar.13104

Ghanizadeh, A., & Moafian, F. (2010). The role of EFL teachers' emotional intelligence in their success. *ELT Journal, 64*(4), 424–435. http://dx.doi.org/10.1093/elt/ccp084

Ginsberg, S. (2003). *Hello, my name is Scott: Wearing nametags for a friendlier society.* Brooklyn, NY: HELLO, my name is Scott!

Ginsberg, S. (2012). *Consistency is far better than rare moments of greatness: Living life without editing yourself.* Brooklyn, NY: HELLO! my name is Scott!

Gnepp, J., Klayman, J., Williamson, I. O., & Barlas, S. (2020). The future of feedback: Motivating performance improvement through future-focused feedback. *PLOS One, 15*(6), Article e0234444. https://doi.org/10.1371/journal.pone.0234444

Goldsmith, M. (2007). *What got you here won't get you there: How successful people become even more successful.* New York: Hyperion.

Goleman, D. (2011). *Leadership: The power of emotional intelligence.* Northampton, MA: More Than Sound.

Gollwitzer, M., Süssenbach, P., & Hannuschke, M. (2015). Victimization experiences and the stabilization of victim sensitivity. *Frontiers in Psychology, 6*, 439. https://doi.org/10.3389/fpsyg.2015.00439

Gomes, B. W. (2017). *Theses Doctoral: The Desire and Struggle for Recognition.* Columbia University Commons. https://doi.org/10.7916/D8765M12

Grant, D., & Green, W. B. (2012). Grades as incentives. *Empirical Economics, 44*, 1563–1592.

Güçer, E., & Demirdağ, S. A. (2014). Organizational trust and job satisfaction: A study on hotels. *Business Management Dynamics, 4*(1), 12–28.

Guinot, J., & Chiva, R. (2019). Vertical trust within organizations and performance: A systematic review. *Human Resource Development Review, 18*(2), 196–227. https://doi.org/10.1177/1534484319842992

Han, Y., & Hong, S. (2019). The impact of accountability on organizational performance in the U.S. federal government: The moderating role of autonomy. *Review of Public Personnel Administration, 39*(1), 3–23. https://doi.org/10.1177/0734371X16682816

Hardavella, G., Aamli-Gaagnat, A., Saad, N., Rousalova, I., & Sreter, K. B. (2017). How to give and receive feedback effectively. *Breathe, 13*(4), 327–333. https://doi.org/10.1183/20734735.009917

Hattie, J. A. C. (2009). *Visible learning: A synthesis of over 800 meta-analyses relating to achievement.* New York: Routledge.

Hattie, J. A. C., & Clarke, S. (2019). *Visible learning: Feedback.* New York: Routledge.

Hebles, M., Trincado-Munoz, F., & Ortega, K. (2022). Stress and turnover intentions within healthcare teams: The mediating role of psychological safety, and the moderating effect of COVID-19 worry and supervisor support. *Frontiers in Psychology, 12*, Article 758438. https://doi.org/10.3389/fpsyg.2021.758438

Heifetz, R., Grashow, A., & Linsky, M. (2009). *The practice of adaptive leadership: Tools and tactics for changing your organization and the world*. Boston: Harvard Business Press.

Heifetz, R., & Laurie, D. L. (2001, December). The work of leadership. *Harvard Business Review*. Accessed at https://hbr.org/2001/12/the-work-of-leadership on November 3, 2023.

Hepler, R. (2023, January 11). Adjustment mechanisms: Definition, types & uses. *Study.com*. https://study.com/academy/lesson/adjustment-mechanisms-definition-types-uses.html

Heshmat, S. (2015, April 23). What is confirmation bias? *Psychology Today*. Accessed at www.psychologytoday.com/us/blog/science-of-choice/201504/what-is-confirmation-bias on March 15, 2024.

Hodel, L., Formanowicz, M., Sczesny, S., Valdrová, J., & von Stockhausen, L. (2017). Gender-fair language in job advertisements: A cross-linguistic and cross-cultural analysis. *Journal of Cross-Cultural Psychology, 48*(3), 384–401.

Huang, S.-C., Jin, L., & Zhang, Y. (2017). Step by step: Sub-goals as a source of motivation. *Organizational Behavior and Human Decision Processes, 141*, 1–15.

Hyatt, M. (2020). *The vision-driven leader: 10 questions to focus your efforts, energize your team, and scale your business*. Grand Rapids, MI: Baker Books.

Impelman, C. (2018, June 20). *Never mistake activity for achievement*. Accessed at www.thewoodeneffect.com/activity-achievement on November 3, 2023.

Imran, A., Ahmad, S., Nisar, Q. A., & Ahmad, U. (2014). Exploring relationship among rewards, recognition and employees' job satisfaction: A descriptive study on libraries in Pakistan. *Middle-East Journal of Scientific Research, 21*(9), 1533–1540.

Jagtap, P. (2016). Teacher's role as facilitator in learning. *Scholarly Research Journal for Humanity Sciences and English Language, 3*(17), 3903–3905.

Johnson, L. B. (2007). *A White House diary*. Austin, TX: University of Texas Press.

Kang, S. H. K. (2016). Spaced repetition promotes efficient and effective learning: Policy implications for instruction. *Policy Insights From the Behavioral and Brain Sciences, 3*(1), 12–19. https://doi.org/10.1177/2372732215624708

Kaplan, R. S., & Norton, D. P. (2005, October). The office of strategy management. *Harvard Business Review*. Accessed at https://hbr.org/2005/10/the-office-of-strategy-management on November 3, 2023.

Karge, B. D. (2023). *Watch, listen, ask, learn: How school leaders can create an inclusive environment for students with disabilities.* Bloomington, IN: Solution Tree Press.

Kauffmann, D., & Golan, C. (2017). The mediating effect of interpersonal trust on virtual team's collaboration. *International Journal of Knowledge Management, 13*(3), 20–37. https://doi.org/10.4018/IJKM.2017070102

Keague, S. (2012). *The little red handbook of public speaking and presenting.* CreateSpace Independent Publishing Platform.

Keeney, R. L. (2020). *Give yourself a nudge: Helping smart people make smarter personal and business decisions.* New York: Cambridge University Press.

Key Differences. (2016). *Difference between assessment and evaluation.* Accessed at https://keydifferences.com/difference-between-assessment-and-evaluation.html on November 3, 2023.

Kim, T.-Y., Wang, J., & Chen, J. (2018). Mutual trust between leader and subordinate and employee outcomes. *Journal of Business Ethics, 149*, 945–958. https://doi.org/10.1007/s10551-016-3093-y

King, M. L., Jr. (1960, September 25). *"The Negro and the American dream," excerpt from address at the annual Freedom Mass Meeting of the North Carolina State Conference of Branches of the NAACP* [Speech]. Charlotte, North Carolina. Accessed at https://kinginstitute.stanford.edu/king-papers/documents/negro-and-american-dream-excerpt-address-annual-freedom-mass-meeting-north on November 3, 2023.

Kiran, D. R. (2017). *Total quality management: Key concepts and case studies.* Cambridge, MA: Butterworth Heinemann.

Klimecki, O. M. (2019). The role of empathy and compassion in conflict resolution. *Emotion Review, 11*(4), 310–325. https://doi.org/10.1177/1754073919838609

Kluger, A. N., & Itzchakov, G. (2022). The power of listening at work. *Annual Review of Organizational Psychology and Organizational Behavior, 9*, 121–146. https://doi.org/10.1146/annurev-orgpsych-012420-091013

Kopzhassarova, U., Akbayeva, G., Eskazinova, Z., Belgibayeva, G., & Tazhikeyeva, A. (2016). Enhancement of students' independent learning through their critical thinking skills development. *International Journal of Environmental and Science Education, 11*(18), 11585–11592.

Kotter, J. P., & Whitehead, L. A. (2010). *Buy-in: Saving your good idea from getting shot down.* Boston: Harvard Business Review Press.

Levine, E. E., Roberts, A. R., & Cohen, T. R. (2020). Difficult conversations: Navigating the tension between honesty and benevolence. *Current Opinion in Psychology, 31*, 38–43. https://doi.org/10.1016/j.copsyc.2019.07.034

Lin, L. (2015). Exploring collaborative learning: Theoretical and conceptual perspectives. *Investigating Chinese HE EFL Classroom* (pp. 11-28). Berlin: Springer-Verlag.

Liu, D., Jiang, K., Shalley, C. E., Keem, S., & Zhou, J. (2016). Motivational mechanisms of employee creativity: A meta-analytic examination and theoretical extension of the creativity literature. *Organizational Behavior and Human Decision Processes, 137*, 236–263.

Liu, H., Geng, J., & Yao, P. (2021). Relationship of leadership and envy: How to resolve workplace envy with leadership—A bibliometric review study. *Journal of Intelligence, 9*(3), 44. https://doi.org/10.3390/jintelligence9030044

Lokhorst, A. M., Werner, C., Staats, H., van Dijk, E., & Gale, J. L. (2013). Commitment and behavior change: A meta-analysis and critical review of commitment-making strategies in environmental research. *Environment and Behavior, 45*(1), 3–34. https://doi.org/10.1177/0013916511411477

Lumineau, F., & Schilke, O. (2018). Trust development across levels of analysis: An embedded-agency perspective. *Journal of Trust Research, 8*(2), 238–248. https://doi.org/10.1080/21515581.2018.1531766

Lynn, A. B. (2008). *The EQ interview: Finding employees with high emotional intelligence.* New York: AMACOM.

Mart, C. T. (2013). A passionate teacher: Teacher commitment and dedication to student learning. *International Journal of Academic Research in Progressive Education and Development, 2*(1), 437–442.

Masters, G. N. (2022, August 8). *Reimagining the purpose of assessment* [Keynote]. Australian Council for Educational Research Conference 2022, Melbourne, Australia.

Mather, V. (2016, August 19). U.S. women go from gaffe to gold in 4×100 relay. *The New York Times.* Accessed at www.nytimes.com/2016/08/20/sports/olympics/women-4x100-relay-usa-results-jamaica.html on November 3, 2023.

Maurer, R. (2002). *Why don't you want what I want? How to win support for your ideas without hard sell, manipulation, or power plays.* Portland, OR: Bard Press.

Maxwell Leadership [@Maxwell_Leaders]. (2018, February 23). Leaders become great not because of their power, but because of their ability to empower others [Post]. X. Accessed at https://twitter.com/JohnCMaxwell/status/967069491686494209 on November 3, 2023.

McDaniel, M. A., Hartman, N. S., Whetzel, D. L., & Grubb, W. L., III. (2007). Situational judgment tests, response instructions, and validity: A meta-analysis. *Personnel Psychology, 60*(1), 63–91. https://doi.org/10.1111/j.1744-6570.2007.00065.x

Mehta, R., & Zhu, M. (2016). Creating when you have less. *Journal of Consumer Research, 42*(5), 767–782.

Michigan State University. (2016, March 1). Hey boss: Workers prefer consistent jerk to loose cannon. *ScienceDaily*. Accessed at www.sciencedaily.com/releases/2016/03/160301131113.htm on February 3, 2024.

Millman, D. (2006). *Way of the peaceful warrior: A book that changes lives*. Tiburon, CA: Kramer.

Mitchell, M. (2013). Teacher enthusiasm: Seeking student learning and avoiding apathy. *Journal of Physical Education, Recreation and Dance, 84*(6), 19–24. https://doi.org/10.1080/07303084.2013.779536

Moen, R. (2009, September). Foundation and history of the PDSA cycle. In *Asian Network for Quality Conference, Tokyo*. https://www.deming.org/sites/default/files/pdf/2015/PDSA_History_Ron_Moen.pdf

NAACP. (n.d.). *The 1963 march on Washington: A quarter million people and a dream*. Accessed at https://naacp.org/find-resources/history-explained/1963-march-washington on November 3, 2023.

Nagashibaevna, Y. K. (2019). Students' lack of interest: How to motivate them? *Universal Journal of Educational Research, 7*(3), 797–802. https://doi.org/10.13189/ujer.2019.070320

National Center for Urban School Transformation. (n.d.). *America's Best Schools award winners*. Accessed at https://ncust.com/previous-americas-best-urban-schools-award-winners on November 3, 2023.

New International Version Holy Bible. (1978). Grand Rapids, MI: Zondervan.

New World Encyclopedia. (n.d.). *Vilfredo Pareto*. Accessed at www.newworldencyclopedia.org/entry/Vilfredo_Pareto on August 20, 2023.

Ng, T. W. H. (2015). The incremental validity of organizational commitment, organizational trust, and organizational identification. *Journal of Vocational Behavior, 88*, 154–163. https://doi.org/10.1016/j.jvb.2015.03.003

Paulo, A. (2014). Harnessing assessment's power to improve students' learning and raise achievements: What and how should teachers do? *International Journal of Learning, Teaching and Educational Research, 8*(1), 136–148.

Pearson, J., Naselaris, T., Holmes, E. A., & Kosslyn, S. M. (2015). Mental imagery: Functional mechanisms and clinical applications. *Trends in Cognitive Sciences, 19*(10), 590-602.

Peifer, C., Schönfeld, P., Wolters, G., Aust, F., & Margraf, J. (2020). Well done! Effects of positive feedback on perceived self-efficacy, flow and performance in a mental arithmetic task. *Frontiers in Psychology, 11*, Article 1008. https://doi.org/10.3389/fpsyg.2020.01008

Primeau, M. (2021, September 15). Your powerful, changeable mindset. *Stanford Report*. Accessed at https://news.stanford.edu/report/2021/09/15/mindsets-clearing-lens-life on March 4, 2024.

Prøitz, T. S., Mausethagen, S., & Skedsmo, G. (2017). Data use in education: Alluring attributes and productive processes. *Nordic Journal of Studies in Educational Policy, 3*(1), 1–5.

Pugwash Conferences on Science and World Affairs. (1955, July 9). *Statement: The Russell–Einstein Manifesto*. Accessed at https://pugwash.org/1955/07/09/statement-manifesto on November 3, 2023.

Punke, H. (2013, June 28). *Best practices for developing an employee recognition program*. Accessed at www.beckershospitalreview.com/hr/best-practices-for-developing-an-employee-recognition-program.html on March 4, 2024.

Qasserras, L., Asmae, A., Qasserras, M., & Anasse, K. (2023). The effects of grades on the motivation and academic performance of Moroccan high school students. *International Journal for Multidisciplinary Research, 5*(2), 1–10.

Quote Investigator. (2018, October 9). *If we treat people as if they were what they ought to be, we help them become what they are capable of becoming*. Accessed at https://quoteinvestigator.com/2018/10/09/capable/#f+20373+1+2 on March 4, 2024.

Rahim, M. A., & Daud, W. N. W. (2013). Rewards and motivation among administrators of University Sultan Zainal Abidin (UniSZA): An empirical study. *International Journal of Business and Society, 14*(2), 265–286.

Rahman, S., & Majumder, A. A. (2015). Is it assessment of learning or assessment for learning? *South East Asia Journal of Public Health, 4*(1), 72–74.

Raymond, J. (2016). *Good authority: How to become the leader your team is waiting for*. Washington, DC: Ideapress.

Reininger, M. (2012). Hometown disadvantage? It depends on where you're from: Teachers' location preferences and implications for staffing schools. *Educational Evaluation and Policy Analysis, 34*(2), 127–145. https://doi.org/10.3102/0162373711420864

Roghanizad, M. M., & Bohns, V. K. (2017). Ask in person: You're less persuasive than you think over email. Journal of Experimental Social Psychology, 69, 223–226. https://doi.org/10.1016/j.jesp.2016.10.002

Rone, N. A., Guao, N. A. A., Jariol, M. S., Jr., Acedillo, N. B., Balinton, K. R., & Saro, J. M. (2023). Students' lack of interest, motivation in learning, and classroom participation: How to motivate them? *Educational Psychology, 7*(1), 636–645.

Rosenthal, R., & Jacobson, L. (1968). Pygmalion in the classroom. *The Urban Review, 3,* 16–20.

Ruff, H. J. (n.d.). *Howard Ruff: Quotes to live by.* Accessed at www.howardruff.com/ruff-quotes on November 3, 2023.

Ryan, R. M., & Deci, E. L. (2017). *Self-determination theory: Basic psychological needs in motivation, development, and wellness.* New York: Guilford Press.

Sah, K. P. (2013). Assessment and test in teaching and learning. *Academic Voices: A Multidisciplinary Journal, 2*(1), 28–32.

Sahay, A. (2019). Strategic thinking: My encounter. *IBA Journal of Management and Leadership, 10*(2), 7–14.

Schildkamp, K., Karbautzki, L., & Vanhoof, J. (2014). Exploring data use practices around Europe: Identifying enablers and barriers. *Studies in Educational Evaluation, 42,* 15–24. https://doi.org/10.1016/j.stueduc.2013.10.007

Schmid, E. A., Verdorfer, A. P., & Peus, C. (2019). Shedding light on leaders' self-interest: Theory and measurement of exploitative leadership. *Journal of Management, 45*(4), 1401–1433. https://doi.org/10.1177/0149206317707810

Schwab, K., Moseley, B., & Dustin, D. (2018). Grading grades as a measure of student learning. *SCHOLE: A Journal of Leisure Studies and Recreation Education, 33*(2), 87–95.

Schwantes, M. (2017, October 17). Steve Jobs once gave some brilliant management advice on hiring top people. Here it is in 2 sentences. *Inc. Magazine.* Accessed at www.inc.com/marcel-schwantes/this-classic-quote-from-steve-jobs-about-hiring-employees-describes-what-great-leadership-looks-like.html on November 3, 2023.

Scofield, C. I. (Ed.). (1996). *The Old Scofield study Bible, KJV* (Large print ed.). New York: Oxford University Press.

Scopelliti, I., Morewedge, C. K., McCormick, E., Min, H. L., Lebrecht, S., & Kassam, K. S. (2015). Bias blind spot: Structure, measurement, and consequences. *Management Science, 61*(10), 2468–2486.

Scott, S. (2004). *Fierce conversations: Achieving success at work and in life, one conversation at a time.* New York: New American Library.

Scott, S. (2017). *Fierce conversations: Achieving success at work and in life, one conversation at a time.* New York: New American Library.

Seneca, L. A. (2018). *Moral letters to Lucilius.* CreateSpace Independent Publishing Platform.

Şener, S., & Çokçalışkan, A. (2018). An investigation between multiple intelligences and learning styles. *Journal of Education and Training Studies*, 6(2), 125–132. https://doi.org/10.11114/jets.v6i2.2643

Serin, H. (2018). A comparison of teacher-centered and student-centered approaches in educational settings. *International Journal of Social Sciences and Educational Studies*, 5(1), 164–167. ISSN 2409-1294

Shallenberger, S., & Shallenberger, R. (2020). *Start with the vision: Six steps to effectively plan, create solutions, and take action.* Heber City, UT: Star Leadership.

Siebert, J. U., Kunz, R. E., & Rolf, P. (2021). Effects of decision training on individuals' decision-making proactivity. *European Journal of Operational Research*, 294(1), 264–282. https://doi.org/10.1016/j.ejor.2021.01.010

Society for Human Resource Management. (2016). *Employee job satisfaction and engagement: Revitalizing a changing workforce.* Alexandria, VA: Author. Accessed at www.shrm.org/topics-tools/news/employee-relations/survey-respect-work-boosts-job-satisfaction on February 17, 2024.

Spetzler, C., Winter, H., & Meyer, J. (2016). *Decision quality: Value creation from better business decisions.* Hoboken, NJ: John Wiley & Sons.

Srulovici, E., & Drach-Zahavy, A. (2017). Nurses' personal and ward accountability and missed nursing care: A cross-sectional study. *International Journal of Nursing Studies*, 75, 163–171. https://doi.org/10.1016/j.ijnurstu.2017.08.003

Stanford GSB Staff. (2007, August 1). Robert Joss: "Leadership is not about you." *Insights by Stanford Business.* Accessed at www.gsb.stanford.edu/insights/robert-joss-leadership-not-about-you on November 3, 2023.

Stangel, L. (2016, October 14). Three problems with top-down teams (and how to fix them). *Insights by Stanford Business.* Accessed at www.gsb.stanford.edu/insights/robert-joss-leadership-not-about-you on March 4, 2024.

Stieger, S., Lewetz, D., & Willinger, D. (2023). Face-to-face more important than digital communication for mental health during the pandemic. *Scientific Reports*, 13, 8022. https://doi.org/10.1038/s41598-023-34957-4

Summitt, P. (1999). *Reach for the summit: The definite dozen system for succeeding at whatever you do.* New York: Broadway Books.

Tehseen, S., & Hadi, N. U. (2015). Factors influencing teachers' performance and retention. *Mediterranean Journal of Social Sciences*, 6(1), 233–244. https://doi.org//10.5901/mjss.2015.v6n1p233

Touro University Worldwide. (2015, January 3). *Top-down vs. bottom-up management styles.* Accessed at www.tuw.edu/business/top-down-bottom-up-management on March 4, 2024.

Trivedi, A. (2013, August 22). *A study of literature review on individual accountability.* Accessed at https://ssrn.com/abstract=2314551 on March 4, 2024.

van Loon, M. H., & Roebers, C. M. (2017). Effects of feedback on self-evaluations and self-regulation in elementary school. *Applied Cognitive Psychology, 31*(5), 508–519.

von Goethe, J. W. (1824). *Wilhelm Meister's Apprenticeship and Travels* (T. Carlyle, Trans., Vol. 2, Book VIII, Chapter IV, p. 93). Chapman and Hall. Retrieved from https://quoteinvestigator.com/2018/10/09/capable/#f+20373+1+2

Vyas, S. (2021). An analysis of adjustment level among higher secondary school students. *IOSR Journal of Nursing and Health Science, 10*(3), 44–48.

Walston, J., & Conley, M. (2022). *Practical measurement for continuous improvement in the classroom: A toolkit for educators* (REL 2023–139). Washington, DC: Institute of Education Sciences. Accessed at https://ies.ed.gov/ncee/rel/Products/Publication/100841 on March 4, 2024.

Wang, S., Rubie-Davies, C. M., & Meissel, K. (2018). A systematic review of the teacher expectation literature over the past 30 years. *Educational Research and Evaluation, 24*(3–5), 124–179. https://doi.org/10.1080/13803611.2018.1548798

Warrilow, G. D. (2017). The effects of feedback modality on performance (Master's thesis, Western Michigan University). *Master's Theses.* https://scholarworks.wmich.edu/masters_theses/905

Weinstein, C. S., & Novodvorsky, I. (2015). *Middle and secondary classroom management: Lessons from research and practice* (5th ed.). New York: McGraw Hill Education.

Westerlund, A., Nilsen, P., & Sundberg, L. (2019). Implementation of implementation science knowledge: The research-practice gap paradox. *Worldviews on Evidence-Based Nursing, 16*(5), 332–334. https://doi.org/10.1111/wvn.12403

Whyte, W. H., Jr. (1952). *Is anybody listening? How and why U.S. business fumbles when it talks with human beings.* New York: Simon & Schuster.

Wisniewski, B., Zierer, K., & Hattie, J. (2020). The power of feedback revisited: A meta-analysis of educational feedback research. *Frontiers in Psychology, 10,* Article 3087. https://doi.org/10.3389/fpsyg.2019.03087

Woods, P. J., & Copur-Gencturk, Y. (2024). Examining the role of student-centered versus teacher-centered pedagogical approaches to self-directed learning through teaching. *Teaching and Teacher Education, 138,* Article 104415. https://doi.org/10.1016/j.tate.2023.104415

Wouters-Soomers, L., Van Ruysseveldt, J., Bos, A. E. R., & Jacobs, N. (2022). An individual perspective on psychological safety: The role of basic need satisfaction and self-compassion. *Frontiers in Psychology, 13*, Article 920908. https://doi.org/10.3389/fpsyg.2022.920908

Yaeger, D. (2016, March 13). Timeless lessons from John Wooden, the greatest coach of all time. *SUCCESS Magazine*. Accessed at www.success.com/timeless-lessons-from-john-wooden-the-greatest-coach-of-all-time on March 1, 2024.

Yu, M.-C., Mai, Q., Tsai, S.-B., & Dai, Y. (2018). An empirical study on the organizational trust, employee-organization relationship and innovative behavior from the integrated perspective of social exchange and organizational sustainability. *Sustainability, 10*(3), 864. https://doi.org/10.3390/su10030864

Zeffane, R., & Melhem, S. B. (2018). Do feelings of trust/distrust affect employees' turnover intentions? An exploratory study in the United Arab Emirates. *Middle East Journal of Management, 5*(4), 385–408. Accessed at www.inderscience.com/offers.php?id=95582 on November 3, 2023.

Zenger, J., & Folkman, J. (2014, January 15). Your employees want the negative feedback you hate to give. *Harvard Business Review*. Accessed at https://hbr.org/2014/01/your-employees-want-the-negative-feedback-you-hate-to-give on March 4, 2024.

Zhu, X. S., Wolfson, M. A., Dalal, D. K., & Mathieu, J. E. (2021). Team decision making: The dynamic effects of team decision style composition and performance via decision strategy. *Journal of Management, 47*(5), 1281–1304.

INDEX

A

absence of investment, 21
accountability, 8, 69–70, 107
    as a positive thing, 176–179
    defined, 176
    difference between a culture of accountability and a culture of nonaccountability, 185–186
    establishing a culture of, 110, 175–192
an accountable leader's actions, 182–183
    adjusting your mindset, 183
    focus relentlessly on relationships, 183
    making sure you do your part, 183
an accountable leader's mindset, 182
    consequences should be taught and sustained, 182
    employees want to do a good job and succeed, 182
    relationships are the ultimate tool for influence the performance of others, 182
acknowledgment, 187–188
action mindset, 16
action steps, 7, 94
actionable feedback, 149–150
active listening, 147
    ensuring clarity, 96
    investing in people, 12, 16, 22
Adams, R. J., 14
adapting to changing circumstances, 123
adaptive challenges, 37, 48–49, 57, 164
    root cause analysis, 122
adaptive learning, 55
adaptive teaching
    feedback, 54
    reflective activity, 58

adjusting and improving, 68–69, 72, 77, 163–164
    difference between, 164–166
    key points, 170–171
    reflective activity, 172–173
    six questions for adjustment reflection, 168–170
    when to make adjustments, 166–167
adjusting your mindset, 183
adopting a culture of feedback from the top, 148
advocating for adjustment and improvement, 8
aeronautical decision-making thought process, 64–65
affirmation, 187
allowing for ways to give feedback anonymously, 147
allowing others to engage in the knowledge, 132–133
applying emotional intelligence in the interview process, 198–200
applying research effectively, 13–15
the art of teaching, 48
artifacts, 195–196
the "assessment and evaluation are the same thing" myth, 39
the "assessment is one-way communication" myth, 41
assessments, 7
    diagnostic, 40
    formative, 40
    myths about, 41–42
    summative, 40
the "assignments turned in late should not count for full credit" myth, 43–44
avoiding planning for the same of planning, 108

B

Bartoletta, T., 127
Basic assumptions, 195–196

becoming a leader, 62–63
beginning with vision, 88–90
behavioral interviews, 206
    questions, 199–200
being accountable and giving rewards, 69–70, 72, 78, 175–176
    accountability as a positive thing, 176–179
    difference between cultures of accountability and nonaccountability, 185–186
    establishing culture of accountability, 175, 179–183
    key points, 188–189
    reflective activity, 190–192
    reward and recognition, 187–188
    when ownership is dormant, 183–184
being consistent, 20–21, 83
being specific, 83
benchmarks, 156–157
biggest lessons of investing in others, 10
    applying research effectively, 13–15
    paying attention to the process, 10–11
    investing in people, 11–13
blame game. See shifting the blame game
Bowie, T., 127
brainstorming sessions, 195
Branch, G. F., 194
building trust, 134
buy-in. See fostering buy-in

C

calendar tools, 105
candidate demonstrates no evidence that they researched your organization, 203–204
candidate doesn't take responsibility for mistakes, 204
candidate is disrespectful, arrogant, or overly self-assured, 203
candidate is not enthusiastic, 203
candidate shows up late, 202
candidate speaks badly about their previous employer, 203
candidate's most recent supervisor is not listed as a reference, 204–205
candidate's résumé does match with their responses, 202
celebrating achievements, 8, 18–19
challenges in shaping student achievement, 7
Cheshin, A., 69
chronological fashion feedback, 152
chunking, 95–96, 165–166
Churchill, W., 89
clarifying statements, 85
clarifying the consequence of decisions, 175–176
clarifying the mission, 65, 72–73, 81–82, 93–95
    beginning with vision, 88–90
    defining clarity, 82–85
    distinguishing a mission from a vision, 92
    ensuring clarity, 85–87
    fostering buy-in, 95–97
    key points, 100
    prioritizing consistency, 97–99
    reflective activities, 101–102
    sustaining the vision, 90–92
clarity in accountability, 186, 189
classroom success. See re-envisioning classroom success
climate
    defined, 194–195, 207
    vs. culture, 194–197
coercion, 135
collaboration
    focusing on, 134
    learning, 30, 34
    fostering, 7, 11–12
Collins, J., 95
committing to the high road, 22–23
communicating progress, 7, 97
confirmation bias, 16–17
conflict resolution, 8
connection, 7
consequence
    defined, 177–178
    should be taught and sustained, 182
consistency. See being consistent; prioritizing consistency
consistently monitoring, 123
cooperative learning, 29
Copur-Gencturk, Y., 29
core beliefs, 31–32
Covey, S. R., 22
crafting your values, 107
creating a sustainable environment for success, 70, 209–210
critical-thinking skills. See fostering critical thinking skills
criticism, 166–167
"culture eats strategy for breakfast" (Drucker), 194
culture. See organizational culture

D

the "data inform best decisions" myth, 39–40
data vs. information, 39–40
data-based decisions, 8
day-to-day recognition, 188
decision making (see also planning strategically and making decisions), 29
    aeronautical thought process, 64–65, 104
    effective, 110–112
    effective, 123
    individual and collective, 111
    influenced by biases, 63
    leadership cycle, 63–64, 66
    roots and fruits of the process, 114–121
declaring explicit accountability, 107
defining clarity, 82–85
    being consistent, 83
    being specific, 83
    establishing a vision, 82–83
    holding your team accountable, 83
    sharing your vision, 83
defining innovation
defining measurement and monitoring, 143–144

defining success, 7, 9–10
defining your vision, 107
delegating, 66, 132, 184
Deming, W. D., 15
dependent learners. See ensuring learning for independent and dependent learners, 32–33
descriptive feedback, 50–51
determining desired outcomes, 107
determining what can be controlled, 105–106
diagnostic assessment, 40
the difference between a culture of accountability and a culture of nonaccountability, 185–186
    recognizing that beliefs drive actions, 185
    shifting the focus from finding faults to finding solutions, 185
    moving from assuming and informing to ensuring and empowering, 185
the difference between adjustment and improvement, 164–166
differentiation, 3–4
disconnect between candidate's activity and evidence of their impact, 202–203
discrediting/dismissing opposing viewpoints, 135
distinguishing a mission from a vision, 92
Drucker, P., 194
Dweck, C. S., 44–45
dynamic nature of leadership, 8

E

educating others, 132
effective communication, 25, 34
80/20 rule, 105–106, 115–116, 123
Eisenhower Matrix, 105
embracing change, 8
embracing diverse perspectives, 7, 11–12, 16–17
emotional intelligence (EQ)
    applying in the interview process, 198–200
    defined, 112
    gauging, 201
    importance in hiring, 206
    importance in leadership, 8
    incorporating, 112–114, 123
    questions in the interview, 199–200
    relationship management, 114
    self-awareness, 113
    self-management, 114
    social awareness, 114
emotional security. See leadership and emotional security
empathy, 7, 18
emphasizing persuasion and reason, 134
employees want to do a good job and succeed, 182
empowering learners, 7, 25–26
    ensuring learning for independent and dependent learners, 32–33
    key points, 34
    managing individual expectations, 28–30
    re-envisioning classroom success, 30–32
    reflective activity, 35
    what it means to ensure learning, 26–28

empowering yourself and others, 66–67, 72, 75, 127–128, 184
    impact without imposition, 133–135
    key points, 138–139
    leadership and emotional security, 135–136
    reflective activity, 140
    relay race, 127–128, 137–138
    two focus areas of empowerment, 128–133
empowerment, 8
    defined, 128
empowerment of others, 128, 131–133, 139
    allowing others to engage in the knowledge, 132–133
    delegating, 132
    educating, 132
    encouraging, 132
encouraging diversity, 205–206
encouraging others, 132
encouraging self-acknowledgment, 27–28
engaging the right team, 123
ensuring buy-in, 7
ensuring clarity, 85–87, 100–102
ensuring learning, 3
    clarifying what it means, 26–28
    for independent and dependent learners, 32–34
ensuring success by investing in others, 22–23
ensuring the right people fill the right seats, 205–206
Escalante, J., 89–90
establishing a culture of accountability, 110, 175, 179–180, 210
    an accountable leader's actions, 182–183
    an accountable leader's mindset, 182
    seeds of the culture, 181–182
    three major accountability inhibitors, 180–181
    two questions that impact the process, 180
establishing a vision, 82–83
establishing key performance indicators, 108
establishing quality instruction and learning, 37
    feedback, 49–56
    focusing on action over learning, 44–45
    key points, 56–57
    misconceptions about learning assessment, 39–44
    outcomes and assessments of ensuring learning, 38–39
    reflective activities, 58–60
    a tale of two mindsets, 45–47
    two types of challenges, 47–49
establishing relevance, 25–27, 34
the "everything a learner does needs a grade" myth, 42
evidence of learning, 1–2
examining the interview process, 197–198
    applying emotional intelligence, 198–200
    shaking it up, 200
exchange zone, 137
excuses instead of execution, 181, 189
experimentation discouraged by rigid constraints, 45
expressing gratitude, 18–19

F

favoritism, 177
feedback, 7–8
    adaptive learning, 51, 54
    adaptive learning, 55
    adaptive teaching, 51, 54
    adaptive teaching, 54
    adjustment reflection, 169
    descriptive, 37
    descriptive, 50–51
    diversity in, 134
    empowering yourself and others, 140
    establishing quality instruction and learning, 49–51
    giving, 149–154
    holding people accountable, 184
    in action, 55–56
    input and, 96–97
    measuring and gathering, 67–68, 141–162
    misaligned, 171
    one-way written analysis, 50
    prescriptive, 37, 50–51
    quadrants, 51
    receiving, 146–149
    seeking, 20–21empowering learners, 31
    technical learning, 53
    technical teaching, 51–52
    understanding, 144–146
    when to make adjustments, 166–167
feedback quadrant, 51, 58–59
feedback sandwich, 151–152
Felix, A., 127–128, 137
the five whys method, 117–121
fixed mindset, 46, 57
    working around time and change, 104–105
focusing, 110
    on action over learning, 44–45
    on busyness rather than on impact, 181, 189
    on collaboration and shared goals, 134
    on impact, 8
    on long-term benefits and sustainability, 134
    on personal gain, 135
    on relationships, 183
    on teaching vs. on learning, 60
Folkman, J., 150
formal recognition, 187
formative assessment, 40
Fortnite, 46
fostering a culture of open communication, 8
fostering accountability, 66, 69–70
fostering buy-in, 95–97, 99
    chunking, 95–96
    communicating progress, 97
    feedback and input, 96–97
    listening, 96
    transparent and honest dialogue, 95
fostering clarity, 25
fostering collaboration, 7, 11–12
fostering critical-thinking skills, 8, 29
fostering ownership, 8

G

Gabriel, A. S., 69
Gandhi, M., 88
Gardner, E., 127–128, 137
Garfield High School (Los Angeles, Calif.), 89–90
Geng, J., 135
Ginsberg, S., 98
giving effective feedback, 149
    actionable, 149–150
    chronological fashion, 152
    feedback sandwich, 151–152
    goal-referenced, 149
    ongoing, 151
    Pendleton model, 152–153
    praise, 153–154
    timely, 150–151
goal setting
    shared, 134
    SMART goals, 107
    sub-goals, 10–11, 93–94
goal-referenced feedback, 149
Goldsmith, M., 13
Goleman, D., 112
Good Authority (Raymond), 184
Good to Great (Collins), 95
the "grades and test scores maximize motivation and learning" myth, 43
grades, 38–39
    not always needed, 42
    vs. assessment, 39, 41–42, 56
growth mindset, 7, 57
    accountability, 184
    self-empowerment, 130
    vs. fixed, 46–47
    working around time and change, 104–105

H

Hadi, N. U., 69
Han, Y., 69
handling rejection, 4–5
Hanushek, E. A., 194
Harvard Business Review, 104, 150
having a process for managing feedback, 148
helicopter management, 156
helping teams build a habit around feedback, 147
Heshmat, S., 16
hiring with precision, 193–194
    applying emotional intelligence, 198–200
    examining the interview process, 197–198
    key points, 206–207
    shaking up the interview process, 200–206
    with climate and culture in mind, 194–197
holding people accountable, 83, 184
holistic development of young minds, 6–7
homework, 41–42
Hong, S., 69
How Expert Pilots Think (Adams), 14
how to invest in people, 15–16
    being consistent, 20–21
    ensuring success by investing in others, 22–23
    prioritizing personal interactions, 17–20

recognizing the consequences of not investing in others, 21
understanding how experience and beliefs inform performance, 16–17
Huang, S.-C., 10

I

identifying red flags in an interview, 202–205
    candidate demonstrates no evidence that they researched your organization, 203–204
    candidate doesn't take responsibility for mistakes, 204
    candidate is disrespectful, arrogant, or overly self-assured, 203
    candidate is not enthusiastic, 203
    candidate shows up late, 202
    candidate speaks badly about their previous employer, 203
    candidate's most recent supervisor is not listed as a reference, 204–205
    candidate's résumé does match with their responses, 202
    there is a disconnect between candidate's activity and evidence of their impact, 202–203
impact without imposition, 133–135
    bad power-seeking behaviors, 134–135
    building trust, 134
    emphasizing persuasion and reason, 134
    focusing on collaboration and shared goals, 134
    focusing on long-term benefits and sustainability, 134
    promoting transparency and ethical practices, 134
    respecting diverse perspectives and feedback, 134
inconsistency, 98–99
increasing your investment in your team, 210
independent learners. See ensuring learning for independent and dependent learners, 32–33
individual and collective decision making, 111
informal recognition, 187
informed decision making, 7
initiatives, 94
innovation. See defining innovation, 84–85
insecurity, 139
institutions of learning, 2–4, 7, 34
interviewing. See examining the interview process
intimidation, 135
intricacies of quality instruction, 7
introducing feedback training, 147–148
investing in people, 7, 9–10
    biggest lessons, 10–15
    how to, 15–23
    key points, 23
    reflective activity, 24
inviting the right team, 109
irresponsibility, 8
    damage it does, 183–184, 189
Itzchakov, G., 22

J

Jacobson, L., 28
Jin, L., 10
Jobs, S., 157
Joss, R., 20
journey of leadership, 4–6

K

Kaplan, R. S., 104
Keague, S., 105
keeping plans flexible, 109
key performance indicators, 108
key points, 8
    adjusting and improving, 170–171
    being accountable and giving rewards, 188–189
    clarifying the mission, 100
    empowering learners, 34
    empowering yourself and others, 138–139
    establishing quality instruction and learning, 56–57
    hiring with precision, 206–207
    investing in others, 23
    leadership cycle, 72
    measuring and gathering feedback, 158–159
    planning strategically and making decisions, 123
key results, 94
King, M. L. Jr., 88–89, 136
Klimecki, O. M., 22
Kluger, A. N., 22

L

lack of metrics to track improvement, 156–157
lack of time and attention, 154–156
Leadership (Goleman), 112–114
leadership and emotional security, 135–136
leadership cycle, 7, 61–63
    adjusting and improving, 163–173
    analysis, 73–79
    being accountable and giving rewards, 175–192
    clarifying the mission, 81–102
    creating a sustainable environment for success, 70
    empowering yourself and others, 127–140
    graphic, 62
    key points, 72
    learning, 64–70
    measuring and gathering feedback, 141–162
    planning strategically and making decisions, 103–125
    processing as part of leadership, 63–64
    reflective activity, 73–79
    skipping steps, 70–72
    to create a culture of sustainable success, 209–210
leadership thinking game, 13–14
learning the leadership cycle, 64–65
    adjusting and improving, 68–69
    being accountable and giving rewards, 69–70

clarifying the mission, 65
empowering yourself and others, 66–67
measuring and gathering feedback, 67–68
planning strategically and making decisions, 66
lesson demonstration, 201
Liu, H., 135

M

making decisions effectively, 110–112
    individual and collective decision making, 111
making it easy to give feedback, 146–147
making promises/commitments you cannot keep, 135
making sure you do your part, 183
making time for reflection, 11
managing individual expectations, 28
    limitations of the term students, 28–29, 34
    potential of the term learners, 29–30, 34
Mandela, N., 89
manipulating information, 135
Mart, C. T., 29
Maurer, R., 96
Maxwell, J. C., 66
measuring and gathering feedback, 8, 67–68, 72, 76, 141–142
    defining measurement and monitoring, 143–144
    giving effective feedback, 149–154
    key points, 158–159
    receiving feedback, 146–149
    reflective activities, 160–162
    skipping the step, 154–158
    understanding feedback, 144–146
mentoring, 12
micromanagement, 156
milestones, 93
Mindset (Dweck), 45–46
mindset. See also fixed mindset; growth mindset
    role in determining outcomes, 68–69
    working around time and change, 104–105
mini-missions, 93–95
misaligned measurement, 171
misconceptions about learning assessment, 39
    assessment and evaluation are the same thing, 39
    assessment is one-way communication, 41
    assessments are for grading, 41–42
    assignments turned in late should not count for full credit, 43–44
    data inform best decisions, 39–40
    everything a learner does needs a grade, 42
    grades and test scores maximize motivation and learning, 43
    most assessments are summative, 40
mission clarity. See clarifying the mission
modeling accountability, 184
Moghanizad, M., 86
monitoring constantly, 109
Moran, C. M., 69
the "most assessments are summative" myth, 40
motivation
    discouraged by rigid constraints, 43–45
    importance of, 29
    relevance and, 25–27
moving from assuming and informing to ensuring and empowering, 185

N

Nation's Report Card
    widespread decline on, 10
National Assessment of Educational Progress (NAEP), 10
Norton, D. P., 104

O

Obama, B., 19, 89
observation, 38
ongoing feedback, 151
open-ended questions, 152–153
Organizational Behavior and Human Decision Processes, 10
organizational culture vs. climate, 194–197
    defined, 195, 207
    defining, 196–197
outcomes and assessments of ensuring learning, 38–39
overcoming resistance, 8

P

Pareto, V. F. D., 105
Parks, R., 89
paying attention to the process, 10–11
Pendleton model feedback, 152–153
performance tasks, 38
personal reflection, 8
plan, do, study, act (PDSA) cycle, 15
planning for impact, 108–109
planning in place of action, 180, 189
planning strategically and making decisions (see also strategic planning; decision making), 66, 72, 74, 103–104
    addressing the roots and fruits of the decision-making process, 114–121
    determining what can be controlled, 105–106
    incorporating emotional intelligence, 112–114
    key points, 123
    making decisions effectively, 110–112
    redefining strategic planning, 107–108
    reflective activities, 124–125
    using root cause analysis, 121–122
    using the seven principles, 108–110
    working around time and change, 104–105
planning time, 124
positive feedback vs. praise, 154
possibility maps, 117, 119–120
power-seeking behaviors, 134–135
praise, 153–154
    can be detrimental, 166–167
    vs. positive feedback, 154
prescriptive feedback, 50–51
prioritization frameworks, 105
prioritizing consistency, 83, 97–99

prioritizing personal interactions, 17–20
proactive behavior, 186
proactive learning, 8
problem-solving skills, 8
    empowering learners, 29–30
processing as part of leadership, 63–64
professional learning community (PLC), 71
promoting transparency and ethical practices, 134
Punke, H., 187
purpose of school, 1–2
    institutions of learning, 2–4
    journey of leadership, 4–6

Q

questions
    for a behavioral interview, 199–202
    for a culture of accountability, 190–192
    for adjustment reflection, 168–170
    for clarification, 85, 87
    open-ended, 152–153
    reflective, 172–173
    that impact the accountability process, 180

R

Raymond, J., 184
receiving feedback, 146–149
    adopting a culture of feedback from the top, 148
    allowing for ways to give anonymously, 147
    having a process for managing, 148
    helping teams build a habit around feedback, 147
    introduce feedback training, 147–148
    making it easy to give, 146–147
    showing that you will act on it, 148
recognition (see also rewards and recognition), 8, 18–19
    of responsible behavior, 184
    three methods, 187–188
recognizing that beliefs drive actions, 185–186
recognizing the consequences of not investing in others, 21
red flags. See identifying red flags in an interview
re-envisioning classroom success, 30–32
reflection for action, 152
reflective activities, 8
    adjusting and improving, 172–173
    being accountable and giving rewards, 190–192
    clarifying the mission, 101–102
    empowering learners, 35
    empowering yourself and others, 140
    establishing quality instruction and learning, 58
    establishing quality instruction, 58–60
    investing in others, 24
    leadership cycle, 73–79
    measuring and gathering feedback, 160–162
relationships
    are the ultimate tool for influence the performance of others, 182
    focusing relentlessly on, 184
    managing, 114
    the relay race, 127–128, 137–139
relevance. See establishing relevance
research-practice gap, 14, 22
    poor decision making, 63–64
resistance, 164–166, 167, 170
resource allocation, 8
respect, 84
respecting diverse perspectives and feedback, 134
rewards and recognition, 69–70, 187–189, 195
    day-to-day, 188
    formal, 187
    informal, 187
risk taking
    accountability encourages, 186
    deterred by fixed mindset, 46
    discouraged by rigid constraints, 45
Rivkin, S. G., 194
Roebers, C. M., 27
root cause analysis, 121–122
    example problem, 121–122
root causes of issues, 7, 123
roots and fruits of the decision-making process, 114–121
    possibility maps, 117, 119–120
Rosenthal, R., 28

S

scheduling time to build relationships, 12, 17–18
seeds of a culture of accountability, 181–182
self-acknowledgment. See encouraging self-acknowledgment
self-assessment, 31
self-awareness, 113
self-empowerment, 128–131, 139
self-fulfilling prophecies, 28
self-management, 114
self–responsibility, 8
Seneca, L. A., 92
setting clear goals, 123
seven principles of strategic planning, 108–110
    avoiding planning for the sake of planning, 108
    establishing a culture of accountability, 110
    focusing, 110
    inviting the right team, 109
    keeping plans flexible, 109
    monitoring constantly, 109
    planning for impact, 108–109
The 7 Habits of Highly Effective People (Covey), 22
shaking up the interview process, 200–202
    ensuring the right people fill the right seats, 205–206
    identifying red flags, 202–205
sharing your vision, 83
shifting the blame game, 184, 189
shifting the focus from finding faults to finding solutions, 185
shiny object syndrome, 99
showing gratitude, 12
showing that you will act on feedback, 148
six questions for adjustment reflection, 168–170

skipping steps in the leadership cycle, 70–72
skipping the feedback step, 154
    lack of metrics to track improvement, 156–157
    lack of time and attentions, 154–156
    monitoring, measurement, and micromanagement, 156
    wasted time, 157–158
SMART goals, 107
social awareness, 114
Society for Human Resource Management, 131
"Step by Step" (Huang et al.), 10
strategic planning (see also planning strategically and making decisions), 7, 66, 125
    crafting your values, 107
    declaring explicit accountability, 107
    defining your vision, 107
    determining desired outcomes, 107
    establishing key performance indicators, 108
    redefining, 107–108
student autonomy, 29
student reflection, 29
student self-evaluations, 38
student-centered learning, 7, 28–30
students vs. learners, 28–30
students with disabilities, 2
summative assessment, 40
sustainable change, 7
sustaining the vision, 90–92

T

taking credit for others' work/achievements, 135
a tale of two mindsets, 45–46
    fixed mindset, 46
    growth mindset, 46–47
team dynamics, 8, 200–206
team interviews, 205–207
team-building activities, 195
technical challenges, 37, 47–49, 57, 164
    root cause analysis, 122
technical learning
    feedback, 52–53
    sample feedback, 53
Tehseen, S., 69
threats, 135
three major accountability inhibitors, 180–181
    excuses instead of execution, 181, 189
    focus on busyness rather than on impact, 181, 189
    planning in place of action, 180, 189
three methods of recognition, 187–188
time and change, 123
timely feedback, 150–151
time-tracking apps, 105
top-down management, 96–97
town halls with staff, 195
traditional teaching methods, 25
transparent and honest dialogue, 95, 196–197
trivial many, 105
trust, 130
    accountability, 186
    building, 134
two focus areas of empowerment, 128
    empowerment of others, 128, 131–133, 139
    self-empowerment, 128–131
two questions that impact the accountability process, 180
two types of challenges, 47
    adaptive, 48
    in schools, 49
    technical, 47–48

U

unconscious bias in the interview process, 205
uncontrollable factors, 168
understanding change, 7
understanding feedback, 144–146
understanding how experience and beliefs inform performance, 16–17
understanding time, 7

V

validation, 17, 22
values, 195–196
van Kleef, G. A., 69
van Loon, M. H., 27
Vasu, 27
victim sensitivity, 177
vision, 7
    beginning with, 88–90
    distinguishing from a mission, 92
    fostering buy-in, 94–97
    sustaining, 90–92
visualization, 32
vital few, 105
von Goethe, J. W., 21

W

walkthrough model, 50
wasted time, 157–158
What Got You Here Won't Get You There (Goldsmith), 13
what it means to ensure learning, 26
    encouraging self-acknowledgment, 27–28
    establishing relevance, 26–27
when accountability is dormant, 183–184, 189
    empowering and delegating, 184
    holding people accountable, 184
    modeling accountability, 184
    recognizing and rewarding responsible behavior, 184
    shifting the blame game, 184
when to make adjustments, 166–167
will or skill, 168
withholding key details, 135
Wooden, J., 10
Woods, P. J., 29
working around time and change, 104–105

Y

Yao, P., 135
yes, but situations, 85

Z

Zenger, J., 150
Zhang, Y., 10

Implement With IMPACT
Jenice Pizzuto and Steven Carney
Learn how to build an implementation team that will bridge the implementation gap and prevent the adopt-and-abandon cycle that often comes with change. The IMPACT framework provides distinct stages and human- and learning-centered design elements to help you achieve quick, tangible wins and sustainable, scalable results.
BKG093

The Principal's Backpack
Nancy Karlin Flynn
In *The Principal's Backpack*, Nancy Karlin Flynn draws on her background as a hiker and her years of experience leading schools to provide concrete ideas and practical tips on how to not only survive but thrive as a school leader.
BKG117

Moving Beyond Busy
Greg Curtis
Break the cycle of endless busywork to achieve sustainable change. With the support of *Moving Beyond Busy*, you will learn how to commit to a few clear, learning-focused goals—and then act on them—using the input-output-impact (I-O-I) framework.
BKF854

Be the Driving Force
Don Parker
Learn how to sustain your passion for leadership and maintain your focus on equity. This essential leadership guide offers research-based strategies, action steps, and reflection questions to help leaders become the driving force for schoolwide equitable practices.
BKG090

Solution Tree | Press

Visit SolutionTree.com or call 800.733.6786 to order.

Wait! Your professional development journey doesn't have to end with the last pages of this book.

We realize improving student learning doesn't happen overnight. And your school or district shouldn't be left to puzzle out all the details of this process alone.

No matter where you are on the journey, we're committed to helping you get to the next stage.

Take advantage of everything from **custom workshops** to **keynote presentations** and **interactive web and video conferencing**. We can even help you develop an action plan tailored to fit your specific needs.

Let's get the conversation started.

Call 888.763.9045 today.

SolutionTree.com